A Pratical Introduction to French Phonetics

Nicholson

BIBLIOLIFE

A PRACTICAL INTRODUCTION

TO

FRENCH PHONETICS

*FOR THE USE OF ENGLISH-SPEAKING STUDENTS
AND TEACHERS*

BY

G. G. NICHOLSON, B.A., B.C.L.

OF BALLIOL COLLEGE, OXFORD
LECTURER IN FRENCH AND GERMAN AT THE UNIVERSITY OF SYDNEY

MACMILLAN AND CO., LIMITED
ST. MARTIN'S STREET, LONDON

1909

GLASGOW: PRINTED AT THE UNIVERSITY PRESS
BY ROBERT MACLEHOSE AND CO. LTD.

PREFACE

In the revision that modern language teaching has under-
gone during the last quarter of a century two facts have been
firmly established · first, that the pronunciation of a modern
foreign language should be taught with great care from the
outset ; and, secondly, that pronunciation can neither be
taught nor learned to the best advantage without the aid
of phonetics [1] There is, moreover, to use the words of
Dr. Breul, 'a growing conviction that the teaching of
modern languages in our secondary schools should hence-
forth as a rule not be entrusted to foreigners but to duly
qualified English men and women.' [2] But whether the
language he teaches be his native speech or not, the
teacher can no longer afford to dispense with a phonetic
training. [3] For however successful he may be without the
aid of phonetics, he can always improve his results with
such aid. Especially is this true when it is his lot to
teach French to English-speakers. He can then hardly
allow the pupil to carry over a single sound from his

[1] See *The Teaching of Modern Foreign Languages and the Training
of Teachers*, by Karl Breul, Cambridge, 1906 ; *How to teach a Foreign
Language*, by O. Jespersen, London, 1904 ; and *The Sounds of English*,
by Henry Sweet, Oxford, 1908

[2] *Op. cit* p. 37.

[3] 'Phonetics makes us independent of native teachers   It is certain
that a phonetically-trained Englishman who has a clear knowledge of
the relations between French and English sounds can teach French
sounds to English people better than an unphonetic Frenchman . .
who is unable to communicate his pronunciation to his pupils, and,
perhaps, speaks a vulgar or dialectal form of French himself' (Sweet's
Sounds of English, p 92).

own language without modification. And yet the sounds
of French often resemble English sounds so far that the
learner will fail to detect any difference even when he is
assured that the sounds are not the same. It is obvious,
then, that every means of fixing the identity of a sound
will be helpful. Now phonetics enables the teacher to
fortify the appeal to the ear with an appeal to the reason,
and often to the senses of touch and sight. In correcting a
faulty pronunciation he no longer rests content with a
repetition of the right sound. He tells the pupil exactly
why his pronunciation is wrong, and what he must do in
order to rectify it. The pupil has then the immense
advantage of knowing when he is wrong, even though his
ear may still not appreciate the difference between the right
and the wrong sound, and even when the teacher is not
there to help him. Like sounds thus acquire distinguishing
marks, cases of mistaken identity become less common, and
the training of the ear is greatly accelerated. Where, on the
other hand, the foreign sound has no analogue in English,
and can be produced only by bringing the organs of speech
into positions which are quite unfamiliar to the learner and
which at first probably demand a considerable effort on his
part, the teacher can spare him the tedious task of discovery.

To the self-taught student, *a fortiori*, phonetics is in-
valuable. Even if he be most favourably situated for the
acquisition of the foreign tongue, by residence in the
country where it is spoken, a reasoned knowledge of
the sounds will render his progress much more rapid and
much more sure. He will know what sounds to expect,
he will know when the pronunciations he hears are
abnormal and not to be imitated, he will be quicker to
detect his own faults, he will know from what cause they
proceed, and how to amend them.[1]

[1] See Sweet's *Sounds of English*, p. 92.

In the first part of this book I have endeavoured to fix
the identity of each sound in standard French by (i) giving
a list of its traditional spellings, (ii) defining the position of
the organs of speech necessary for its production, and (iii)
explaining its relations to other sounds, usually its nearest
English analogues.   Where the pronunciation of the latter
fluctuates, reference is made to the most important variations, including those current in America and Australia.
Occasion is everywhere taken to warn the student against
the errors into which he will be most likely to fall.

The second part deals with the factors which control the
combination of sounds in connected speech.   One needs
only an elementary acquaintance with the language to be
aware that a knowledge of these factors is of vital importance.   Here, again, wherever they seemed likely to be helpful,
comparisons have been drawn between the two languages

It was at first my intention to add a running com-
mentary explaining the growth and origin of the sounds of
modern French   The pages of history are here peculiarly
alluring and enlightening   But the book being designed
for a practical mission, it seemed, on reflection, prudent
to resist this temptation.   The scholar would no doubt
be interested to observe how the very numerous diphthongs
of Old and Middle French gradually passed over into other
sounds, leaving not a single survivor, how the diverse
spellings of a sound originated ; how elision became more
and more common as linking grew more and more rare ;
but a solution of these and like problems did not appear
to be so helpful as to warrant my diverting attention from
the main purpose.   To master the pronunciation of a foreign
language is no light task, and the student's forces need to
be economized

I frankly own that this little treatise would never have
seen the light had not the works of Professor Paul Passy,

of M. l'abbé Rousselot, of Professor Viëtor and Dr. Sweet been already in existence. I also express my general indebtedness to most other works of repute on French Phonetics, of which I must be content to mention but one : Dr. Quiehl's *Französische Aussprache und Sprachfertigkeit* (4th ed. Marburg, 1906), an admirable contribution on the teaching of French in German schools. Yet, in spite of my debts, I trust it will be found that the book is not a 'compilation from foreign works.' I have unhesitatingly resorted to all good sources for help and succour, but I have ventured to differ from authority in print whenever it seemed at variance with authority in speech : in all such cases my opinion has been corroborated by careful observation and experiment in the great laboratory of French, Paris itself. On some chapters, particularly Elision and Linking, the authorities in print were distressingly silent, and I was compelled to embark on long courses of investigation. The materials thus gathered I have endeavoured to present in the way which seemed most suited to English needs.

The attempt has been greatly facilitated by generous help and encouragement both in Sydney and Paris, and, in particular, by the constant and wise counsels of my wife, without whose aid the work would not have been undertaken. For this counsel, encouragement and help I tender my best thanks.

G. G. N.

PARIS, *Easter*, 1908.

The author owes a special debt of gratitude to Dr. E. J. Trechmann, M.A., his predecessor at the University of Sydney, now of London, for revision of the proofs and valuable suggestions.

G. G. N.

SYDNEY, 1909.

CONTENTS

		PAGE
INTRODUCTION	- - - - - - - -	I

PART I

THE INDIVIDUAL SOUNDS

CHAPTER

I. THE VOWELS

1 The different kinds of Vowels	- - -	9
2. The French and English Vowel-systems compared - - - - - - - - -		12
3. The Normal Oral Vowels - - - -		13
4. The Abnormal Oral Vowels - - - -		27
5. The Nasalized Vowels—General - - -		32
6. The Nasalized Normal Vowels - - -		34
7. The Nasalized Abnormal Vowel - - -		37

II. THE DIPHTHONGS (so-called) - - - - 39

III. THE CONSONANTS

1. The different kinds of Consonants - - -		42
2. The French and English Consonant-systems compared - - - - - - -		43
3. The Stops or Explosives - - - -		44
4. The Nasal Consonants - - - - -		54
5. The Continuants or Fricatives - - -		57

PART II

THE SOUNDS IN COMBINATION

CHAPTER   PAGE

I. UNITS OF SPEECH (Sentence, Sound-group, Stress-
group, Syllable) - - - - - - - 6c

II. LINKING - - - - - - - - - 7?

III. ELISION - - - - - - - - - 11?

IV. ASSIMILATION - - - - - - - - 14?

V. TRANSITION (Glides) - - - - - - 15?

VI. ACCENTUATION - - - - - - - - 16?

VII. QUANTITY - - - - - - - - - 17?

VIII. PITCH - - - - - - - - - 18?

INDEX - - - - - - - - - 18?

INTRODUCTION

FRENCH orthography, like English, is radically defective
The language contains at least thirty-seven distinct sounds,
not reckoning differences in length, stress and pitch, or
other occasional modifications. To represent these sounds
accurately and unambiguously, there should be a similar
number of symbols. Not only, however, is the equipment
of symbols very inadequate, but those that exist are
employed with bewildering inconsistency. Thus the sign *e*
may stand for an 'open *e*,' as in *avec*; for a 'close *e*,' as in
parler; or for the so-called 'mute *e*,' as in *petit*. It may
even be an idle sign, without any corresponding sound,
as in *beau* and *comme*. Combined with another vowel-sign
it is used to indicate other simple sounds, when further
inconsistencies result. Thus *eu* represents three different
sounds in *leur*, *yeux*, and *il eut*; while the first of these
three sounds is also represented by *œ*, as in *œil*, by *ue*, as in
cueillir; by *œu*, as in *cœur*. The incoherence is emphasized
by the phenomenon of nasalization. We find, for example,
the signs *un*, *um* standing for the nasalized form of the
vowel in *leur* and not for a nasal *u*, the signs *aim*, *ain*, *ein*,
im, *in* and *en*, as in *faim*, *pain*, *sein*, *simple*, *fin*, *bien*,
standing for a nasalized vowel which does not exist in
French in its pure or oral form; and the signs *am*, *an*, *em*,
en, *aon* for a nasalized *a*, as in *champ*, *tant*, *temps*, *vent*,
paon.

F P.   A   Œ

The accents, too, which might have served to extend the capacity of the French alphabet, only increase the confusion. While an isolated *è* would naturally stand for 'open *e*,' *à* is never used for the 'open *a*,' nor *ò* for the 'open *o*.' Likewise *ê* would regularly stand for a long 'open *e*,' but it represents a short 'open *e*' in *vous êtes*, and is often pronounced as a half-long 'close *e*,' in *vêtu*. The symbol *â* indicates, in many cases, a long 'open *a*,' as in *âme*; but it represents a short 'close *a*' in the first and second persons plural of the past definite tense of verbs of the first conjugation, *e.g. aimâmes, aimâtes*. On the other hand *ô*, as a rule, stands for a 'close *o*,' sometimes long, as in *hôte*, sometimes half-long, as in *hôtesse*; but in *hôtel, rôti*, is pronounced as a short 'open *o*.' Placed over the vowels *i* and *u*, which are always close in French, the circumflex accent becomes merely a sign of length; yet *î* and *û* often denote short sounds, as in *qu'il fît, qu'il fût*, and the long *i* and *u* more often than not, as in *tige, ruse*, bear no accent.

This confusion extends to the consonants. Take *s* as an example. This sound is represented by *s* in *sang*, by *ss* in *tasse*, by *ç* in *leçon*, by *c* in *place*, by *sc* in *scène*, by *t* in *nation*, by *x* in *soixante*, and, along with *k*, by *x* in *exprès* and by *xc* in *excellent*: while the sign *s* is used not only for the sound *s* but also for *z*, as in *cause*, or idly, without any sound-value, as in *il est*.

Further, not only is there confusion between the vowels, on the one hand, and the consonants, on the other, *inter se*: we constantly find vowel-signs representing consonantal sounds. Thus the *u* in *huit*, the *i* in *bien*, the *ou* in *oui* are consonants. Still more complex is the confusion in words like *roi*, *foi*, *loi*, where the vowel-signs *oi* do duty for a consonant and a vowel '*a*' that is not readily suggested by either of the signs.

From the foregoing we may conclude, first, that the

traditional spelling is no safe guide to pronunciation ; and, secondly, that even if the traditional alphabet were applied more consistently it would be, at best, a very clumsy means of indicating the precise sounds of the language. The latter result may be illustrated a little more directly. How, for example, using the traditional signs, should we distinguish between the open and the close sounds of the vowel *eu* ? The least objectionable method would be to employ an accent for one of the two sounds, say the circumflex, placed over the sign *u* (*i.e.* *eû*), to denote the close vowel. This symbol has the disadvantage of containing three signs to represent one sound, and of suggesting to the mind, by the accent placed over one of them—and it must be placed over one of the signs unless new type is cast—that there are two distinct sounds. Moreover, practical experience has shown that the use of the accent to indicate the quality of a vowel clogs the mental process by which the sign is converted into a sound, and frequently results in the production of the wrong sound. What is required or desirable is a simple sign that will at once and directly suggest the right idea, and thus enable the learner to devote all his attention to the realization of that idea, namely, the production of the sound.

Objections to phonetic methods of the kind indicated might be multiplied. But enough has been said to show the need for some more adequate equipment of symbols. This need has been met by the International Phonetic Association, whose phonetic alphabet will be adopted in the present work. This alphabet has the threefold merit of utilizing familiar material, of having been adopted by nearly all the later writers on phonetics, and of representing each sound by but one sign. Whatever defects it has, and it is not put forward as the perfect realization of an ideal, it is adopted with confidence as the best that has yet been devised. It has stood the practical test of nearly a quarter of a century, and the testimony of those who have employed it is generally to the effect that a knowledge of it is very easily acquired by the average schoolboy.

As applied to French and English this alphabet may be set forth as follows :[1]

Sign.	French.	English.
a	*patte* [pat], *part* [paːr]	*high* [haɪ] ; sometimes in *ask* [aːsk]
ɑ	*pas* [pɑ], *pâte* [pɑːt]	*far* [fɑː], *part* [pɑːt]
ɑ̃	*tant* [tɑ̃], *tante* [tɑ̃ːt]	
ɒ		*not* [nɒt], *all* [ɒːl]
æ		*cat* [kæt], *ash* [æʃ]
e	*dé* [de], *plaisir* [pleziːr]	*day* [dɛe] [dɛɪ], Scotch [deː]
ɛ	*fait* [fɛ], *fête* [fɛːt]	*fell* [fɛl], *fare* [fɛː] [fɛːə]
ɛ̃	*fin* [fɛ̃], *feinte* [fɛ̃ːt]	
ə	*le* [lə], *leçon* [ləsɔ̃]	*sofa* [soofə], *labour* [lɛɪbə]
ʌ		*but* [bʌt], *cut* [kʌt]
ɐ		*bird* [bɐːd], *fur* [fɐː]
i	*si* [si], *assise* [asiːz]	*sea* [sɪi], *seize* [sɪiz]
ɪ		*sit* [sɪt], *pity* [pɪtɪ]
o	*chaud* [ʃo], *chose* [ʃoːz]	*show* [ʃoo], *shows* [ʃooz]
ɔ	*note* [nɔt], *nord* [nɔːr]	*note* [nɔot], *door* [dɔː] [dɔoə]

---

[1] The letters of the phonetic alphabet should be named only by their sounds ; but those which are not readily pronounced apart may be articulated with an [ə]. Thus [t] will be called [tə] and not [tɪi], as in English, nor [te], as in French ; [s] will be named by the hissing sound it represents and not by the customary [ɛs] ; [u] will be denoted by the sound traditionally written *ou* in French and not by the alphabetical name current in English [juu] or French [y]. To avoid misunderstanding, phonetic signs will, throughout the book, be enclosed in square brackets. For the sign [ː] see page 7.

Sign.	French.	English.
ɔ̃	*non* [nɔ̃], *monde* [mɔ̃ːd]	
œ	*seul* [sœl], *sœur* [sœːr]	
œ̃	*un* [œ̃], *humble* [œ̃ːbl]	
ø	*peu* [pø], *heureuse* [œrøːz]	
u	*tout* [tu], *tour* [tuːr].	*do* [duu], *few* [fjuu]
ʊ		*put* [pʊt], *true* [tɹuu]
y	*tu* [ty], *mur* [myːr]	
b	*beau* [bo], *robe* [rɔb]	*bow* [boo], *rob* [ɹɒb]
d	*doux* [du], *rude* [ryd]	*do* [duu], *rude* [ɹuud]
ð		*then* [ðɛn], *with* [wɪð]
f	*faire* [fɛːr], *sauf* [soːf]	*fare* [fɛːə], *loaf* [loof]
g	*gai* [ge], *dogue* [dɔg]	*gay* [gɛɪ], *dog* [dɒg]
h	*harpe* [harp] [arp]	*harp* [hɑːp]
j	*yeux* [jø], *veille* [vɛːj]	*you* [juu], *view* [vjuu]
k	*car* [kaːr], *lac* [lak]	*car* [kɑː], *lack* [læk]
l	*lent* [lɑ̃], *bal* [bal]	*long* [lɒŋ], *ball* [bɒːl]
m	*mode* [mɔd], *dime* [dim]	*mode* [mood], *dim* [dɪm]
n	*nappe* [nap], *canne* [kan]	*nap* [næp], *can* [kæn]
ɲ	*signe* [siɲ], *signer* [siɲe]	
ŋ		*sing* [sɪŋ], *singer* [sɪŋgə]
p	*pire* [piːr], *tape* [tap]	*peer* [piiə], *tap* [tæp]
r	*rare* [raːr], *tort* [tɔːr]	
ʀ	*rare* [ʀɑːʀ], *tort* [tɔːʀ]	
ɹ		*rare* [ɹɛːə], *merry* [mɛɹɪ]
s	*sot* [so], *masse* [mas]	*so* [soo], *mass* [mæs]
ʃ	*chou* [ʃu], *ruche* [ryʃ]	*shoe* [ʃuu], *rush* [ɹʌʃ]
ʒ	*joue* [ʒu], *cage* [kaːʒ]	*judge* [dʒʌdʒ], *leisure* [lɛʒə]
t	*tas* [tɑ], *site* [sit]	*tar* [tɑː], *sit* [sɪt]

6 FRENCH PHONETICS

Sign.	French.	English.
θ		*thin* [θɪn], *through* [θɹuu]
v	*ville* [vil], *rêve* [rɛɪv]	*veal* [vɪil], *rave* [ɹɛɪv] [ɹèɪv]
w	*oui* [wi], *bois* [bwɑ]	*we* [wɹi], *win* [wɪn]
ɥ	*puis* [pɥi], *huit* [ɥit]	
z	*zèle* [zɛl], *gaz* [gɑɪz]	*zeal* [zɪil], *gaze* [gɛɪz]

The use of the same sign for both languages must not
be taken to imply identity between the sounds. In nearly
all such cases, on the contrary, there are differences which
cannot be neglected and which will be discussed in due
course. But to employ double symbols for sounds which
are essentially the same would mean a great complication
of the alphabet for a very slight advantage.

To the alphabet we may append a list of the signs which
are used to indicate either certain occasional modifications
of the regular sounds or certain additional sounds of rare
occurrence in French and English:

? the glottal-stop heard in German before accented
initial vowels, as in *Abart* [ʔɑpʔɑɪrt].

ʰ the sound of breathing.

ᴒ the sound produced by the vibration of the vocal
chords, briefly 'voice.'

ᵒ placed over or under a letter indicates that it is
devocalized: *e.g. quatre* [katɹ̥], *pied* [pʃe].

ᵛ placed over or under a letter indicates that it is
vocalized: *e.g. masse de gens* [maṣ də ʒɑ̃].

ı placed under a letter indicates that it has syllabic
value: *e.g. able* [ɛɪbl̩].

ˋ placed over a vowel indicates that it is pronounced
with relaxed organs and is, therefore, more open:
e.g. méchant [mèʃɑ̃].

ˊ placed over a vowel indicates that it is closer and is
pronounced with tenser organs.

ː placed after a vowel or consonant indicates that it
    is long *e.g. art* [aːr], *salle* [salː].
· placed after a vowel indicates that it is half-long: *e.g.*
    enfant [ã·fã].
′ placed *before* a syllable indicates that it is accented :
    when necessary a strong accent may be indicated
    by doubling or even trebling the sign : ″ or ‴

It has been said that the French language is built
up out of some thirty-seven sounds. Strictly speaking,
however, there is no limit to the number, for each sound
is subject to infinite variations. The least change in the
method of production theoretically entails a modification
of the sound. Yet we are justified in speaking of a norm
or standard pronunciation, to which the individual sounds
have reference, and which they are supposed to reproduce.
In all languages this normal pronunciation varies with
the locality These variations often extend to the educated
classes among English-speaking people, and render the
selection of a norm for our language no easy task. But
no such difficulty arises in connection with French. The
standard is found, by common consent, in the pronunciation of the educated classes in Paris, subject to one possible
modification in favour of more general usage where the
Parisian practice is at variance with that of the educated
classes in other parts of the country. Reference will be
made to this modification in defining the individual sounds.

PART I

THE INDIVIDUAL SOUNDS

CHAPTER I

THE VOWELS

1. The different kinds of vowels.

All vowels are essentially variations of one simple kind of sound, that produced by vibration of the vocal chords.[1] Their differentiation is wholly due to the shape of the cavity in which the resonance takes place. This cavity may consist either of the mouth alone or of the mouth and nose combined. In the former case the velum, or pendent end of the soft palate, acting like a valve, rises and closes the passage to the nose either entirely, or at least so effectually that all the voice is deflected into the mouth. Vowels produced in this way may be called *Oral* Vowels or *Pure* Vowels. If the velum is lowered (but not so far as to touch the tongue and thus close the

[1] The two vocal chords stretch horizontally from back to front across the larynx or upper part of the windpipe. Each of them, throughout its whole length, is connected, on the outer side, with the walls of the larynx by an elastic membrane. The breath can, therefore, pass only between the chords. This space or passage, which is called the *glottis*, can be narrowed or closed by bringing the chords together. If the chords are brought together and the breath forced between them, they vibrate and produce the sound which is known as *voice*.

passage to the mouth) the voice will pass into both nose
and mouth, which being now in direct communication
with each other may be regarded as forming one complex
cavity.   Vowels produced with such a resonance-chamber
are known as *Nasal* Vowels or, more exactly, *Nasalized*
Vowels.

As the nose-cavity has a fixed form, all further distinctions
must be due to modifications in the shape of the mouth.
These modifications are effected chiefly by movements of
the tongue and lips, and on the relative positions of these
organs is based the classification of vowels as normal
and abnormal.   If the positions of the tongue and lips
are such that they each tend towards the production of
the same characteristics they are said to be normal, and
the vowel that they produce is called a *Normal* Vowel.
If, on the other hand, they counteract each other, and
thus give rise to a mixed vowel-sound, they are considered
abnormal, and the resulting sound is described as an
Abnormal Vowel.   In pronouncing the series [i–e–ɑ–o–u]
in the given order, it will be observed (1) that the tongue,
which in articulating [i] is well forward in the mouth and
presses against the sides of the front palate, falls a little
and recedes a little for [e], lies flat on the floor of the
mouth for [ɑ], is drawn back and rises towards the back
palate for [o] and reaches its extreme backward position for
[u]; (2) that as the tongue moves backward the lips move
forward and are rounded; (3) that the pitch of the voice
falls at each step, [i] being the vowel of highest and [u]
the vowel of lowest pitch in the series.   Both tongue and
lips contribute towards this lowering of the pitch.   The
vowels in question are, therefore, Normal.   Suppose,
however, that while the tongue is in its forward position
for [i], the lips, instead of being held against the teeth
(thus helping to raise the pitch), are thrust forward as

for [u] (thus counteracting the effort of the tongue to produce a high-pitched vowel): the relative positions are then said to be Abnormal, and an Abnormal vowel-sound [y] is heard, whose pitch is neither as low as that of [u] nor as high as that of [i]. Taking then as our starting-point the positions for [ɑ] when the tongue lies as flat as possible on the floor of the mouth, we may say that the movement of the lips is normal if they draw back to the teeth in proportion as the tongue advances (for by this means they will assist in raising the pitch), and move forward and contract in proportion as the tongue recedes (because they thus help to lower the pitch). If, on the contrary, the lips are thrust forward and rounded when the tongue is in a forward position, or held back to the teeth when the tongue is in a backward position, they may be said to defeat the effort of the tongue, in which case the positions of the organs and the sound uttered may be regarded as abnormal.

Finally, every vowel may be *close* or *narrow* and *open* or *wide*. These terms refer to the distance between the palate and the articulating part of the tongue. The organs are tense in producing a narrow vowel, and relaxed in producing a wide one. Thus *i* is open or wide in Eng. *sit* [sɪt], close or narrow in Fr. *site* [sit]; *e* is open or wide in Eng. *dare* [dɛːə], close or narrow in Fr. *dé* [de]; *u* is open or wide in Eng. *full* [fʊl], close or narrow in Fr. *foule* [ful]. It is sometimes necessary to distinguish a third species, intermediate between the close and open sounds : such a vowel may be called *half-open* or *half-wide*. This middle sound is indicated phonetically by the sign [ˋ] placed over the close vowel. An approximation to the middle and close sounds is often heard in the diphthongs in *seat* [slit], *day* [dèe], *fool* [fùul].

2. The French and English vowel-systems compared.

Nearly all the vowels of English, and the bulk of the French vowels, are normal oral vowels. Comparing the normal lip and tongue movements in the two languages we find that, while in French they are carried out with almost mathematical precision to their fullest extent, English practice shows with regard to each organ, but especially with regard to the lips, a relaxation of effort. Hence the individual normal vowel-sounds of English and French are rarely ever quite the same : the one or two sounds that can be practically identified are those which make the smallest demands upon the tongue and lips, particularly the latter ; and the more effort a specific sound requires, the less the correspondence between the two languages. The long close vowels [iː] [eː] [oː] [uː], the four sounds which necessitate the greatest efforts of tongue and lips, are generally replaced in modern English by diphthongs in which, as a rule, neither element has exactly the close vowel-sound. In their short form these vowels have ceased to exist in English, their places having been taken by the corresponding open sounds. French, on the other hand, which possesses both long and short close vowels, has no open *i* or open *u* and no diphthongs. The vowels of English secondary and weak syllables have either been reduced to the colourless [ə] or are at least normally open. In the pretonic syllables of French, open and close vowels retain their values. Compare Eng. *revolution* [ɹɛvəluʊʃn̩] [ɹɛvəljʊuʃn̩] and Fr. *révolution* [revɔlysjɔ̃], Eng. *arithmetic* [əɹɪθmətɪk] and Fr. *arithmétique* [aritmetik], Eng. *opposition* [ɒpəzɪʃn̩] and Fr. *opposition* [ɔpozisjɔ̃]. It is true that the organs of speech are not quite so tense, even in French, in producing vowels which bear a secondary or weak accent, and therefore that close vowels in these

positions tend to become half-open, but the close vowel
is not transformed into an open one, and neither close
nor open vowels are reduced to [ə].

In additional to its normal vowels, French possesses
several abnormal and nasalized vowels. The nasalization
of vowels occurs in English only as a dialectal peculiarity.
All the French abnormal vowels are formed by the projection of the lips when the tongue is in a forward position.
The one English vowel which is sometimes described as
abnormal, the [ʌ] in *cup* [kʌp], if rightly so described, has
that character because the lips are idle when the tongue
occupies a backward position.

This comparison of the two vowel-systems may serve to
warn the student that in learning French he will have to
contend with a characteristic slackness of the organs of
speech. It should, in particular, put him on his guard
against carrying English vowels over into French, against
the diphthongizing and lengthening of short close vowels,
against the opening of close vowels in unaccented syllables,
and the blurring of unaccented vowels in general.

3. The Normal Oral Vowels.

The general relations between the members of this series
of vowels may be indicated by means of the following
diagram :

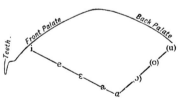

The falling and rising line is that described by the
articulating part of the tongue as it moves from its extreme

forward to its extreme backward position in the mouth; and the place of each vowel marks its locality of articulation and consequent order in the series. Thus [i] is produced with the tongue in its extreme forward position, when it bunches up close to the front part of the hard palate. For the next vowel [e] the bunch recedes a little and falls a little. The movement continues for [ɛ] and [a]. When [ɑ] is reached the tongue lies flat on the floor of the mouth. The backward movement being continued, the back part of the tongue begins to bunch up towards the back palate, and [ɔ] [o] and [u] are produced in turn.

The curved brackets indicate that articulation of the last three vowels cannot be effected without rounding of the lips. For the same reason these vowels are sometimes described as 'rounded vowels.'

The series may be divided into two groups [i–e–ɛ–a] being classed as Front Vowels and [ɑ–ɔ–o–u] as Back Vowels. The individual vowels are then described as follows: [i] High-Front-Narrow Vowel; [e] Mid-Front-Narrow Vowel; [ɛ] Mid-Front-Wide Vowel; [a] Low-Front-Narrow Vowel; [ɑ] Low-Back-Wide Vowel; [ɔ] Mid-Back-Wide Vowel; [o] Mid-Back-Narrow Vowel; [u] High-Back-Narrow Vowel.

High-Front-Narrow Vowel or Close i.

Phonetic sign : [i].

Traditional spellings :

1. *i*, as in *signe* [siɲ]·;
2. *î*, as in *dîme* [dim];
3. *ie*, as in *folie* [fɔli];
4. *y*, as in *cygne* [siɲ];
5. *ee*, as in *spleen* [splin].

Articulation. The jaws being normally so close together that the upper front-teeth just overlap, without touching, the lower ones, the tip of the tongue touches the inside of the

lower front-teeth and its sides press upwards against the upper
gums, and outwards against the molars, bringing its face as
close to the middle of the hard palate as possible without
creating consonantal friction. The corners of the mouth
being drawn back, the lips are held against the teeth.

Explanation. This is the vowel-sound that is heard in
the Scotch pronunciation of *dear* [diːr]. The English
sound which is commonly supposed to correspond to [iː]
is in reality a diphthong of which the first and stressed
element is a more open sound [i] or [ɪ], and the second,
unstressed element sometimes a closer sound approaching
the consonant [j] in *yes* [jɪs] : *seat* [sìjt] [sɪit], *breeze* [bɹìjz]
[bɹiiz]. This [ɪ] is articulated with the tongue just touching
the upper gums, and a shade less forward in the mouth than
for [i]. In uttering the English diphthong the tongue,
therefore, moves forward and begins to press against the
gums after the sound is attacked. The movement of the
tongue is accompanied by an upward movement of the lower
jaw which can be easily observed with the aid of a mirror.
For the vowel [iː] the tongue must be well forward and press
against the gums from the outset, and the jaws must not
move : *brise* [briːz].

The shorter English sound is the vowel [ɪ] : *sit* [sɪt].
This sound, the High-Front-Wide Vowel or open *i*, does
not exist in French, the [i] requiring the same pressure
of the tongue as [iː] : Fr. *site* [sit].

Hence Fr. *qui* [ki] is not to be pronounced as Eng. *key*
[kɹi], nor Fr. *six* [sis] as Eng. *cease* [sɹis], nor Fr. *il* or *île*
[il] as Eng. *ill* [ɪl] or *eel* [ɹil], nor Fr. *pire* [piːr] as Eng. *peer*
[pɹiə] and [pɹɪə], nor Fr. *lire* [liːr] as Eng. *leer* [lɹiə] [lɹɪə], nor
Fr. *oui* [wi] as Eng. *we* [wɹi].[1]

----

[1] The French and English consonants in the examples, even though
represented by the same sign, are not absolutely identical. See under
Consonants.

The lips should be kept back against the teeth, though not necessarily further back than for the next vowel [e]. If they are allowed to protrude, as generally they do in English, they will cloud the sound. French [i] is clear and bright.

In unaccented syllables the [i] is often a shade less close than it is under the accent. The English-speaking student will, however, do well to neglect this fact for two reasons : first, because the close sound is not incorrect in this position ; secondly, because his natural tendency will be to relax the organs overmuch and to produce [ɪ], a sound which must be rigorously avoided in French. Compare Fr. *fini* [fini] and Eng. *finish* [fɪnɪʃ], Fr. *miracle* [mirɑːkl] and Eng. *miracle* [mɪɹəkl], Fr. *dissémination* [disemina'sjɔ̃] and Eng. *dissemination* [dɪsɛmɪnɛɪʃ n̩]. Still less may unaccented [i] be reduced to [ə]: compare Fr. *direct* [dirɛkt] with Eng. *direct* [dɪɹɛkt] [dəɹɛkt] [daɪɹɛkt].

Mid-Front-Narrow Vowel or Close e.

Phonetic sign : [e].

Traditional spellings :

      1. *é*, as in *pénétré* [penetre] ;

      2. *e*, as in *aimer* [ɛ'me], *et* [e] ;

      3. *ê*, as in *revêtu* [rəve'ty] [rəvɛ'ty] ;

      4. *ai*, as in *aurai* [ɔre], *gai* [ge] ;

      5. *ay*, as in *pays* [pei] ;

      6. *ais*, as in *je vais* [ʒə ve] [ʒə vɛ].

Articulation. The tongue being spread out presses firmly upwards against the molars, and sometimes comes into the gentlest possible contact with the gums. The jaws are normally a little less close together than for [i] : there is an interval between the upper and lower front-teeth wide enough to admit a finger-nail. The tip of the tongue touches the inside edge of the lower front-teeth. The corners of the mouth are drawn back, the lips being thus held against the teeth.

Explanation. This vowel is of the same quality as the [eː] in the Scotch pronunciation of *day* [deː]. Its supposed analogue in English is really a diphthong, the exact nature of which varies with the locality and even with the speaker. In the North of England it generally takes the form [ei], but the first, and often also the second, element shows a tendency to open more and more the further South we go. The diphthong thus becomes [èi] [ɛɪ] or even [ɛe]. The pronunciations [ɛɪ] [ɛe] are regularly heard in America and Australia.[1] The first element is, therefore, ordinarily a more or less open sound: *gay* [gèi] [gɛɪ] [gɛe]. Now [ɛ] is articulated with the tongue just touching the molars, and for the half-open sound [è] this contact becomes gentle pressure. The English diphthong, then, generally begins with the tongue touching or very gently pressing against the molars, and at the end of the sound the tongue either presses more firmly against the teeth [ɛe], or falls between the teeth and touches [ɛɪ] or presses against the gums [èi]. The movement of the tongue is accompanied by a movement of the lower jaw which can be observed with the aid of a mirror. For the vowel [e] the tongue must from the outset press firmly against the upper molars: *gai* [ge]. This vowel, in French, is—except occasionally in emphatic speech[2]— always short or half-long. The English-speaking student

---

[1] The uneducated classes in Australia carry the tendency still further, and pronounce [æɪ] [aɪ]: *cake* [kæɪk] [kaɪk]. This pronunciation, which is also one of the characteristics of Cockney, is still felt to be decidedly vulgar. It nevertheless threatens to spread both in London and in Australia, and has already become one of the vices of speech with which the teacher has to contend.

[2] See pp. 169 ff. and 180.

F.P.   B

must carefully avoid lengthening or diphthongizing it. Compare Fr. *été* [ete] and Eng. *eighty* [ɛɪtɪ].

The short English sound is [ɛ] : *petty* [pɛtɪ]. The English-speaker's tendency will be to substitute this [ɛ] for [e] in unaccented syllables with the spelling *e*, to pronounce, for example, *était* [etɛ] as·[ɛtɛ]. Such pronunciations are not unknown in vulgar French, but must be avoided by the student. It is true that the [e] of an unaccented syllable is often articulated with slightly-relaxed organs, but it remains clearly distinguishable from [ɛ].

It is helpful to note that this [e] is much more akin to the English [ɪ] than to [ɛ]. The vowels in *d'été* [dete] sound somewhat like those in *ditty* [dɪtɪ]. This is so because [ɪ] is formed with the tongue touching the upper gums lightly, and when the tongue is pressed against the teeth for [e] it bulges up till it comes very nearly into the same position.

The lips should not be allowed to deaden the sound by protruding.

Hence Fr. *mes* [me][1] differs widely from Eng. *may* [mɛɪ], Fr. *les* [le][1] from Eng. *lay* [lɛɪ], Fr. *ses, sais* [se][1] from Eng. *say* [sɛɪ], Fr. *dé* [de] from Eng. *day* [dɛɪ], Fr. *nez* [ne] from Eng. *nay* [nɛɪ]. Compare further the first vowel-sound in Fr. *maison* [me'zɔ̃] [mè'zɔ̃] and Eng. *mason* [mɛɪsn̩], Fr. *plaisir* [ple'ziːr] and Eng. *pleasure* [plɛʒə].

The traditional names of the letters *b, c, d, g, p, t* and *v* in French should be pronounced [be] [se] [de] [ʒe] [pe] [te] [ve] and not [bɛɪ] [sɛɪ] [dɛɪ], etc. The latter false pronunciation is inevitably suggested by the spellings 'bay,' 'say,' 'day,' etc., usually found in French grammars for English-speaking students.

---

[1] The plural article and the plural possessive pronouns are regularly heard with [e] in conversational French : [me] [te] [se] [le]. In the reading of poetry and elevated prose the open sound is preferred : [mɛ] [tɛ] [sɛ] [lɛ].

Mid-Front-Wide Vowel or Open e.

Phonetic sign : [ɛ].

Traditional spellings :

1. *è*, as in *collège* [kɔlɛɪʒ] ;
2. *e*, as in *tel* [tɛl], *valet* [valɛ], *il est* [il ɛ] ;
3. *ê*, as in *tête* [tɛ:t] ;
4. *é*, as in *chanté-je* [ʃɑ̃'tɛɪʒ] ;
5. *ei*, as in *peine* [pɛn] ;
6. *ai*, as in *chaise* [ʃɛɪz] ;
7. *aie*, as in *craie* [krɛ] ;
8. *ais*, as in *mais* [mɛ], *aimais* [ɛ'mɛ] ;
9. *ait*, as in *trait* [trɛ], *aimait* [ɛ'mɛ].

Articulation. The tongue being spread out touches gently the upper molars. The jaws are considerably wider apart than for [e], the interval between the lower and upper front-teeth being at least large enough to admit an ordinary lead-pencil. The tip of the tongue remains in contact with the lower front-teeth. The lips are not allowed to protrude.

Explanation. This vowel, requiring less tension of the organs, exists in English both as a long and as a short sound : *fare* [fɛɪ] [fɛə], *pair*, *pear* [pɛɪ] [pɛə], *sell* [sɛl], *net* [nɛt], *met* [mɛt]. Compare the French *faire* [fɛ:r], *paire* [pɛ:r], *selle* [sɛl], *net* [nɛt], *mettes* [mɛt].

The English sound is, however, not always given its real value. A mincing speaker will sometimes pronounce [è] or even [e] in place of the short [ɛ]: the mouth not being sufficiently opened, the tongue presses against the teeth ; *bed* [bɛd] then becomes [bèd] or [bed]. This pronunciation is more common in the South than in the North of England. For [ɛ] the mouth must be well opened and the tongue must not press against the teeth.

In its longer form this vowel occurs in English only

before the letter *r*. This letter, when not followed by a vowel, no longer represents a consonantal sound; it has been reduced to the vowel [ə] or has dropped away altogether. We say *air* [ɛɪ] [ɛɪə], but *airing* [ɛɪɹɪŋ] or [ɛɪəɹɪŋ]. The vowel [ə] must be rigorously avoided in similar positions in French: compare the French *air* [ɛːr] and *airain* [ɛˈrɛ̃].

Special care must be taken with a final [ɛ]. This sound never being final in English, the tendency is to produce a diphthong in that position. Observe then that *fait* is not to be pronounced [fɛə] or [fɛɪ] but [fɛ]—like the Eng. *fell* without the final consonant. Even here, there is need to repeat the warning: keep the organs of speech rigidly in the one position during the enunciation of a vowel.

In unaccented syllables [ɛ] must not be reduced to [ə]: compare Fr. *perspective* [pɛrspɛktiːv] and Eng. *perspective* [pəspɛktɪv] [pʊspɛktɪv].

Low-Front-Narrow Vowel or Close **a.**

Phonetic sign : [a].

Traditional spellings :

        1. *a*, as in *salle* [sal], *gage* [gaːʒ] ;

        2. *â*, as in *parlâmes* [parlam] ;

        3. *e*, as in *femme* [fam] ;

        4. *i*, as in *toi* [twa].

Articulation. The tongue being spread out touches gently the upper middle or back molars. The jaws are normally a little wider apart than for [ɛ]. The tip of the tongue remains in contact with the lower front-teeth. The corners of the mouth are slightly retracted, the lips being thus prevented from protruding.

Explanation. A certain confusion which exists among the *a*-sounds in English renders the explanation of this sound by analogy somewhat difficult. We may, however,

begin by distinguishing it both from the [ɑ] in *father*
[fɑːðə] and from the [æ] which is heard (in all but Northern
pronunciation) in *man* [mæn], *ash* [æʃ]. The English [ɑ]
approaches closely to the [ɑ] in *pas*, the French vowel
next to be defined : it is a more open sound than [a]. The
vowel [æ] differs little from a very open [ɛ], and is generally
heard as such by French ears that have not been trained
phonetically. In some of the most popular ' English
courses' for French students the learner is even directed
to pronounce *man* as '*menne*,' and our word *gentleman*
generally becomes in a French mouth [dʒɛntəlmɛn]. This
is, of course, seriously incorrect ; but it is no less incorrect
to substitute the English [æ] for the French [a]. The
latter sound lies between [æ] and [ɑ]. Now an intermediate sound is often heard in English : *e.g.* in *after*,
ask, class, demand; and as the first part of the diphthong in
high, I. Unfortunately the pronunciation of these and
other words in which the sound occurs is not stable, the
intermediate *a* being supplanted often, and especially in
the South of England and in Australia, by [ɑ] and sometimes, especially in the midland counties, by [æ]. The
existence of this middle English *a* is, therefore, not
recognized by Professor Viëtor. On the other hand,
Professor Hempl regards it as the standard in the words
given, and in many others.[1] The sound is identified
by Professor Hempl with the French [a], but it is generally
somewhat more open [à], being strictly equivalent to the
French vowel only when the latter occurs in unaccented
syllables. The English-speaker to whom this English
middle *a* is familiar can arrive at the French [a] by
increasing the tenseness of the organs of speech. In spite

[1] Professor Hempl is responsible for the English pronunciations in
the *International French-English and English-French Dictionary*
published by T. C. and E. C. Jack, London.

of the close analogy between this English [à] and the French [a] experience has shown that the English-speaking student is more inclined to carry over [æ] and [ɑ]. As [æ] is always short in English and [ɑ] usually long, the tendency is to substitute [ɑ] for [aː] and [æ] for [a], substitutions which are equally objectionable. Compared with [ɑ] the vowel [a] has a bright ring and sounds forward in the mouth: it differs from [æ] in being a decided *a*-vowel. The sound will lose its characteristic clearness if the lips are not held back to the teeth.

The student should, therefore, carefully distinguish Fr. *hache* [aʃ] from Eng. *ash* [æʃ], Fr. *patte* [pat] from Eng. *pat* [pæt], Fr. *panne*, [pan] from Eng. *pan* [pæn], Fr. *fade* [fad] from Eng. *fad* [fæd] ; and the vowel of Fr. *parc* [park], *part* [paɪr], *car* [kaːr], *carte* [kart] from that of Eng. *park* [pɑːk], *part* [pɑːt], *car* [kɑː], *cart* [kɑːt]. The *a* in *Paris* [pa'ri] resembles neither that in *starry* [stɑːɹɪ] nor that in *parry* [pæɹɪ]. Contrast also *Marie* [ma'ri] with *mar* [mɑː] and *marry* [mæɹɪ].

In unaccented syllables [a] must never be reduced to [ə] as [æ] and [ɑ] so often are in English : compare Fr. *marine* [marin] with Eng. *marine* [məɹiin], Fr. *adresse* [adrɛs] with Eng. *address* [ədɹɛs], Fr. *parade* [parad] with Eng. *parade* [pəɹeɪd].

Low-Back-Wide Vowel or Open a.

Phonetic sign : [ɑ].

Traditional spellings :

1. *a*, as in *passe* [pɑːs], *pas* [pɑ] ;
2. *â*, as in *marâtre* [marɑːtr] ;
3. *am*, as in *condamner* [kɔ̃'dɑ'ne] ;
4. *i*, as in *trois* [trwɑ].

Articulation. The tongue is drawn back a little from the front teeth and held as low as possible in the mouth.

The mouth is wide open, though not to the physical limit. The lips not being held back, the corners of the mouth are carried slightly forward by the opening of the jaws.

Explanation. This is essentially the common English vowel of *far*, *father*, produced with more open mouth. It is important to open the mouth well, because the orifice thus assumes a more circular form than is the case with the English sound, and the rounder opening gives the French vowel its distinctive character, that is, a sound slightly, but only slightly, akin to the rounded vowel [ɔ]. Great care must be taken not to exaggerate this kinship: the lips must not be consciously rounded, otherwise a sound closely resembling the vowel in *all* [ɒːl] will be produced, and this is to be avoided. All that is necessary for the correct articulation of the French [ɑ] is to pronounce the [ɑ] of *far* [fɑː] with the mouth wide open. With this slight difference the vowel of the following pairs of words is the same: Fr. *âme* [ɑːm], Eng. *arm* [ɑːm]; Fr. *pâte* [pɑːt], Eng. *part* [pɑːt].

The [ɑ] must not be lengthened when it is final: compare Fr. *pas* [pɑ] with Eng. *par* [pɑː], Fr. *tas* [tɑ] with Eng. *tar* [tɑː].

In Southern English this [ɑː] is sometimes diphthongized, the lower jaw rising a little as the sound comes to an end. This must be avoided in French.

Mid-Back-Wide Vowel or Open o.

Phonetic sign: [ɔ].

Traditional spellings:

      1. *o*, as in *comme* [kɔm], *port* [pɔːr];

      2. *ô*, as in *hôtel* [ɔtɛl], *rôti* [rɔti];

      3. *au*, as in *aurai* [ɔre];

      4. *u*, as in *pensum* [pɛ̃'sɔm], *album* [albɔm], *rhum* [rɔm].

Articulation. The tongue being drawn further back than for [ɑ] bunches up towards the soft palate : its tip sinks till it occupies a position just behind and not quite in contact with the bottom of the lower front gums. The corners of the mouth are thrust forward a little and the lips are slightly rounded.

Explanation. The tendency of the English-speaker is to identify this [ɔ], when short, with the *o* in *not* [nɒt]; when long, with the *o* in *cord* [kɒːd]. These sounds differ widely from the French. In producing the English vowels, which are the long and the short forms of the same sound, the tongue is not so far back in the mouth (its tip being just behind the intersection of the lower front teeth and gums), and the lips are idle. It is, therefore, much more open than the French [ɔ]. In French ears it sounds, as it really is, akin to the *a*-vowels. The English-speaking student must pay special heed to the position of the lips in pronouncing the French vowel.

A close approximation to [ɔ] is heard as the first element of the diphthong in the Southern English pronunciation of *note* [nɔot] [nɔʊt] and sometimes even as a long vowel in *more* [mɔː] [mɔːə], *door* [dɔː] [dɔːə].[1] This sound, how-ever, is a little closer than the French.

The following pairs of words may be compared : Fr. *note* [nɔt] and Eng. *not* [nɒt], Fr. *corde* [kɔrd] and Eng. *cord* [kɒːd], Fr. *sorte* [sɔrt] and Eng. *sort* [sɒːt], Fr. *sotte* [sɔt] and Eng. *sot* [sɒt], Fr. *vote* [vɔt] and Eng. *vote* [vɔot] [vɔʊt], Fr. *port* [pɔr] and Eng. *port* [pɔːt] [pɔoət], Fr. *Paul* [pɔl] and Eng. *Paul* [pɒːl].

An unaccented [ɔ] must not be reduced to [ə] : compare Fr. *morose* [mɔroːz] with Eng. *morose* [məɹoos], Fr. *possède* [pɔsɛd] with Eng. *possess* [pəzɛs], Fr. *Cologne* [kɔlɔɲ] with

---

[1] These words are also pronounced [mɔ̀oə] [dɔ̀oə] or [mɔ̀ʊə] [dɔ̀ʊə].

Eng. *Cologne* [kɔlɔon], Fr. *proportion* [prɔpɔrsjõ] with Eng. *proportion* [pɹəpɔɹʃn].

Mid-Back-Narrow Vowel or Close o.

Phonetic sign : [o].

Traditional spellings :

1. *o*, as in *dos* [do], *dossier* [do'sje] ;
2. *ô*, as in *hôte* [oːt] ;
3. *au*, as in *cause* [koːz] ;
4. *eau*, as in *peau* [po].

Articulation. The tongue being drawn considerably further back than for [ɔ] rises fairly close to the soft palate. The lips are energetically thrust forward and rounded : they now meet each other for at least one-third of their width on each side, leaving only a small oval aperture.

Explanation. French [o] is identical in quality with the long Scotch *o* : *no* [noː]. In English the treatment of close *o* is analogous to that of close [e] : thus [oː] becomes in the North of England [ou] and in the South [ðʊ] [ɔʊ] or even [ɔo]. The pronunciations [ɔʊ] [ɔo] are common in America and Australia. Vulgarly, particularly in Southern England and in Australia, this diphthong takes the form [æʊ] or [aʊ], *oh no!* being pronounced [æʊ næʊ]. Hence, in place of the simple vowel a diphthong is heard in English of which the stressed element is generally a more open sound, and the unstressed a sound varying between [o] and [u] : *boat* [boot] [boʊt]. During the enunciation of the English sound the lips and tongue change their positions : the shifting of the tongue can be easily felt, and the movement of the lips can be seen with the aid of a mirror. There will be a strong tendency to carry this practice over into French. This must be

corrected: the organs must be in position from the outset
and must retain the same positions throughout. The
position of both lips and tongue being one of high tension
much greater effort is demanded than in English. Care
must be taken not to lengthen a short [o].

Distinguish Fr. *côte* [koɪt] from Eng. *coat* [kout], Fr. *rose*
[roɪz] from Eng. *rose* [rouz], Fr. *beau* [bo] from Eng. *bow*
[bou], Fr. *sot* [so] from Eng. *so, sew* [sou], Fr. *chaud* [ʃo]
from Eng. *show* [ʃou], Fr. *dos* [do] from Eng. *dough* [dou],
Fr. *mot* [mo] from Eng. *mow* [mou], Fr. *eau* [o] from
Eng. *oh* [ou].

The vowel must be given its proper value in unaccented
syllables: compare Fr. *position* [pozisjɔ̃] with Eng. *position*
[pəzɪʃn̩], Fr. *opposition* [ɔpozisjɔ̃] with Eng. *opposition*
[ɒpəzɪʃn̩].

High-Back-Narrow Vowel or Close **ou.**

Phonetic sign: [u].

Traditional spellings:

>   1. *ou*, as in *tout* [tu];
>   2. *où*, as in *où* [u];
>   3. *oû*, as in *goût* [gu].

Articulation. The tongue is drawn back further than
for [o] and bunches up as close to the soft palate as
possible without creating consonantal friction. The lips are
energetically thrust forward and rounded, forming a still
smaller and now almost circular opening.

Explanation. This [u] is heard, in its long form, in the
Scotch pronunciation of *poor* [puːr]. The treatment of [u]
in English is analogous to that of [i], the High-Front-
Narrow vowel. The English sound which is commonly
supposed to correspond to [uː] is a diphthong of which
the first and stressed element is a more open sound: *true*

[ɹùu] [ɹʊu]. The positions of the lips and tongue when the English sound is begun are, therefore, not as extreme as those required for [u] and these organs only approach their extreme positions just as the sound ends. For the vowel [u] the tongue must be right back and the lips right forward from the outset, and they must retain these positions rigidly : *rouge* = [ruːʒ] and not, as the word is pronounced by English-speakers, [ɹʊuʒ].

The shorter English sound is the open vowel [ʊ]: *pull* [pʊl]. This sound, the High-Back-Wide vowel, is not used in French. The short French [u] requires the same lip and tongue positions as the long [uː]. Care must be taken not to lengthen a final [u].

Distinguish Fr. *coup* [ku] from Eng. *coo* [kʊu], Fr. *doux* [du] from Eng. *do* [dʊu], Fr. *chou* [ʃu] from Eng. *shoe* [ʃʊu], Fr. *tour* [tuːr] from Eng. *tour* [tuːə] [tʊuə], Fr. *route* [rut] from Eng. *root* [ɹʊut].

The vowel must be given its full value in unaccented syllables : compare the French pronunciation of *Touraine* [turɛn] with the English [tuɹɛın].

4. The Abnormal Oral Vowels.

The relations between the Abnormal and the Normal Oral Vowels may be indicated by means of the diagram :

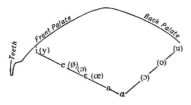

All four are Rounded Front-Vowels : [y] has the tongue-position for [i] and the lip-position for [u] ; [ø] the tongue-position for [e] and the lip-position for [o]; [ə] the tongue-position for [è] and the lip-position for [ò]; [œ] the tongue-position for [ɛ] and the lip-position for [ɔ].

High-Front-Narrow-Round Vowel or Close French u.

Phonetic sign : [y].

Traditional spellings :

       1.　*u*, as in *du* [dy] ;

       2.　*û*, as in *sûr* [syːr] ;

       3.　*eu*, as in *eus, eu* [y] ;

       4.　*eû*, as in *qu'il eût* [kil y].

Articulation.　The tongue is in the position for [i]: the lips are thrust forward and rounded as for [u].

Explanation.　This sound has no analogue in English. The tongue is placed to articulate the normal vowel of highest pitch; the lips are placed to articulate the normal vowel of lowest pitch : the result is an abnormal vowel of lower pitch than [i] but of higher pitch than any other abnormal vowel.

In the absence of phonetic hints this vowel usually gives the English-speaker much trouble.　Its formation, however, is so simple that he can arrive at an exact knowledge of the sound without the assistance of a teacher.　The best way to practise the sound, in the first instance, is to project the lips vigorously as for [u] and while keeping them in this position (if necessary with the aid of a mirror) to try and pronounce [i].　This will at first need an effort, because the tongue is normally drawn back when the lips are thrust forward.　The student must, therefore, make sure that his tongue does move forward into the position for [i].　If the tongue and lips are in the proper positions he cannot fail to produce the right sound.　But if, for instance, the tongue only reaches the position for [ɪ], a German sound, the vowel [ʏ] in *Hütte* [hʏtə], will be produced. Another way of arriving at the [y] is to place the tongue in the position for [i] and, while keeping it in that position, to project the lips as for [u]. Much practice will be required before the vowel can be produced instinctively. The exercises [u—y, u—y, u—y] and [i—y, i—y, i—y] are recommended : in the former the lips will remain stationary and the tongue will move from its extreme backward to its extreme forward position ; in the latter the tongue will be stationary and the lips will move from their extreme backward to their extreme forward position. When the sound has once been mastered, the positions of tongue and lips must be assumed simultaneously, that is, both tongue and lips must be thrust forward together. It is a common mistake of English-speaking students to produce [iʏ], the lips not being forward when the sound begins, and the tongue being drawn back a little as the lips are projected.

Mid-Front-Narrow-Round Vowel or Close eu.

Phonetic sign : [ø]

Traditional spellings :

            1. *eu*, as in *dieu* [djø] ;

            2. *œu*, as in *œufs* [ø] ;

            3. *eue*, as in *queue* [kø] ;

            4. *eux*, as in *eux* [ø].

Articulation. The tongue being in the position for [e] the lips are thrust forward and rounded as for [o].

Explanation. This is the abnormal vowel produced by combining the tongue position for the normal vowel of second highest pitch with the lip position for that of second lowest pitch.

There is no corresponding sound in English. The [ɐ] of *sir* [sɐː], *fur* [fɐː] must on no account be substituted for [ø].

The two sounds are quite different both in acoustic effect and in mode of articulation. The English vowel is formed with the tongue much further back and lower than for [e], and with the lips very slightly projected. In passing from [ɐ] to [ø] both tongue and lips move forward. The French sound demands considerable tension of the muscles towards the front of the mouth, while the English vowel is produced with relaxed organs.

Distinguish Fr. *queue* [kø] from Eng. *cur* [kɐː], Fr. *ceux* [sø] from Eng. *sir* [sɐː], Fr. *feu* [fø] from Eng. *fur, fir* [fɐː], Fr. *peu* [pø] from Eng. *per* [pɐː], Fr. *œufs, eux* [ø] from the vowel in Eng. *her* [hɐː].

Mid-Front-Half-Narrow-Round Vowel or Mute e.

Phonetic sign: [ə].

Traditional spellings:

    1. *e*, as in *je* [ʒə], *devoir* [dəvwaːr];

    2. *ai*, as in *faisant* [fəzɑ̃], *faisait* [fəzɛ].

Articulation. The tongue is in position for a half-open *e* [è] while the lips are thrust forward and rounded as for half-open *o* [ò].

Explanation. The so-called '*e* mute' is essentially a middle, or half-open, *eu*. In acoustic effect it is more akin to [ø] than to the open *eu* [œ] next to be described. In passing from [ø] to [ə] both tongue and lips are relaxed a little; in passing from [œ] to [ə] both tongue and lips advance. The tongue is in a position which it very often occupies in English in the first part of the diphthong that takes the place of [eː]: *day* [dèɪ], *pay* [pèɪ]; the lips are just a little more forward and rounded than for the vowel in the Southern English pronunciation of *door* [dɔː]; they often occupy the position for [ə] in the first part of the diphthong that takes the place of [oː]: *dote* [dòʊt].

The English weak vowel which is represented by the same sign [ə] must not be substituted for the French sound. It is really a relaxed form of the [ɐ] : compare *fur* [fɐː] and *sofa* [sɔʊfə]. Both these sounds are produced with the tongue further back and lower than for the French [ə] ; the forward movement can be felt in passing from the vowel in *fur* [fɐː] to the diphthong in *fay* [fèɪ]. The lips are idle in the English [ə], and almost idle in [ɐ] ; the forward movement of the lips can be observed in passing from the vowel in *fur* [fɐː] to that in the Southern pronunciation of *four* [fɔː], but for the French [ə] they must move a little further forward. It must never be forgotten that the so-called '*e* mute' is produced with rounded lips.

This vowel is always unaccented. If by any chance an accent should fall on an '*e* mute,' it is transformed, usually into [ø] ; sometimes, however, into [œ] : *faites-le* [fɛt lø].

Distinguish Fr. *ce, se* [sə] from Eng. *sir* [sɐː], Fr. *que* [kə] from Eng. *cur* [kɐː], Fr. *me* [mə] from Eng. *myrrh* [mɐː], the *te* in *je te dis* [ʒə tə di] from the *to* in the hastier pronunciation of *to-day* [tədɛɪ].

Mid-Front-Wide-Round Vowel or Open eu.

Phonetic sign : [œ].

Traditional spellings ·

      1. *eu*, as in *leur* [lœːr] [lœr] ;
      2. *œu*, as in *œuf* [œf] ,
      3. *ue*, as in *cueillir* [kœjiːr] ;
      4. *œ*, as in *œil* [œːj].

Articulation. The tongue is in the position for [ɛ] ; the lips are advanced and rounded as for [ɔ].

Explanation. The English vowel in *fur* [fɐː] approaches more closely in acoustic effect to [œ] than to [ə] and [ø].

This is so simply because the positions of the organs
in [ɐ] are more akin to those for [œ]. Still, neither the
effects nor the positions are identical. French [œ] requires
the tongue a little further forward and a little higher,
and a more active cooperation of the lips. Particular
attention should be paid to the lip-position.

Distinguish Fr. *cœur* [kœːr] from Eng. *cur* [kɐː], Fr.
sœur [sœːr] from Eng. *sir* [sɐː], Fr. *peur* [pœːr] from
Eng. *per* [pɐː], Fr. *meurs* [mœːr] from Eng. *myrrh* [mɐː],
and the vowel in *mœurs* [mœrs] [mœːr] from that in *purse*
[pɐːs]. Contrast the syllables of *heureux* [œrø] and *peureux*
[pœrø].

5. The Nasalized Vowels.

All the four nasalized vowels of modern French are
Mid-Wide or Low-Wide vowels. Their relation to the oral
vowels may be indicated by means of the vowel-diagram,
the sign [˜] placed over the vowel denoting that it is
accompanied by nasal resonance:

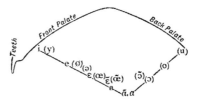

When a vowel is nasalized it does not cease to be
oral. Nasalization consists not in the substitution of one
chamber of resonance for another, but in the extension
of the chamber of resonance to include the nose-cavity.
It is effected merely by lowering the velum. The velum
is the movable end of the soft palate; from the middle
of it hangs the uvula which in shape resembles a small

stalactite. Both velum and uvula can be seen by opening
the mouth in front of a mirror. Behind the velum is
the passage leading up to the nose. While the velum
occupies a neutral position the breath from the lungs
naturally passes into both nose and mouth. The velum
plays an active part in the production of all the vowels
already described in rising and blocking the passage to
the nose. But as it discharges the same function for
all the English vowels (save in America)[1] its action has
hitherto been taken for granted. For the nasalized vowels
this function changes: the velum is now held down, leaving
the nasal passage more or less open. It plays a similar
part in the articulation of the common English nasal
consonants [m] and [n]. But as this movement of the
velum is never associated, in standard English, with vowel
articulation, some difficulty may at first be experienced
in producing the nasalized vowels. That serious mispronunciations may be avoided the student's attention
should be directed to the following two points:

(1) The velum must not be lowered so far as to touch
the tongue. This contact creates the end-consonant in
our word *long* [lɒŋ], and is responsible for very ugly
mispronunciations such as [frɑ̃ŋsɛ] [bjɛ̃ŋ] for [frɑ̃'sɛ]
français, [bjɛ̃] *bien*. Students who find it difficult to avoid
the consonant should practise such words with a long-
sustained nasal vowel. The mistake is generally caused
by the learner directing all his thought to the nasality of
the sound. He must not forget that the vowel is articulated
in the mouth, and must not aim at sending all the voice
through the nose. There is a simple practical method of

[1] The tendency to nasalize pure vowels, especially when followed
by a nasal consonant, is a feature of Australian pronunciation, but
the nasalization is often so faint that it cannot be detected by
untrained ears.

F.P.   C

testing whether the sound produced is a true nasal vowel or the consonant [ŋ]. Close the nostrils by pinching them with the thumb and first finger while the sound is being produced: if the consonant is articulated, the sound will be brought to a sudden end, because the consonant closes the mouth-passage.

(2) A nasal consonant following a nasalized vowel in the same syllable is never sounded in modern French. Its sole purpose is to indicate the nasal quality of the vowel: *chanter* is pronounced [ʃɑ̃'te], not [ʃɑ̃nte]; *tante* [tɑ̃ːt], not [tɑ̃ːnt]; *condition* [kɔ̃'disjɔ̃], not [kɔ̃ndisjɔ̃]; *bombe* [bɔ̃ːb], not [bɔ̃mb]. The nasalization must cease with the vowel-sound; in other words, the velum must rise and block the nasal passage when the lips and tongue proceed to articulate the following consonant. This habit can be acquired by practising such words as *danser, pendant, vampire* with a pause between each syllable: [dɑ̃—se], [pɑ̃—dɑ̃], [vɑ̃—piːr]. Mispronunciations would be much less common if such words were mentally pictured in their phonetic form.

6. The Nasalized Normal Vowels.

Three normal vowels appear in a nasalized form: the Mid-Front-Wide, the Mid-Back-Wide and the Low-Back-Wide. In each case the positions of the organs are slightly modified: for the Front-Nasal the mouth is a little more open, for the Back-Nasals a little less open than in articulating the corresponding oral vowels.

Mid-Front-Wide-Nasal Vowel or Nasal e.

Phonetic sign: [ɛ̃].

Traditional spellings:

      1. *en*, as in *bien* [bjɛ̃], *examen* [egzamɛ̃];

      2. *ein*, as in *sein* [sɛ̃];

3. *in*, as in *fin* [fɛ̃], *foin* [fwɛ̃] ;
4. *ing*, as in *poing* [pwɛ̃] ;
5. *im*, as in *impropre* [ɛ̃'prɔpr] ;
6. *ain*, as in *main* [mɛ̃] ;
7. *aim*, as in *faim* [fɛ̃].

Articulation. The organs are in position for [æ] save that the velum is lowered.

Explanation. Although this vowel is known as the 'nasal *e*' and is phonetically represented by [ɛ̃], it is strictly the nasalized form of the common English vowel in *cat* [kæt], *man* [mæn].

Care must be taken not to pronounce *fin*, *faim* [fɛ̃] as Eng. *fang* [fæŋ] ; nor *sein* [sɛ̃] as Eng. *sang* [sæŋ] ; nor *bain* [bɛ̃] as Eng. *bang* [bæŋ] ; nor *Rhin* [rɛ̃] as Eng. *rang* [ɹæŋ]. Both tongue and lip positions for the vowel in all these words, French and English, are identical : but while the vowel itself is nasalized in French it is followed by a nasal consonant in English.

The English-speaking student should pay particular heed to the pronunciation of words like *indu* [ɛ̃'dy], *pimpant* [pɛ̃'pɑ̃], *simple* [sɛ̃ːpl], *sainte* [sɛ̃ːt], *imberbe* [ɛ̃'bɛrb], *dinde* [dɛ̃ːd], *ingrat* [ɛ̃'gra], *inquiet* [ɛ̃'kjɛ]. The nasal vowel being here followed by a consonant, which is formed in the same or much the same way as one of the English nasal consonants [m] [n] [ŋ], the learner is specially liable to produce one of these consonants after the vowel. The spelling with *m* when the next letter is *p* or *b*, and with *n* when it is *t*, *d* or *g*, forcibly suggests the wrong pronunciation. The learner should, therefore, observe that the pronunciation of the words would not be affected if we substituted *m* for *n* and vice versa, writing *imdu*, *inberbe*, *imgrat*, *sinple*, etc.

Low-Back-Wide-Nasal Vowel or Nasal a.

Phonetic sign : [ɑ̃].

Traditional spellings :

1. *an*, as in *tant* [tɑ̃] ;
2. *am*, as in *champ* [ʃɑ̃] ;
3. *en*, as in *tente* [tɑ̃ːt] ;
4. *em*, as in *temps* [tɑ̃] ;
5. *aon*, as in *taon* [tɑ̃].

Articulation. The tongue is a little further back and the mouth not quite so open as for [ɑ], and the velum is lowered.

Explanation. This vowel is usually described as the nasalized form of the [ɑ] in *father*, or, what is the same thing, of the [ɑ] in *pas* with less open mouth. This description is incorrect : the tongue really occupies a position intermediate between the [ɑ] and [ɒ] positions. The series [ɑ] [ɑ̃] [ɒ] may be illustrated by the words Eng. *tar* [tɑː], Fr. *temps, tant* [tɑ̃], Eng. *taw* [tɒː].

The English-speaking student must be specially warned not to draw the tongue too far back. Common mispronunciations of *temps* are [tɒŋ] [tõ] [tɔ̃]. The latter mistake, [ɔ̃] for [ɑ̃], is often made by the provincial Frenchman, and occasionally by the Parisian. It is at best an affectation which should be carefully avoided by the foreigner.

The velum must not be allowed to touch the tongue : contrast Fr. *temps* [tɑ̃] and Eng. *tongs* [tɒŋz], Fr. *rang* [rɑ̃] and Eng. *wrong* [ɹɒŋ], Fr. *sang* [sɑ̃] and Eng. *song* [sɒŋ], Fr. *lent* [lɑ̃] and Eng. *long* [lɒŋ], Fr. *gant* [gɑ̃] and Eng. *gong* [gɒŋ].

Particular care must be taken not to pronounce a nasal consonant after the vowel in such words as *camper* [kɑ̃'pe], *campagne* [kɑ̃'paɲ], *cambrure* [kɑ̃'bryːr], *pampre* [pɑ̃ːpr], *ambre* [ɑ̃ːbr], *lanterne* [lɑ̃'tɛrn], *lampe* [lɑ̃ːp], *fantaisie* [fɑ̃'tɛzi], *antre* [ɑ̃ːtr].

Mid-Back-Wide-Nasal Vowel or Nasal o.

Phonetic sign : [õ].

Traditional spellings :

1. *on*, as in *ton* [tõ] ;
2. *om*, as in *tomber* [tõ'be].

Articulation. The organs are in position for [ɔ] save that the mouth is a little less open and that the velum is lowered.

Explanation. The projection of the lips will require an effort on the part of the English-speaking student.

He will be very apt to produce the nasal consonant [ŋ] after this vowel : contrast, both in this respect and in respect of the tongue and lip positions for the vowel-sound, Fr. *son* [sõ] and Eng. *song* [sɒŋ], Fr. *long* [lõ] and Eng. *long* [lɒŋ], Fr. *gond* [gõ] and Eng. *gong* [gɒŋ].

No nasal consonant must be heard after the vowel in words like *bombe* [bõːb], *ombre* [õːbr], *rompre* [rõːpr], *nombre* [nõːbr], *tomber* [tõ'be], *tondre* [tõːdr], *fondre* [fõːdr], *combination* [kõ'bina'sjõ], *compote* [kõ'pɔt], *conter* [kõ'te].

7. The Nasalized Abnormal Vowel.

Only one abnormal vowel appears in a nasalized form, the Mid-Front-Wide-Round vowel [œ]. The positions of the tongue and lips undergo no modification.

Mid-Front-Wide-Round-Nasal Vowel or Nasal u.

Phonetic sign : [œ̃].

Traditional spellings :

1. *eun*, as in *jeun* [ʒœ̃] ;
2. *un*, as in *un* [œ̃] ;
3. *um*, as in *humble* [œ̃ːbl].

Articulation. The lips and tongue are in position for [œ] and the velum is lowered.

Explanation. This vowel is not a nasalized *u*, although it is popularly known by that name. It is the nasalized form of the vowel in *heure* [œːr]. Hence the tongue is in the position for [ɛ] while the lips are projected and rounded as for [ɔ].

The provincial Frenchman often, and the Parisian sometimes substitute [ɛ̃] for [œ̃], confusing, for example, *brun* [brœ̃] and *brin* [brɛ̃]. To avoid imitating the mistake the student must be careful to project the lips.

A nasal consonant must not be pronounced after the nasal vowel and in the same syllable.

CHAPTER II

THE DIPHTHONGS (SO-CALLED)

A DIPHTHONG consists of two vowel-sounds pronounced in the same syllable, one of the vowels being usually subordinated to the other in point of both stress and duration. If the accent falls on the first vowel, the combination is called a *falling* diphthong ; if the second element is stressed, the combination is called a *rising* diphthong. The English diphthongs are all of the former kind. Thus in *time* [tɑɪm] [taɪm] [tæɪm], *boy* [bɔɪ], *eight* [ɛɪt] the second element [ɪ] is both short and weak.

If we were to be guided by traditional spelling we should conclude that French contained a large number of diphthongs and even triphthongs : for example, in *peur, peu, coup, cause, pain ; mieux, pied, fier, bien, miauler ; puis, lueur, nuage ; oui, ouate, oiseau, loin.* But such combinations of vowel-signs in a single syllable stand either for a single vowel-sound or for a consonant and a vowel. Thus in *peur* [pœːr], *peu* [pø], *coup* [ku], *cause* [koːz], *pain* [pɛ̃] two or three signs are used for one sound ; in *mieux* [mjø], *pied* [pje], *fier* [fjɛːr], *bien* [bjɛ̃], *miauler* [mjole], *puis* [pɥi], *lueur* [lɥœːr], *nuage* [nɥaːʒ], *oui* [wi], *ouate* [wat], *oiseau* [wazo], *loin* [lwɛ̃] the two or three vowel-signs represent a consonant, [j] [ɥ] or [w], and a single vowel.

The combinations of the so-called semi-vowels [j] [ɥ] [w] with a vowel approach very closely to falling diphthongs, and are often described as such. In standard French, however, the semi-vowels are really fricative consonants. Hence, in none of the above examples do we find two vowels in succession.

On the other hand two successive vowels are heard in *pays* [pei], *poète* [pɔɛit], *chaos* [kao], *noël* [nɔɛl], *fléau* [fleo], *réel* [reɛl], *prier* [prie], *brioche* [briɔʃ], *triage* [triaːʒ], *cruauté* [kryote], *bluet* [blyɛ], *éblouir* [ebluiːr], *trouer* [true]. Here, however, each vowel forms a separate syllable.

It will be found that whenever two or more vowel-signs follow each other the combination belongs to one of the three classes above described, and stands either for a single vowel-sound, or for a consonant and a vowel, or for two vowels forming distinct syllables. There are no diphthongs in modern French.

The letters *ou*, *i* and *u* followed by a vowel and preceded by a group of two or more consonants represent, with few exceptions (*e.g. pluie* [plɥi]), vowel-sounds having syllabic value. But if, being followed by a vowel, they are not preceded by a group of consonants, they regularly stand for the consonants [w] [j] and [ɥ]. Some hesitation, however, prevails in the treatment of verbs like *jouer*, *louer*, *secouer*, *fier*, *nier*, *tuer*, in the indicative present of which the letters in question necessarily represent a vowel : *je joue*, *je fie*, *je tue*, etc. In the phonetic texts published under the auspices of the International Phonetic Association, such words are transcribed with the consonantal sound : *jouer* [ʒwe], *nier* [nje], etc. Yet in deliberate and careful speech the vowel sound is certainly more usual. The words then gain a syllable : [ʒue] [lue] [səkue] [fie] [nie] [tye]. The influence extends to cognate words : *jouissance* [ʒuisɑ̃ːs], *louange* [luɑ̃ːʒ]. The student is strongly recommended to adopt the latter pronunciations, giving such verbs and their derivatives two full vowel-sounds on all occasions.

On the other hand, the endings *-tion*, *-sion* should, at least in conversation and in the reading of prose, be pronounced as single syllables [sjɔ̃] [zjɔ̃] : *émotion* [emosjɔ̃], *illusion* [ilyzjɔ̃] [illyzjɔ̃], in spite of the fact that they count as two syllables in verse.

CHAPTER III

THE CONSONANTS

1. The different kinds of Consonants.

Consonants are speech-sounds produced either by closing the breath-passage or by narrowing it to such an extent that the breath cannot escape without creating audible friction. In the former case they are known as *Stops* or *Explosives*; in the latter, as *Continuants* or *Fricatives*. When the breath is stopped at some point in the mouth, but allowed to pass through the nose, a particular kind of Stop-Consonant is produced which is described as a *Nasal*.

Consonant-sounds of either class (stops or continuants) may be accompanied by vibration of the vocal chords, and we thus arrive at the extremely important distinction between *Breath* (voiceless, surd) and *Voice* (voiced, sonant) consonants. In this respect the consonants tend to form pairs : [b] = voiced [p], d = voiced [t], [g] = voiced [k], [v] = voiced [f], [z] = voiced [s], [ʒ] = voiced [ʃ]. Even those voiced consonants which have no recognized voiceless counterpart in French and English, viz. [m] [n] [ɲ] [w] [ɥ] [j] [r] [l], may, as we shall see in Part II. Chapter IV., in certain circumstances, become voiceless or devocalized. It is very essential that the student should have a clear knowledge of the difference between a Breath and a Voice Consonant. The difference may be demonstrated in various ways.

A simple method is to place the palms of the hands over the ears and to utter first a long-sustained [s] or [f], and then a long-sustained [z] or [v], taking care in each case to avoid pronouncing a vowel-sound along with the consonant. With the voice consonants, just as with any vowel, a more or less forcible humming or buzzing is set up in the ears. If the process be repeated with the palm of the hand resting lightly on the scalp, or with the fingers placed gently on the outer larynx or 'Adam's apple,' a distinct quivering will be felt. This humming, buzzing or quivering is caused by the vibration of the vocal chords, and not by the force of articulation. On the contrary, Breath Consonants are normally produced with greater force than Voice Consonants, and are distinguished from the latter as *hard* from *soft* sounds.

2. The French and English Consonant-systems compared.

Of the twenty-one or twenty-two consonants that are found in French, all save three, [ɥ] [ɲ] [ʀ], belong nominally also to the English system. Yet scarcely a single consonant can be carried over from English to French without some modification. This lack of complete identity between consonant-sounds common to both languages is due chiefly to the comparative slackness of the organs of speech in English articulation. We produce our consonants, generally speaking, like our vowels, with the minimum of effort. If the sound requires the lips to be projected, as in the case of [w], we do not project them as energetically as the French; if it requires a backward position of the tongue, as in the case of [w], the tongue is not drawn so far back, if a forward position, as in the case of [t] or [l], the tongue is not thrust so far forward as in French; if it necessitates closure of the breath-passage, as in the case of [p] [t] and [k], we do not close it as energetically; if it consists in

friction of the breath, as in the case of [s] and [ʃ], the
friction in English is relatively faint; if it is a trilled sound,
[r], the trill approaches the vanishing point in English; if it
is a voiced consonant, such as [b] [v] [n] [ʒ], the vibration
of the vocal chords is weaker and briefer than in French.
The student must, therefore, be prepared for a greater
expenditure of effort than is demanded by his native speech.
Yet it would be a mistake to conclude that mere force will
transform an English consonant into a French one.   The
effort must be rightly directed, and this involves a detailed
discussion of each sound.

3. The Stops or Explosives.

(*a*) The general relations between the consonants of
this class may be shown by means of the following
diagram, the Voice-Stops being printed in fat type:

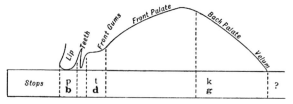

In the case of [p] and [b] the stoppage is produced by
bringing the lips together: they are, therefore, known as
Lip-Stops.   For [t] and [d] the point of the tongue is
applied to the teeth: they are, therefore, called Point-
Teeth-Stops.   The sounds [k] and [g] are Back-Stops,
being articulated by bringing the back part of the tongue
into contact with the back part of the palate.   The sound
[ʔ], which is very rare in French, is formed by closing the
glottis, and is known as the Glottal-Stop.

(*b*) A most important general distinction between the

French and English Breath-Stops lies in the fact that
these sounds are aspirates in English. In articulating the
English [p] [t] and [k], especially when they are followed
by an accented vowel, the breath is allowed to escape
with a slight gasp when the explosion takes place: *pie*
sounds [pʰaɪ], *tie* [tʰaɪ], *kite* [kʰaɪt]. This may be explained
as follows : The glottis (space between the vocal chords)
is wide open in articulating these consonants, and when
the explosion occurs the breath is forced out by the
lung-bellows just as in the process of breathing, but more
energetically. The explosion is, therefore, immediately
followed by a contraction of the chest which can be distinctly felt. At the same time the chords are being
brought together for the articulation of the vowel, and
the friction of the breath against them becomes audible
before the chords vibrate. Where the Stop is not followed
by a vowel the 'breathing' is less noticeable, because
the vocal chords remain apart.

This aspiration must be carefully avoided in French
by closing the glottis when the stop is made by the lips
(for [p]) or tongue (for [t] and [k]).[1] The mouth-cavity
then becomes air-tight, and the breath expelled is only
that contained in the mouth. The explosion is produced
by the muscles of the mouth and not, as in English, by
the lung-bellows. The glottis being closed, no gasp can
intervene between the explosion and the vibration of the
vocal chords. More breath escapes in producing the English
Breath-Stops, but the French Breath-Stops are much clearer
explosives than the English. The explosion is comparable
in English to a puff, in French to a sharp and 'dry'
detonation. The muscles of the mouth are much tenser
than in English.

[1] Professor Passy is of opinion that the breath is controlled without
actually closing the glottis.

(*c*) The general difference between the French and English Voice-Stops, [b], [d], [g], is of another kind. These sounds are not aspirates in either language. They are voiced consonants, and there is no interruption in the vibration of the vocal chords in passing to a following vowel. The voicing of these consonants in the two languages, however, differs in point of (i) volume, and (ii) duration.

The volume of the voice is much greater in French than in English, or, conversely, the buzzing which distinguishes the Voice-Stop from the Breath-Stop is much fainter in English than in French. The distinction between the two sets of sounds thus tends to be less marked in English, and, to prevent confusion, the English-speaker is apt to utter the Voice-Stop more forcibly than the Breath-Stop, thus reversing their normal relations. In French the voiced consonants [b] [d] [g] are pronounced with less force than their voiceless counterparts [p] [t] [k], and are very clearly distinguished from the latter by their richly sonorous character.

The voicing is not only less sonorous in English : it is also of shorter duration. Where the Voice-Stops begin a syllable, vocalization is often not set up until just as the explosion takes place ; and where they end one, vocalization frequently ceases just after the organs are brought together. In an exaggerated way this may be illustrated phonetically by the transcription of *bowl* as [ᵖbɔʊl] and of *sad* as [sædᵗ]. In French, vocalization must start with the closure when these consonants begin a syllable, and, where they end one, it must be well-sustained. The length of time during which vocalization takes place is actually very short, but it is perceptibly longer with [d] than with [g], and with [b] than with [d]. It thus varies in proportion with the size of the resonance-chamber.

The very sonorous character of the Voice-Stops in French has given rise to the opinion that they are really equivalent to [mb] [nd] and [ŋg] respectively. This view is inaccurate: the nasal passage is closed during the articulation of the Voice-Stops, and the buzz is not nasal.

Lip-Breath-Stop.

Phonetic sign : [p].

Traditional spellings :

      1. *p*, as in *pas* [pɑ], *cap* [kap] ;

      2. *pp*, as in *échapper* [eʃape] ;

      3. *b*, as in *absolu* [apsɔly].

Articulation. The lips and the glottis are closed simultaneously, the lips press firmly against each other and are then opened suddenly with a forcible but well-controlled emission of the breath.

This sound is not voiced. The tongue plays no part in its production, and may meanwhile prepare to articulate a following vowel or consonant.

Explanation. In French, as in English, the articulation of [p] may, in certain positions, consist either in only closing or in only opening the organs : thus in the English word *simple* [sɪmpl] the lips, which are already closed for [m], do not open and close again for [p], and in the French word *échappement* [eʃapmɑ̃] the lips do not open between [p] and [m]. Special cases of this kind will be explained in Part II. Chapter V., dealing with the transition from one sound to another.

The difference between the French [p] and the English lies (i) in the tenseness of the mouth-muscles, and (ii) in the control of the breath.

In producing the English [p] the lips are, as a rule, brought lightly together ; they retain their neutral position in other respects, hang loosely away from the teeth, and meet on their moist inner edges. The normal position of the lips in articulating the French [p] is somewhat more perpendicular; they are held a little closer to the teeth, and the contact, which is firm, takes place more towards the dry ridge. If [p] is immediately preceded or followed by a vowel in the same syllable, the exact position of the lips depends upon the vowel. Thus they are held close to the teeth and meet perpendicularly if the vowel is [i], but are projected and meet on their moist edges at a more or less sharp angle if the vowel is [o] or [u]. Generally speaking, they retain or assume as far as possible the position required for the vowel. But in all positions the lips must be tense and the contact firm.

The slight aspiration or gasp which often follows the English [p] must be carefully avoided in French by closing the glottis. (See § 3 (b), p. 44.)

Lip-Voice-Stop.

Phonetic sign : [b].

Traditional spellings :

        1. *b*, as in *bon* [bõ], *courbe* [kurb] ;

        2. *bb*, as in *abbé* [abe].

Articulation. The lips are closed with very gentle pressure, and the vocal chords are simultaneously made to vibrate, producing a resonance in the mouth-cavity. After a fraction of time the lips are suddenly opened with a slight emission of the breath.

The tongue is not actively concerned in producing this sound, and may prepare to articulate a following vowel or consonant.

Explanation. As in the case of [p] the articulation may consist in only closing or only opening the lips.

The position of the lips is again governed by the vowel of the syllable. The lips remain longer in contact, but are less tense than for [p]

The English-speaking student should (i) pay particular heed to the vocalization, which must be sonorous and well-sustained, and (ii) avoid producing [b] more forcibly than [p]. (See § 3 (c), p. 46.)

Point-Teeth-Breath-Stop.

Phonetic sign : [t].

Traditional spellings

1. *t*, as in *tâter* [tɑˈte] ,
2. *tt*, as in *chatte* [ʃat], *attaquer* [atake] ;
3. *th*, as in *rythme* [rɪtm] ;
4. *d*, as in *grand homme* [grɑ̃t ɔm], *vend-elle* [vɑ̃t ɛl]

Articulation. The point of the tongue is pressed firmly against the upper front teeth and gums[1] and the glottis closed ; the tongue is then drawn away suddenly with a forcible though well-controlled emission of the breath.

This sound is not voiced, and the lips, not being concerned in its production, may meanwhile prepare to articulate a following vowel or consonant.

Explanation. In French as in English [t] may, in certain positions, be formed by simply closing (*e g.* Eng. *matlock*, Fr. *matelot*) or simply opening (*e g.* Eng. *canteen*, Fr. *hanneton*) the organs.[2]

The difference between French [t] and English [t] consists (i) in the position of the tongue, (ii) in the tenseness

---

[1] There is contact between tongue and teeth all round, the sides of the back part of the tongue pressing against the lower face of the molars But as this lateral contact takes place also in English, attention need only be directed to the position of the tongue-point.

[2] See Part II. Chap. V. pp. 155 ff.

F.P. D

of the muscles of the mouth, and (iii) in the control of the breath.

For the English [t] the tongue is less forward in the mouth : its tip is curled upwards, and forms a contact with the gums at some distance from the teeth. This gives the consonant a relatively dull, flat sound. In French the point of the tongue must press against the teeth and the gums. Special attention should be given to the group [tr], the [r] not being allowed to influence the articulation of the [t].

The muscles of the tongue are much tenser in French, the contact firmer, the explosion sharper.

The glottis being left open in producing the English [t], a slight [h] is heard after the explosion, as in the case of [p]. This must be carefully avoided in French. (See § 3 (b), p. 44.)

Point-Teeth-Voice-Stop.

Phonetic sign : [d].

Traditional spellings :

      1.   *d*, as in *doux* [du], *fade* [fad] ;

      2.   *dd*, as in *addition* [adisjɔ̃].

Articulation. The point of the tongue is brought into very gentle contact with the upper front teeth and gums, and the vocal chords are at the same instant made to vibrate, producing a resonance in the mouth-cavity. After a fraction of time the tongue is drawn suddenly away with a slight emission of the breath.

The lips, playing no part in the production of this sound, may meanwhile prepare to articulate a following vowel or consonant.

Explanation. As in the case of [t] this sound may be formed by merely closing or merely opening the organs.[1]

[1] See Part II. Chap. V. pp. 155 ff.

French [d] differs from English [d] as follows:

(i) English [d], like English [t], is not a Point-Teeth-Stop: the tip of the tongue is curled upwards and meets the gums at some distance from the teeth. It must be further forward for the French [d], and must be applied to both teeth and gums.

(ii) In English, [d] is often produced with more force than [t]. It is, on the other hand, a softer sound than [t] in French.

(iii) The volume of the voice is greater, and its duration longer in French than in English. (See § 3 (c), p. 46.)

Back-Breath-Stop.

Phonetic sign: [k]

Traditional spellings:

1. *k*, as in *képi* [kepi];
2. *c*, as in *canot* [kano], *bac* [bak];
3. *cc*, as in *baccalauréat* [bakalɔrca];
4. *ch*, as in *archange* [arkɑ̃ːʒ];[1]
5. *cch*, as in *bacchante* [bakɑ̃ːt];
6. *q*, as in *aquarelle* [akwarɛl];
7. *qu*, as in *aquilon* [akilɔ̃], *laque* [lak];
8. *cqu*, as in *acquit* [aki];
9. *x*, as in *Xerès* [kerɛːs], *excès* [ɛksɛ];
10. *g*, as in *long exil* [lɔ̃k egzil].

Articulation. The back part of the tongue is raised and pressed firmly against the palate, and at the same time the glottis is closed. The tongue is then suddenly drawn away from the palate with a forcible but well-controlled emission of the breath.

---

[1] But *architecte* [arʃitɛkt], *patriarche* [patriarʃ], *archer* [arʃe], etc.

This sound is voiceless. The lips, not being actively concerned, may meanwhile prepare to articulate a following consonant or vowel.

Explanation. French [k] differs from English [k] in much the same way as French [p] and [t] differ from English [p] and [t]. The following points should be noted:

(i) In both French and English, the exact point of contact between tongue and palate depends upon the vowel of the syllable. Thus it is considerably further forward with [i] than with [u]. In French, however, it is always further forward than in English.

(ii) The contact is much less vigorous in English. English [k] is a dull, flat, soft sound; whereas French [k] is a very clear, hard and 'dry' explosive, articulated with energy.

(iii) English [k], like English [p] and [t], is articulated with open glottis, and is followed by a slight aspiration which must be carefully avoided in French. (See § 3 (b), p. 44.)

Back-Voice-Stop.

Phonetic sign: [g].

Traditional spellings:

> 1. *g*, as in *gond* [gɔ̃], *suggérer* [sygʒere];
> 2. *gg*, as in *couagga* [kwaga];
> 3. *gu*, as in *guerre*, *guère* [gɛːr], *bague* [bag];
> 4. *x*, as in *exercice* [egzɛrsis];
> 5. *c*, as in *second* [səgɔ̃].

Articulation. The back part of the tongue is raised and pressed gently against the palate, and at the same moment the vocal chords vibrate, producing a resonance in the small cavity behind the point of contact. After a fraction of time the tongue is suddenly drawn away from the palate with a slight emission of the breath.

The lips, not being concerned in the production of this sound, may meanwhile prepare to articulate a following vowel or consonant.

Explanation. French [g] differs from French [k] in the same way as [b] and [d] differ from [p] and [t]. The English-speaking student should be careful (i) to see that the voice is well-sustained and sonorous, and (ii) to avoid pronouncing [g] more forcibly than [k]. (See § 3 (c), p. 46.) At the same time the [g] of standard French, being articulated further forward in the mouth and with greater tenseness of the organs, is a harder sound than the English [g].

Glottal-Stop.

Phonetic sign : [ʔ].

Traditional spelling : None.

Articulation. The vocal chords are brought together and suddenly reopened with a slight explosion.

Explanation. This sound, which forms an integral part of the German consonantal system, occurs in French only in rare cases which will be mentioned in Part II. Chap. V. pp. 162 and 164.

It is found quite exceptionally in English in an exaggerated form : *e.g.* in *Whatever is that?* pronounced with special stress on the syllable *ev* [wɒtʔɛvəɹ ɪz ðæt] ; and in *Shoulder arms!* with stress on the second word [ʃʊuldə ʔɑmz]. In some Northern dialects it often replaces a Point-Stop : thus the people of Glasgow pronounce *water* [wɒʔər].

In German, English and French, it occurs only before a

vowel.   The vowel then, instead of being begun smoothly, is attacked with a slight 'catch.'

4. The Nasal Consonants.

The general relations between these consonants and the Stops already described may be indicated by the diagram :

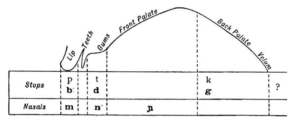

Being all three voiced the nasals are printed in fat type. [m] is a Lip-Stop and [n] a Point-Teeth-Stop.   For [ɲ] the contact takes place between the middle part of the tongue and the hard palate : it may, therefore, be called a Mid-Palate-Stop.

Nasal-Lip-Stop.

Phonetic sign : [m].

Traditional spellings :

      1.   *m*, as in *mal* [mal], *lame* [lam] ;
      2.   *mm*, as in *comment* [kɔmɑ̃], *femme* [fam].

Articulation.   The nasal passage being left open by keeping the velum lowered, the lips are closed with very gentle pressure, and the moment they meet the vocal chords vibrate, producing a resonance in the mouth and nose. After a fraction of time the lips are opened, but with little emission of breath through the mouth.

The tongue is not actively concerned, and may meanwhile prepare to articulate a following vowel or consonant.

Explanation. As with the other lip-stops the position of the lips will be modified by a vowel in juxtaposition with [m] and in the same syllable.

This consonant is very sonorous. Vocalization must begin with the closing of the lips, and it must be well-sustained when the [m] is final. In English the voice is sometimes faint.

In other respects there is no appreciable difference between the French and the English sounds.

Nasal-Point-Teeth-Stop.

Phonetic sign : [n].

Traditional spellings :

1. *n*, as in *non* [nɔ̃], *cane* [kan] ;
2. *nn*, as in *canne* [kan], *donner* [dɔne] ;
3. *mn*, as in *automne* [ɔtɔn], *condamner* [kɔ̃'dɑ'ne].

Articulation. The nasal passage being left open by keeping the velum lowered, the point of the tongue is brought into gentle contact with the upper front-teeth and gums, and at the same moment the vocal chords vibrate, producing a resonance in both mouth and nose. After a fraction of time the tongue is suddenly drawn away from the teeth and gums, but there is little or no emission of breath through the mouth.

The lips, not being actively concerned, may meanwhile prepare to articulate a following vowel or consonant

Explanation. The position of the tongue is precisely the same as for [t] and [d]. The sound should, therefore, not be articulated like the English [n] with the tip of the tongue applied to the gums alone

Attention should be paid to the vocalization, which must begin with the formation of the stop, and, when the consonant is final, be well-sustained. The English [n] is not always quite as sonorous as the French.

Nasal-Mid-Palate-Stop.

Phonetic sign : [ɲ].

Traditional spellings :

1. *gn*, as in *règne* [rɛɲ], *agneau* [aɲo] ;
2. *ign*, as in *oignon* [ɔɲɔ̃], *encoignure* [ɑ̃ˈkɔɲyːr].

Articulation. The nasal passage being left free by keeping the velum lowered, the mouth being slightly open and the tip of the tongue resting against the inside of the lower front-teeth, the face of the tongue, about midway between tip and root, is pressed gently against the hard palate, and at the same moment the vocal chords are made to vibrate, producing in the mouth and nose a resonance which must be sustained until the tongue is withdrawn from the palate.

The lips, not being concerned in the formation of this sound, may meanwhile prepare to articulate a following vowel or consonant.

Explanation. There is no corresponding nasal in English : we pronounce *cañon* [kænjən] or [kænjɒn] ; cf. French *manière* [manjɛːr], *panier* [panje]. English-speakers are, therefore, very apt to substitute [nj] for [ɲ]. This substitution is sometimes made by the French themselves, even by Parisians. It should be avoided, by keeping the tongue in contact with the lower front-teeth. A large part of the face of the tongue must come into contact with the palate, but the point must be held away from the gums.

5. The Continuants or Fricatives.

The diagram being extended to include the Fricatives, all of which, except [f] [s] [ʃ] and [h], are normally voiced, will appear as follows :

	Lip	*Teeth*	*Gums*	*Front Palate*		*Back Palate*	*Velum*
Stops	p b	t d			k̯ g		?
Nasals	m̄	n		ɲ			
Fricatives	w ɥ	f v	l s z ʃ ʒ r̗	ɥ̗ j		w̃ R	h

The Lip-Fricatives [w] and [ɥ] are formed with the cooperation of the tongue ; the position of the latter is suggested by the dotted signs : [w] requires the tongue in its back-position for [u], [ɥ] requires it in its front-position for [i]. Hence [w] is called the Lip-Back and [ɥ] the Lip-Front Fricative. [f] and [v], being formed by the contact of the lower lip with the upper teeth, are Lip-Teeth Fricatives. For [l] the tip of the tongue touches the teeth, and the friction is produced at the sides : it is the Point-Teeth-Lateral Fricative. [s] [z] [ʃ] and [ʒ], being formed by sending the breath along a groove in the blade of the tongue, and against the teeth, are Teeth-Blade consonants. [r] is a Point-Trill ; [R] a Uvula-Trill. [j] has the front part of the tongue brought close to the front part of the palate, and is called a Front-Fricative. [h], being produced by the friction of the breath passing through the glottis, is the Glottal-Fricative.

Lip-Back-Voice-Fricative.

Phonetic sign : [w].

Traditional spellings :

        1. *w*, as in *wallon* [walõ], *tramway* [tramwe] ;

        2. *wh*, as in *whist* [wist], *whig* [wig] ;

        3. *u*, as in *équateur* [ekwatœːr], *lingual* [lɛ̃ˈgwal] ;

        4. *ou*, as in *oui* [wi], *ouest* [wɛst] ;

        5. *o*, as in *toi* [twa], *point* [pwɛ̃], *moyen* [mwajɛ̃],
             poêle [pwaːl] [pwɑːl].

Articulation. The lips being projected still further than
for the vowel [u] and contracted, with tenseness of the
muscles, to form a very small round aperture, and the
tongue being drawn back as for [u], the vocal chords are
instantly made to vibrate, and the organs at once proceed
to form the following vowel.

Explanation. This consonant is very closely allied to
the vowel [u], and is for that reason sometimes called a
semi-vowel. Care should be taken not to pronounce it as
a vowel : it is uttered with the vowel by which it is followed
in one emission of breath, the two sounds together bearing
one even stress-beat and forming one syllable.[1]

It differs considerably from the English [w] in *win* [wɪn],
west [wɛst]. The organs are much tenser in French, the
lips being much further forward and much more contracted,
and the tongue higher and further back in the mouth. It
is still more unlike the voiceless lip-fricative in *whence*
[ẘɛns] [hẘɛns]. The friction of French [w] is faint, and
is often drowned by the voice.

[1] See *Diphthongs*, p. 39.

Lip-Front-Voice-Fricative.

Phonetic sign : [ɥ].

Traditional spelling :

> *u*, as in *huit* [ɥit], *nuance* [nɥãːs].

Articulation. The tongue having assumed the position for [y], and the lips a still more forward and contracted position, the vocal chords are instantly made to vibrate, and the organs at once proceed to form the following vowel.

Explanation. This consonant is related to the vowel [y] just as [w] is to [u], and, like [w], is sometimes called a semi-vowel. Like [w], too, it belongs to the same syllable as the vowel by which it is followed, both sounds being produced with one and the same emission of breath.

The voice often prevents any friction being heard.

There is no sound in English that corresponds even remotely to [ɥ], and, although its acquisition presents no insuperable difficulty, it is nearly always pronounced very badly by English-speakers. The vowel [y] must be first mastered, and should be readily produced before the consonant is attempted.

The English-speaking student needs to be specially cautioned against substituting [w] or [u] for [ɥ]. The initial of *huit* [ɥit] must be carefully distinguished from that of *oui* [wi], and *lui* [lɥi] must not be confounded with *Louis* [lui] [lwi]. Such mispronunciations shock a French ear, and are much more easily avoided than is generally believed. Attention must be paid to the position of the tongue : for both sounds in the group [ɥi] the tongue occupies the same position, viz. that for [i], whereas in the group [wi] it occupies first its extreme backward and then its extreme forward vowel-position. Hence in [ɥi] the *tongue remains stationary*, the change from consonant to vowel being produced by the backward movement of the lips alone : in [wi] we have the same backward movement of the lips, but the *tongue moves forward.* When [ɥ] is followed by some other vowel than [i] the tongue moves *backward*; when [w] is followed by some other vowel than [i] the tongue still always moves forward.

The learner should never forget that to produce [ɥ] he must thrust both tongue and lips right forward.

Lip-Teeth-Breath-Fricative.

Phonetic sign : [f].

Traditional spellings :

1. *f*, as in *fou* [fu], *if* [if] ;
2. *ff*, as in *affaire* [afɛːr], *gaffe* [gaf] ;
3. *ph*, as in *phase* [fɑːz], *épitaphe* [epitaf].

Articulation. The lower lip being applied firmly against the upper teeth, a stream of breath is forced out between lip and teeth. The upper lip is slightly raised to avoid contact with the lower.

The tongue, not being actively concerned, may meanwhile prepare to articulate a following sound.

Explanation. In English, [f] often degenerates into something very like a stop, little or no friction being heard. French [f], which is a decided fricative, may, however, be regarded as equivalent to a carefully uttered English [f].

Lip-Teeth-Voice-Fricative.

Phonetic sign : [v].

Traditional spellings :

1. *v*, as in *vie* [vi], *cave* [kaːv] ;
2. *w*, as in *wagon* [vagɔ̃].

Articulation. The vocal chords being made to vibrate, the lower lip is brought at once into contact with the upper teeth, the breath being then forced out between lip and teeth. The upper lip is slightly raised.

The tongue may meanwhile prepare to articulate a following sound.

Explanation. This sound does not differ appreciably from a careful English [v] Care, however, must be taken in vocalizing a final [v] In English the voice often ceases the moment the lip meets the teeth · *cave* then almost sounds [kɛɪvᶠ] In French the resonance must be sustained The lips should not be pressed firmly against the teeth as for [f]

Point-Teeth-Lateral-Voice-Fricative.

Phonetic sign [l]

Traditional spellings :

1   *l*, as in *lait* [lɛ], *mal* [mal] ;
2   *ll*, as in *allure* [alyːr], *malle* [mal]

Articulation. The tongue assumes exactly the same position as for [t] [d] and [n], save that a narrow opening is left on each side between the tongue and the molars. At the same moment the vocal chords are set vibrating, and the breath is expelled through the lateral openings.

The lips, not being actively concerned, may meanwhile prepare to articulate a following sound

Explanation. The English [l] is produced, like English [t] [d] [n], with the tip of the tongue against the gums at some distance from the teeth , the sound, being thus carried further back in the mouth, has a dull, deep tone as compared with the French [l]. The difference is particularly noticeable when the [l] is final, but it is in all positions greater than that between French and English point-stops The English-speaker must, therefore, be very careful to see that the point of the tongue is in contact with the upper front-teeth.

It is no less important for him to note the lateral position of the tongue. For the French [l] the tongue is spread out and presses upwards against the molars. In English it is

contracted into the shape of a spoon and falls inside the
teeth.   Hence the teeth cannot be brought together in
French, as they can in English, while the tongue retains
the position for [l].

Teeth-(Narrow) Blade-Breath-Fricative.

Phonetic sign : [s].

Traditional spellings :

1. *s*, as in *source* [surs], *fils* [fis] ;
2. *ss*, as in *bossu* [bɔsy], *masse* [mas] ;
3. *c*, as in *ciel* [sjɛl], *place* [plas] ;
4. *ç*, as in *façade* [fasad] ;
5. *sc*, as in *scie* [si], *fasce* [fas] ;
6. *x*, as in *soixante* [swasɑ̃ːt], *dix* [dis], *exprès*
   [ɛksprɛ] ;
7. *t*, as in *nation* [nɑˈsjɔ̃], *péripétie* [peripesi].

Articulation.   The jaws being very close together, the tip
of the tongue touches lightly the lower front-teeth, its face
is raised towards the upper front-gums, its sides press
firmly against the upper molars : a narrow groove is formed
along the centre of the tongue, and the breath being forced
along this groove strikes against the front-teeth and produces a sharp hissing sound.

This consonant is voiceless.   The lips are generally held
fairly close to the teeth, but if the [s] is followed by a
rounded vowel they may be protruded before the completion of the consonant.

Explanation.   For the English [s] the tongue is further
back in the mouth, and points up towards the gums behind
the upper front-teeth ; the muscles being relaxed, the groove
is wider and the resulting sound less clear.   The English-
speaking student must, therefore, be careful to keep the
muscles tense, the groove narrow and the point of the tongue
touching the lower front-teeth.

English [s] is produced with less pressure than English [z]; in French the normal relations are preserved, the voiceless [s] being a hard, the voiced [z] a soft consonant.

Teeth-(Narrow) Blade-Voice-Fricative.

Phonetic sign : [z].

Traditional spellings :

1. *z*, as in *zèle* [zɛl], *gaz* [gɑːz] ;
2. *zz*, as in *lazzi* [lazi] ;
3. *s*, as in *générosité* [ʒenerozite], *base* [bɑːz] ;
4. *x*, as in *dix hommes* [diz ɔm], *Xanthe* [gzɑ̃ːt].

Articulation. The vocal chords being made to vibrate, the tongue assumes the same position as for [s], save that the pressure is reduced and the groove wider.

Explanation. French [z] differs from English [z] in the position of the tongue, and in the volume and duration of the voice. French [z] is a very sonorous consonant. The voice should be heard while the tongue is assuming its position, and must be well-sustained when the [z] is final. In English a final [z] often approaches [zˢ]: *phase* [fɛɪzˢ].

Teeth-(Broad) Blade-Breath-Fricative.

Phonetic sign : [ʃ].

Traditional spellings :

1. *ch*, as in *cher* [ʃɛɪr], *vache* [vaʃ] ;
2. *sh*, as in *shako* [ʃako] ;
3. *sch*, as in *schisme* [ʃism].

Articulation. The mouth being almost closed and the lips slightly projected in the form of a trumpet-bell, the tongue is drawn back a little from the position for [s], its point and face are raised close to the gums and front palate, its sides press against the upper molars and gums, producing a broad groove along the front part of the blade : the breath is then forced vigorously along the groove, and strikes against the front teeth.

The sound is voiceless.

Explanation. English [ʃ] in *shine* differs considerably from the French sound, the difference being due to the slackness of the muscles of the tongue, the more backward position of the tongue, the feebleness of the breath-emission and the neutral position of the lips.

French [ʃ] is a hard consonant produced with greater pressure than its voiced counterpart [ʒ]. The friction is more emphatic than in English. The degree in which the lips are projected is not constant; but they are never quite idle.

Teeth-(Broad) Blade-Voice-Fricative.

Phonetic sign: [ʒ].

Traditional spellings:

    1. *j*, as in *jour* [ʒuːr];

    2. *ge*, as in *geôle* [ʒoːl], *gageure* [gaʒyːr], *juge* [ʒyːʒ];

    3. *g*, as in *gigot* [ʒigo], *largeur* [larʒœːr].

Articulation. The vocal chords being set in vibration, the organs assume the positions for [ʃ] with slight modification due to diminished tenseness of the muscles.

Explanation. The English [ʒ] in *measure* [mɛʒə], *leisure* [lɛʒə] is far from equivalent to the French [ʒ]. The latter requires a more forward position of the tongue, more emphatic friction and much more generous vocalization. The vocal chords vibrate as the tongue is assuming its position, and the buzz must be well-sustained when the consonant is final: Fr. *cage* [kaːʒ] must not be pronounced [kaːʒ']. The tongue must not be pressed firmly against the palate as with [ʃ].

The [ʒ] is not modified by a preceding [d]. Compare the English words *adjective, adjacent,* with the French *adjectif, adjacent.* The syllabication of the English words is [ædʒ-ək-tɪv] [ə-dʒɛɪ-sənt], that of the French [ad-ʒɛk-tɪf] [ad-ʒa-sũ]. In English [d] and [ʒ] are mutually modified by their combination in the same syllable: in French the sounds are separated and retain their individual values.

Point-Trill-Voice-Fricative.

Phonetic sign [r].

Traditional spellings

1. *r*, as in *rare* [rɑːr], *ver*, *vers*, *vert* [vɛːr],
2. *rr*, as in *carreau* [karo], *verre* [vɛːr],
3. *rh*, as in *rhume* [rym], *rhum* [rɔm];
4. *rrh*, as in *arrhes* [aːr], *catarrhe* [kataːr].

Articulation. The point of the tongue is turned upwards and brought loosely against the angle formed by the front gums and the hard palate: the vocal chords are then made to vibrate, and the breath being forced out between the tongue and the gums sets the tongue vibrating As it vibrates it strikes rapidly against the gums

The lips, not being actively concerned, may meanwhile prepare to articulate a following vowel or consonant.

Explanation In English this [r] must be regarded as dialectal it is heard regularly only in Ireland and Scotland, though its use as an initial in the North of England is not uncommon. Elsewhere (in the South of England, in America and in Australia) [ɹ] alone is heard. This [ɹ] is regularly formed with the same tongue-position as [r] but without the trill: it is subject to slight variations, but is normally a mere fricative, like [v] If *bevy* [bɛvɪ] be compared with *berry* [bɛɹɪ] it will be found that the tongue strikes against the angle of the gums for [ɹ] in much the same way as the lip strikes the teeth for [v]. The English [ɹ], save occasionally in the North of England, is pronounced only before a vowel rat [ɹæt], *tray* [tɹɛɪ], *far away* [fɑːɹ əwɛɪ] In other positions it has been lost

altogether in the South of England and in Australia, though
its place is sometimes taken by the vowel [ə] : *far* [fɑː], *farm*
[fɑːm], *bird* [bʊːd], *pair* [pɛː] or [pɛɪə], *fire* [faɪə]. In the
North of England when *r* follows a vowel the tongue is
curled upwards towards the gums, but often fails to form a
contact with them ; the vowel-sound is then modified, but
no consonant is heard : these pronunciations may be indicated by placing [ɹ] over the vowel : *part* [pɑ̇ːt], *third* [θ̇ʊ̇ːd].
The final [ɹ] is treated in a similar way in America, but the
tongue being here curled further back towards the hard
palate, the modification of the vowel is more emphatic.

There are several species of *r* in French. The tongue-
point [r] is the only one admitted by the 'Conservatoire de
Musique et de Déclamation,' which fixes the standard for
artistic singing and elocution in Paris ; and is regularly
heard on the stage of the Comédie Française. It is very
common among the educated classes in other parts of
France. But it is not the characteristic Parisian *r*. The
latter is known as the 'uvular *r*,' or 'r grasseyée,' and is
represented phonetically by the sign [ʀ]. It is articulated as
follows : The point of the tongue is curved downwards and
pressed against the inside of the lower front-teeth, the
back part of the tongue is slightly raised, and the velum
(pendant end of the soft palate) lowered until the uvula
lies forward on the tongue : the vocal chords are then set
vibrating, and the breath being expelled sets, in some cases,
the uvula, in others, the back of the tongue and the contracted edges of the throat in vibration. [ʀ] which, like [r],
is thus normally a trilled consonant, sometimes degenerates
into an ordinary fricative indistinguishable from the *g* in the
German word *Wagen*, when the latter is pronounced as a
fricative and not as a back-stop. This modification, which
is indicated by the sign [ʁ], is considered faulty.

It is a mistake to imagine that the 'uvular *r*' is an indis-

pensable mark of good French pronunciation, or even that it
is the only *r* heard in the streets of Paris It is not recommended by any of the authorities. Moreover, the native-born
Parisian, who uses the [ʀ] himself, will not detect anything
peculiar in the tongue-point [r], correctly produced. The
French [r] must be trilled, but not forcibly. An emphatic [r]
or [ʀ] is either vulgar, or, like the Irish [r] in English, dialectal.

In French, the *r* is sounded as a rule in all positions: compare Fr. *marche* [marʃ] and Eng. *march* [maːtʃ], Fr. *car* [kaːr]
and Eng. *car* [kaː], Fr. *pour* [puːr] [pur] and Eng. *poor* [puːə]
[puuə], Fr. *pire* [piːr] and Eng *peer* [piːə] [piiə], Fr. *partie*,
parti [parti] and Eng. *party* [paːti], Fr *personne* [pɛrsɔn] and
Eng.*person* [pɐsṇ]. A final *r* is, however, not pronounced (i) in
infinitives of the 1st conjugation, *e.g. trouver* [truve], *fier* [fie];
(ii) in all but monosyllabic nouns and adjectives in *-er* and *-ier*,
except *amer* [amɛir], *e g.archer* [arʃe], *danger*[dɑ̃ʒe],*léger*[leʒe],
ménager [menaʒe], *rentier* [rɑ̃'tje], *chapelier* [ʃapəlje], *premier*
[prəmje], *altier* [altje], but *fer* [fɛir], *cher* [ʃɛir], *fier* [fjɛir]; (iii)
in *monsieur* [məsjø], *messieurs* [me'sjø], *volontiers* [vɔlɔ̃'tje],
and many proper names, *e.g. Tanger* [tɑ̃'ʒe], *Poitiers* [pwatje]

Front-Voice-Fricative.

Phonetic sign : [j].

Traditional spellings :

      1. *i*, as in *bien* [bjɛ̃], *dieu* [djø] ,

      2. *y*, as in *yeux* [jø], *foyer* [fwaje] ;

      3 *il*, as in *émail* [emaːj], *bail* [baːj] ;

      4. *ille*, as in *paille* [paːj], *fille* [fiːj]

Articulation. The tongue occupies the position for [i],
save that the blade is brought right up to the palate. The
vocal chords vibrate, and the breath is expelled between
palate and tongue

The lips may meanwhile prepare to articulate a following
vowel.

Explanation. The sound being closely related to [i] is sometimes called a semi-vowel. It differs little from the English [j] in *yes* [jɛs] [jɪs], though the muscles of the tongue are usually somewhat tenser in producing the French sound. The latter should not be sustained, and the friction should be faint.

[j] has supplanted the 'liquid *l*' [λ] save in the South of France and Switzerland. Pronunciations with [λ], constantly recommended by Littré, must now be regarded as dialectal.

Glottal-Breath-Fricative.

Phonetic sign : [h].

Traditional spelling : *h*, as in *aha !* [ɑhɑ].

Articulation. The vocal chords are brought close together, and the breath is expelled between them with audible friction and gradually increasing force, until the following vowel is heard.

Explanation. In standard French [h] is produced only under the influence of emotion : it is thus heard regularly in interjections such as *oho ! he !* and occasionally in expressions like *je hais* [ʒə hɛ], *une honte* [yn hɔ̃ːt], *la haine* [la hɛːn], *aheurter* [ahœrte]. It may even be introduced vulgarly where there is no corresponding letter, as in *Attention !* [hatɑ̃'sjɔ̃].[1]

Its use in provincial French (*e.g.* in Normandy and Brittany) is more common.

The student will do well, as a rule, to regard the *h aspirée* as a mere sign showing that neither elision nor linking is permissible.

This French [h] is strictly equivalent neither to the German nor to the English aspirate. The former is begun with the maximum force ; the latter is attacked like the French [h], with gradually increasing force, but there is a diminution of effort before the vowel is reached.

[1] See also Part II. Chap. V. p. 163.

PART II
THE SOUNDS IN COMBINATION

CHAPTER I

UNITS OF SPEECH

(SENTENCE, SOUND-GROUP, STRESS-GROUP, SYLLABLE)

THE combination of speech-sounds in connected discourse
brings them under the influence of new factors which may
modify their nature or even control their existence. If we
pronounce the words *The fear of an attack*, first separately,
as they are taught to the child : [ðɪɪ] [fɪiə] [ɔv] [æn] [ætæk],
and then continuously, as they would be spoken by an
adult : [ðə fɪɪəɪ əv ən ətæk], it will be seen that in the
combination several of the sounds are altered, a new sound
[ɪ] is heard before *of*, and the accented syllables of *fear*
and *attack* are uttered with a greater stress and at a higher
pitch than any of the other syllables in the expression.
Changes of a similar kind take place in French.

From the grammatical and orthographical points of view a
sentence is made up of so many separate words, and,
because we recognize these units as they are spoken, and see
them as we read, we are apt to conclude that they have also
phonetic individuality, the spaces between the written words
being represented in speech by a series of short pauses

This conclusion has no foundation in fact. The simple
sentence takes the form of an uninterrupted stream of
sound. Phrases like *The night is far spent, Il y est
arrivé* are as continuous as the single words *insuperable,
inévitablement.* In more or less complex sentences,
however, one may pause to take breath or to make the
meaning clear, or for both of these purposes at the same
time. Take, for example, the following sentence: *En
révoquant l'édit de Nantes Louis XIV porta un coup
désastreux au commerce de son pays, car les protestants
s'expatrièrent en foule et portèrent à l'étranger les secrets des
arts et des industries de France.* To utter such a sentence
without a break would be a mere *tour de force*: one
is practically compelled to make a pause, were it only for
the purpose of drawing breath. At the same time it is only
by pausing that the meaning can be adequately expressed.
We must at least make a break at the word *pays,* and
we shall probably find it advisable to make others. The
sentence might be conveniently divided into the following
groups: *En révoquant l'édit de Nantes — Louis XIV porta
un coup désastreux au commerce de son pays, — car les
protestants s'expatrièrent en foule — et portèrent à l'étranger
les secrets des arts et des industries de France.* In deliberate
utterance the length of the groups might be reduced still
further by pausing at the words *désastreux* and *étranger.*
The unbroken succession of speech-sounds between any two
such pauses is called a *sound-group,* and it is generally
within the limits of such a sound-group that the new factors
affecting sounds in combination operate. The sentence
may consist of one or several sound-groups, but the sound-
group should not contain more than one sentence.

No mechanical rules can be laid down for the division of
the complex sentence into sound-groups. It depends upon
circumstances, such as the character of the phrase—whether

it be ceremonious or conversational, the occasion on which it is uttered, the speaker's age, intellectual power and habits of speech. The schoolboy will, in speaking, generally form shorter groups than the educated adult, and in a formal address there will be greater deliberation and more frequent pauses than in familiar conversation. It should, however, be observed that pauses are, as a rule, justifiable only when they coincide with what may be called a junction in the meaning of the phrase. Punctuation is neither a sufficient nor an infallible guide. On the one hand, as reference to the example analysed will show, a pause may often be made where there is no punctuation-mark. On the other, although the full stop, the colon and the semi-colon necessitate a pause, the comma should sometimes be ignored. Thus, in the expression : *Dans cette fameuse Préface de Cromwell, qui fut, en France, le programme de la révolution littéraire* ... (Koschwitz's *Parlers parisiens*, p. 81, line 1), the linking of *fut* with *en*, [ki fyt ã frãɪs], is obligatory in spite of the intervening comma. Linking, again, is often advisable in expressions like *Puis, il ajouta*, etc., *Mais, il avait*, etc. In *Mais, au fur et à mesure qu'on s'éloigne de la capitale* ... (*Parlers parisiens*, p. 47, l. 1) and in *Puis, elle se sentait soulevée* ... (*Parlers parisiens*, p. 13, l. 12) the majority of Koschwitz's readers[1] link the ' *Mais* ' and the ' *Puis* ' to the following word. MM. Rousselot, Jean Passy and Adolphe Rambeau, who, as we shall see in the next chapter, link very sparingly, all read [pətiz afame], in spite of the ellipse, in the following line from Alfred de Musset's *Nuit de Mai* : *Ses petits, affamés, courent sur le rivage* (*Précis de Prononciation française*, p. 199, l. 24 ; *Chrestomathie française*, p. 191, l. 12). In English, too, the comma is often disregarded even by careful readers, for instance, before and after such words as *however, therefore, nevertheless*.

[1] For an account of these readings see the following chapter.

The traditional rule enjoining a pause at every comma is consequently not valid for either language.

Although all the sounds forming a sound-group are uttered without a break, it will be observed that they are not all pronounced with the same force or at the same pitch. Their treatment in these respects, which is by no means the same in French as in English, will be discussed at a later stage. For the present it is only necessary to note that by means of these variations the ear is enabled to detect certain subdivisions of the sound-group. Thus in the first half of the sentence which has been taken as an example, the following sub-groups may be easily discriminated : *En révoquant — l'édit de Nantes — Louis XIV — porta un coup désastreux — au commerce — de son pays.* These divisions are suggestive of the bars in a piece of music. They are distinguishable, in spite of the continuity of the stream of sound, by the recurrence of relatively strong beats or accents, and are for that reason called *stress-groups*. The ictus in French falls on the last full[1] syllable of each group. The analogy between stress-groups and musical bars is, however, not thoroughgoing, for the former are of variable length. They impart rhythm to the phrase but derive their origin from the thought expressed rather than from the mere form of the words. They consist, in general, of two or three words so intimately connected with each other as to be more or less unintelligible when separated. In very slow delivery, for instance in dictating, stress-groups may become sound-groups separated from each other by actual pauses.

If we attempt to analyse the stress-group we find that the next phonetic element is the *syllable*. Syllables in speech correspond very closely to notes in music. They vary in timbre, length, pitch and stress. But differences in timbre,

---

[1] The term 'full syllable' is meant to exclude the '*e* mute.'

duration and pitch are not essential. We may have two successive syllables, as well as two successive notes, of identical value in these three respects. The distinction between the syllables or notes in that case can lie only in an abrupt change in intensity. It is possible to have two successive notes or syllables bearing an equal stress, but there is a fraction of time between them when the stress is suddenly diminished. For the present purpose this may be illustrated by the group *awe or fear* [ɒː ɒ fiːə]. It will be found impossible to divide the continuous sound [ɒ] into two syllables without varying more or less abruptly the intensity of utterance.

The analogy between syllable and note ultimately fails because the syllable may consist of one or more consonants and a vowel, that is, of two or more successive sounds. These sounds, however, though they may have different degrees of sonority, must be of such a nature that they can all be uttered with one and the same expulsion of breath

We need not enter into further detail to show that it is of vital importance for the learner of a language to know how the successive elements of a sound-group are themselves grouped into syllables   Now the French and English languages differ nowhere more than in their syllabic structure. The French system, which, unlike the English, strongly favours open syllables, that is, syllables ending with a vowel-sound, may be summarized as follows :

(i) A single consonant standing between two vowels always forms a syllable with the second vowel : *indivisibilité* [ɛ̃-di-vi-zi-bi-li-te], *civiliser* [si-vi-li-ze], *inusité* [i-ny-zi-te], *mathématiques* [ma-te-ma-tik], *piller* [pi-je], *profiter* [prɔ-fi-te]

(ii) In groups of two or more consonants of which the last is a 'liquid': [l] [r] or a 'semi-vowel' · [w] [ɥ] [j], the

two, or, in groups of more than two, the last two, form a
syllable with the vowel which follows: *tableau* [ta–blo],
montrer [mɔ̃–tre], *devoir* [də–vwaːr], *religion* [rə–li–ʒjɔ̃], *pitié*
[pi–tje], *menuisier* [mə–nɥi–zje], *parfois* [par–fwa], *affreux*
[a–frø], *rallier* [ra–lje]. The groups [rl] [lr] form exceptions: *parler* [par–le]. Similarly, where the last consonant
is neither a liquid nor a semi-vowel, the group will be
divided between the two syllables: *tristesse* [tris–tɛs],
gouverner [gu–vɛr–ne], *brusquement* [brys–kə–mɑ̃], *carton*
[kar–tɔ̃], *percer* [pɛr–se], *victime* [vik–tim].

(iii) Even three consonants are carried over to the vowel
following if the second is a liquid and the third a semi-
vowel: *recroiser* [rə–krwɑ–ze], *refroidir* [rə–frwɑ–diːr],
instruit [ɛ̃s–trɥi].

(iv) A consonant never forms a syllable by itself. In
English words like *people* [piːpl̩], *given* [gɪvn̩], *spasm* [spæzm̩],
the [l] [n] and [m] have a syllabic value. In French the
words *peuple, tourne, spasme* are pronounced either in single
syllables [pœpl̩] [turn] [spasm̩], or in two syllables, by
sounding the [ə] after the consonants in question: [pœ–plə]
[tur–nə] [spaz–mə].

(v) Every syllable contains one, and only one, vowel.
In this respect traditional orthography is often much at
variance with modern pronunciation, two or three vowel-
signs being used to denote a single vowel-sound or a
consonant and a vowel: *beau* [bo], *craie* [krɛ], *fouet* [fwɛ],
oui [wi], *poid* [pwa], *poêle* [pwaːl], *loin* [lwɛ̃], *lui* [lɥi], *rien*
[rjɛ̃], *dieu* [djø], *mieux* [mjø].

On the other hand, two or three successive vowel-signs
occasionally represent two independent syllables: *chaos*
[ka–o], *crier* [kri–e], *plier* [pli–e], *créé* [kre–e], *poésie* [pɔ–e–zi],
cruelle [kry–ɛl], *brouette* [bru–ɛt].

The above rules for syllabication have been illustrated
by isolated words; so complete, however, is the unity of

the sound-group that they usually apply even between words
within its limits :

Peut-être est-il encore en vie [pø–tɛ–trɛ–tɪ–lɑ̃–kɔ–rɑ̃–vi],
rendre un service [rɑ̃–drœ̃–sɛr–vis],
corps à corps [kɔ–ra–kɔːr],
vers une heure [vɛ–ry–nœːr],
une honnête aisance [y–nɔ–nɛ–tɛ–zɑ̃ːs],
une étude approfondie [y–ne–ty–da–prɔ–fõ–di],
table à jouer [ta–bla–ʒu–e],
reste à savoir [rɛs–ta–sa–vwaːr],
porte ouverte [pɔr–tu–vɛrt],
chers amis [ʃɛr–za–mi],
ordre inattendu [ɔr–dri–na–tɑ̃–dy]

The regularity of the syllabic structure of the sound-group
must nevertheless not be exaggerated. In deliberate speech,
a rigid application of the rules between words would sometimes be pedantic and unnatural Thus a final consonant
would hardly be grouped with a following initial [l] or [r] :
cette reine will be pronounced [sɛt–rɛɪn] rather than [sɛ–trɛɪn],
toute la terre [tut–la–tɛːr] rather than [tu–tla–tɛɪr], *ce n'est que
la vérité* [sə–nɛk–la–ve–ri–te] rather than [sə–nɛ–kla–ve–ri–te]
Even in the body of words in which the elision of an 'e
mute creates a group of consonants ending in a liquid, the
group is not always sounded with the following vowel: *matelot*
[ma–tlo] or [mat–lo], *bibelot* [bi–blo] or [bib–lo], *lapereau*
[la–pro] or [lap–ro]. Again, although a final consonant is
generally carried over to an initial vowel in the same sound-
group, it is often sounded with the preceding syllable when
the latter bears an accent, that is, ends a stress-group or
is emphatic : *Quel homme !* [ˈkɛl–ɔm].
The phonetic syllabication of French, which, as we have
seen, proceeds with almost mathematical regularity, contrasts
strikingly with that of our own language. In English a single

consonant between two vowels belongs, as often as not, to the
first: compare *common* [kɒm–ən], *essence* [ɛs–əns], *abbot*
[æb–ət], *alley* [æl–ɪ]ˑwith *attack* [ə–tæk], *irate* [ɑɪ–ɹɛɪt], *at any
rate* [ə–tɛn–ɪ–ɹɛɪt], *an ass* [ə–næs], less usually [ən–æs].
Such a consonant often seems to be a kind of link between
the two syllables, belonging to neither of them in particular:
without [wɪ–ð–aʊt], *setting* [sɛ–t–ɪŋ], *student* [stjʊu–d–ŋt].
The learner must be careful not to carry over these habits of
speech into the foreign language. If *comment* be pronounced
[kɔm–ɑ̃] instead of [kɔ–mɑ̃], *commun* [kɔm–œ̃] instead of
[kɔ–mœ̃], *abbé* [ab–e] instead of [a–be], *aller* [al–e] instead
of [a–le], French ears will often hear a double consonant.[1]

The phonetic syllabication of French is also at variance
with its own system of graphic syllabication. While, for
instance, custom forbids the separation of *l'homme* by
writing *l'* at the end of one line and *homme* at the beginning
of the next, it sanctions the separation of *notre* and *homme*,
and prohibits the carrying over of the *l* in *un animal énorme*
to the following line, although the connection in the latter
cases [nɔ–trɔm] [œ̃–na–ni–ma–le–nɔrm] is quite as close as
that between *l'* and *homme*. The eye, in short, demands a
departure from the strict phonetic syllabication wherever it
would impair the identity of the word.

On the other hand, the word is not a phonetic unit. It
may, of course, become a sound-group in itself, as, for
example, the imperative: *Donne l*, or *Personne* in a negative
answer without a verb. But when, as is usually the case, it
forms part of a composite group, its individuality, in point
of sound, is merged in the latter. Thus *à prendre* has the
same sound-value as *apprendre*, *il apprit* the same as *il a
pris*, *trop heureux* the same as *trop peureux*, *de voir* the
same as *devoir*, *qui l'a vu* the same as *qu'il a vu*. The
mind alone, by its power of interpretation, is capable of

---

[1]On double sounds see Chap. V. p. 156.

distinguishing the words in a sound-group. And it can do so unerringly only after much training in reading and writing. Ability to speak a language and knowledge of the meaning conveyed are, in themselves, insufficient. An illustration of the fact is found in one of Thérèse's letters to Jean-Jacques Rousseau which has survived, and which contains examples like the following : *Mesiceuras ancor mieu re mies* for *Mais il sera encore mieux remis.*

Words lose their identity in the sound-group, not only by the absence of 'blanks' between them, but often because they no longer sound precisely as they did when isolated. In French, indeed, they undergo manifold modifications. They may lose a syllable, as, for example, *tenir* [təniːr] in the group *à tenir* [a tniːr]. They may gain one, as *table* [tabl] in *table ronde* [tablə rɔ̃ːd]. They may lose a consonant, as *quatre* [katr] in *quatre morceaux* [kat mɔrso], or *neuf* [nœf] in *neuf places* [nœ plas], and to this change may be added the modification of a surviving consonant, as in *maître d'hôtel* [mɛˈt dɔtɛl], where the voiceless [t] of *maître* is at least partially assimilated to the following voiced consonant. They may gain a consonant, like *petit.* [pəti] in *petit enfant* [pətit ɑ̃ˈfɑ̃], or the final consonant may be assimilated, as in *tasse de thé* [tɑˈs də te]. Or a vowel may be transformed into a consonant, involving sometimes the loss of a syllable which formed a monosyllabic word : *Il y a, Ça y est, Où est-il?* becoming in hasty speech [il ja] [sa jɛ] [wɛt il]. And over and above all these modifications are changes in the length of vowels and consonants, differences of pitch and stress, and the displacement of the normal accent under the influence of emotion. Clearly, then, a knowledge of the individual sounds and of dictionary pronunciations needs to be supplemented by an acquaintance with the factors that control sounds in combination and bring about these changes.

CHAPTER II

LINKING

LINKING or liaison, in its wider sense, is the carrying over of a consonant or group of consonants at the end of a word to form a syllable with the initial vowel or semi-vowel of the next word in the sound-group. The term is, however, generally limited in French grammars to the carrying over of otherwise mute consonants, as in *petit enfant* [pətit ɑ̃'fɑ̃], and, as the linking of a consonant which would be sounded even if not carried over is merely an aspect of the syllabic structure of the phrase which has already been discussed, it will be convenient to use the term in its narrower sense.

Linking is possible only between words belonging to one and the same sound-group, the final consonant and initial vowel being pronounced together as one syllable precisely as if they were both in the body of the same word. Hence no pause can be made either before or after the consonant: *nos amis* must be pronounced [nozami], not [no, zami], nor [noz, ami]; *vingt et un ans* must be pronounced [vɛ̃teœ̃nɑ̃], just as if it were a single word, and, as we shall see at a later stage, the tonic accent will fall, not on the word *ans*, but on the syllable [nɑ̃]. 'There is nothing more laughable,' says Professor Passy,[1] 'than an ill-made liaison. *C'est une idée* pronounced [sɛt, ynide] suggests the hiccups. A

---

[1] *Les Sons du Français*, 6th ed., p. 41.

teacher used to pronounce phrases like *la première est excessivement facile*, making a pause after *est*. [la prəmjɛːrɛ, tɛːksɛsiːvmɑ̃ fasil]. There would be a general outburst of laughter every time.'

In certain cases, however, the resuscitated consonant is not carried over to the following initial vowel but closes the preceding syllable. This happens only where the resuscitation is obligatory, and the second of the two words in question contains more than one syllable with displaced accent upon the first.[1] Thus in the phrase *L'œuvre de Shakespeare est amorale*, the initial [a] of *amorale* being accented, is attacked with a glottal-stop, and thus clearly separated from the preceding consonant: [lœːvrə də ʃekspiːr ɛt ʔamɔral].[2]

Liaisons of this kind are very rare exceptions, and the learner, in his endeavour to follow the rule, is apt to lay undue stress upon the syllable that forms the link between two words. He must be on his guard against this tendency. To be good, linking must be effected without the least trace of effort. A laborious liaison is a discord in the place of a grace-note.

Not every word that begins with a vowel-sound admits of linking. Those words which are spelled with an initial 'h aspirate' form some of the exceptions. This *h* need not, and generally should not, be pronounced, but whether it be pronounced or not, no linking can take place. We must say [le ero] = *les héros*, [œ̃ grɑ̃ ero] = *un grand héros*, [le ɛn] [le hɛn] = *les haines*. Another class of exceptions consists of words beginning with a semi-vowel: [w] [ɥ] or [j]. Some of these words may be linked: *e.g. les oies* [lez wɑ], *les huîtres* [lez ɥitr], *les yeux* [lez jø] Linking is admissible with nearly all words in [wa] and [wɛ̃], *e.g.*

[1] See pp. 170 ff.
[2] The above example was heard at a public lecture in Paris.

oiseau, oisif, oing, oindre; but it must be regarded as exceptional in all other cases. In doubt, reference should be made to a dictionary. Whenever a word beginning with a semi-vowel does not admit of linking, and whenever the linking of such a word is optional or variable, the fact is carefully noted in the valuable dictionary with phonetic script published by T. C. and E. C. Jack.

With the exception of [f], which sometimes changes to [v] in the word *neuf* [nœf], and [s] in *six* [sis] and *dix* [dis], which always becomes [z], all consonants that would be sounded in the isolated word preserve their original sound when carried over: *qu'il rende un service* [kil rɑ̃'d œ̃ sɛrvis], *fils aîné* [fis ene], *tous ensemble* [tus ɑ̃'sɑ̃ːbl], *les lis éclatants* [le lis eklatɑ̃], *attentif à tout* [atɑ̃'tif a tu]. A final [s] may, in the reading of elevated prose and verse, be pronounced [z] or, in the plural of a word of which it is heard in the singular, [sz]: *tous ensemble* [tuz ɑ̃'sɑ̃ːbl], *les lis éclatants* [lɛ lisz eklatɑ̃], *les mœurs antiques* [lɛ mœrz ɑ̃'tik] [lɛ mœrsz ɑ̃'tik]. The [v] liaison of *neuf* has been definitely preserved only in expressions of constant recurrence, such as *neuf ans* [nœv ɑ̃], *neuf heures* [nœv œːr], *neuf enfants* [nœv ɑ̃'fɑ̃]; elsewhere modern usage is not settled, though it favours the [f] liaison: *neuf écoliers* [nœf ekɔlje], *neuf amis* [nœf ami] rather than [nœv eɔklje], [nœv ami]. A latent consonant, on the other hand, is sometimes resuscitated in a modified form. These exceptions are *d*, which is pronounced as [t]; *g*, which is pronounced as [k]; *s* and *x*, which sound as [z]. Examples: *il rend un service* [il rɑ̃t œ̃ sɛrvis], *grand homme* [grɑ̃t ɔm], *un long exil* [œ̃ lɔ̃k egzil], *un long hiver* [œ̃ lɔ̃k ivɛːr], *les os* [lez o] [lez oːs] [lez ɔs], *beaux habits* [boz abi].

When, in linking, a nasal vowel evolves a nasal consonant, the vowel more often than not loses its nasal character.

[ɔ̃] is regularly denasalized, as in *bon ami* [bɔn ami], not [bɔ̃n ami]; it remains nasal, exceptionally, in the pronoun

on, and sometimes in *ton*, *son*, *mon* : *on arrive* [ɔ̃n ariːv],
mon ami [mɔn ami] or [mɔ̃n ami], *son argent* [sɔn arʒɑ̃] or
[sɔ̃n arʒɑ̃]. [ɛ̃] generally loses its nasality save when it is
spelled *in* : *en plein air* [ɑ̃ plɛn ɛɪr] rather than [ɑ̃ plɛ̃n ɛɪr] ;
certain homme [sɛrtɛn ɔm] rather than [sɛrtɛ̃n ɔm], *ancien
officier* [ɑ̃'sjɛn ɔfisje] rather than [ɑ̃'sjɛ̃n ɔfisje] ; but *le divin
Épicure* [lə divɛn epikyːr], *le malin esprit* [lə malɛn ɛspri].
Exceptions are *bien* and *rien* in which the nasal vowel is
usually preserved : *bien aimable* [bjɛ̃n ɛ'mabl], *je ne com-
prends rien à tout cela* [ʒə n kɔ̃'prɑ̃ rjɛ̃n a tu sla]. Littré's
recommendation to denasalize the vowel in these two words
is contrary to current usage.

The denasalization of [œ̃] is optional : *un homme* may be
pronounced [œ̃n ɔm] or [œn ɔm]. The pronunciation [yn
ɔm], which is heard occasionally, should not be imitated.

Hence the only vowel that never sacrifices its nasality is
[ɑ̃] : *il en est* must be pronounced [il ɑ̃n ɛ], *en attendant*
[ɑ̃n atɑ̃'dɑ̃].

The question remains : When does linking take place?
When is a latent final consonant resuscitated? The answer
depends in the main upon three considerations, namely,
the standard of speech, the relation between the two words,
and the requirements of euphony and sense. As linking
generally implies a knowledge of orthography, it is to be
associated with the idea of learned and careful utterance.
It is, therefore, much more frequent in reading than in
speaking, more frequent in the reading of lofty prose than
in that of colloquial passages, while it becomes the rule in
the recitation of serious verse. Conversely, it may be said
that linking becomes more and more unusual according as
the tone, style, matter and occasion become less formal, less
ceremonious. In the ordinary intercourse of everyday life,
it easily becomes a sign of bad taste, denoting pedantry,
affectation, the desire to appear 'cultured,' to speak

F.P. F

'correctly.' Hence, in conversation, as Professor Passy points out, it is only the class of people intermediate between the educated and the illiterate who link profusely. And naturally enough, in their ignorance, they link not only in the wrong place, but with the wrong consonant, using [z] for [t] or vice versa. To this perhaps is due, in some measure, the growing tendency among the educated towards a more sparing use of liaison in familiar and colloquial speech. Hence, too, it will be easily understood that, in the matter of linking, sins of omission are regarded with more indulgence than sins of commission, and that, in difficult cases, the student will be wise to apply the maxim enjoining inaction in case of doubt.

There are, however, certain liaisons which must be regarded as obligatory on all occasions. These are as follows :

(i) Between an article, demonstrative adjective, possessive adjective or numeral and an adjective or noun following : *les hommes* [lez ɔm], *des amis* [dez ami], *un an* [œn ɑ̃], *cet enfant* [sɛt ɑ̃'fɑ̃], *mon ami* [mɔn ami], *ses ailes* [sez ɛl], *leurs armes* [lœrz arm], *les autres* [lez oːtr], *deux ours* [dø'z uːr], *trois cents hommes* [trwɑ sɑ̃z ɔm], *plusieurs horloges* [plyzjœrz ɔrlɔːʒ], *quelques aunes* [kɛlkəz oːn].

Similarly, in the pronominal expressions, *les uns* [lez œ̃], *les unes* [lez yn] ; but not in the elliptical, *vers les une heure* [vɛr le yn œːr], nor in *les un, les huit, les onze* [le œ̃] [le ɥit] [le ɔ̃z].

(ii) Between an adjective and a noun following : *les petits enfants* [le ptiz ɑ̃'fɑ̃], *un grand ours* [œ̃ grɑ̃t urs], *un gros homme* [œ̃ groz ɔm], *de mauvaises herbes* [də mɔvɛ'zz ɛrb].

(iii) Between a verb and a pronoun (subject or object) or a pronoun and a verb : *ils attendent* [ilz atɑ̃ːd], *nous arrivons* [nuz arivɔ̃], *vous aimez* [vuz ɛ'me], *il en a* [il ɑ̃n a], *en a-t-on*

[ɑ̃n atɔ̃], *pour vous aider* [pur vuz ɛ'de], *nous y sommes* [nuz
i sɔmˌ], *vas-y* [vaz ı], *joignons-y* [ʒwaɲɔ̃z i], *perd-il* [pɛrt ilˌ],
plaît-ıl [plɛt il], *sont-elles* [sɔ̃t ɛl], *prends-en* [prɑ̃z ɑ̃], *voit-on*
[vwat ɔ̃], *allez-vous-en* [ale vuz ɑ̃], *tout est bien* [tut ɛ bjɛ̃], *je
les ai* [ʒə lez e]. In *c'est à vous à jouer* the pronoun *vous*
is neither the subject nor the object of *jouer*, and the final
consonant remains mute : [sɛt a vu a ʒue] Between *les
uns* and a verb liaison is generally avoided : *les uns enten-
dırent* [lez ɶ̃ ɑ̃'tɑ̃'dıːr] (*Parl. par.* 65, 7)

(iv) Between the auxiliaries *avoir* and *être* and the past
partıcıple of any verb : *ıl est aımé* [il ɛt ɛ'me], *nous sommes
occupés* [nu sɔmz ɔkype], *on avaıt entendu* [ɔ̃n avɛt ɑ̃'tɑ̃'dy],
ıls ont appris [ilz ɔ̃t apri], *vous avez eu* [vuz avez y].

In familiar conversation this rule is occasionally neglected
Pronuncıatıons like the following are not uncommon *nous
étions arrivés* [nuz etjɔ̃ arive], *nous avons eu* [nuz avɔ̃ y],
tu as eu [ty a y].

(v) Between *être* and its complement : *c'est un saint* [sɛt
ɶ̃ sɛ̃], *il est en vılle* [il ɛt ɑ̃ vil], *ıl étaıt à Parıs* [il etɛt a
pa'rı], *c'est à moı* [sɛt a mwa], *elle est aımable* [ɛl ɛt ɛ'mabl],
c'est amusant [sɛt amy'zɑ̃], *soyez ındulgents* [swajez ɛ̃'dylʒɑ̃].
Exceptions belong to careless conversatıon : *vous êtes un
polısson* [vuz ɛt ɶ̃ pɔlisɔ̃] in place of the more dignified [vuz
ɛtz ɶ̃ pɔlisɔ̃]

(vi) Between the common short adverbs and an adjec-
tıve or adverb : *très utile* [trɛz ytıl], *bıen égal* [bjɛ̃n egal]
fort élégant [fɔrt elegɑ̃], *tout entier* [tut ɑ̃'tje], *trop avancé*
[trɔp avɑ̃'se], *assez ıntıme* [asez ɛ̃'tim], *plus harmonıeux*
[plyz armɔnjø], *moins ével* [mwɛ̃z elve], *pas encore* [pɑz
ɑ̃'kɔːr].

In less careful speech *pas*, *plus* and *jamais* are often not
linked.

(vıı) Between a preposition and ıts complement : *en
Angleterre* [ɑ̃n ɑ̃'glətɛːr], *en écoutant* [ɑ̃n ekutɑ̃], *dans une*

heure [dũz yn œːr], *sans abri* [sãz abri], *sans entrer* [sãz ã'tre], *devant eux* [dəvãt ø], *chez elle* [ʃez ɛl], *sous un arbre* [suz œn arbr].

The only exceptions to this rule are *vers, envers* and *selon* : in the first two the [z] is rarely carried over, *e.g. vers elle* [vɛr ɛl] rather than [vɛrzɛl] ; *selon* is never linked, *e.g. selon elle* [səlõ ɛl].

In careless speech the final consonant of *depuis, pendant* and *après* often remains mute. The authors of the *Chrestomathie*[1] give the liaison as optional even in reading : *depuis un siècle* (61, 36); *pendant un temps* (93, 21); *après avoir détruit les Mameluks* (109, 23). The student is recommended to avoid these negligent pronunciations in reading, save, perhaps, in cases like the second example where linking may be avoided on grounds of euphony.

(viii) Between the conjunction *quand* and the word following : *quand il viendra* [kãt il vjɛ̃'dra], *quand on en a* [kãt õn ãn a]. This liaison is neglected only in vulgar speech. (See the *Chrestomathie*, p. 137, l. 3.)

(ix) Between the relative *dont* and the word following : *l'homme dont il parle* [lɔm dõt il parl].

(x) Between words forming compound expressions of a fixed and invariable form : *de mieux en mieux* [də mjøz ã mjø], *de pis en pis* [də piz ã pi], *de plus en plus* [də plyz ã ply], *de temps en temps* [də tãz ã tã], *de temps à autre* [də tãz a oːtr], *plus ou moins* [plyz u mwɛ̃], *mot à mot* [mot a mo], *pied à terre* [pjet a tɛːr], *tôt ou tard* [tot u taːr], *tout à coup* [tut a ku], *tout à fait* [tut a fɛ], *tout à l'heure* [tut a lœːr], *tout au plus* [tut o ply], *tout au moins* [tut o mwɛ̃], *pot-au-feu* [pɔt o fø], *pot à eau* [pɔt a o], *mort aux rats* [mɔrt o ra], *suer sang et eau* [sye sãk e o], *quant à* [kãt a], *pas à pas* [pɑz a pɑ], *un à un* [œ̃n a œ̃], *les États-Unis* [lez etaz yni], *les Champs-Élysées* [le ʃãz elize]. In these and like locutions the liaison has been consecrated by long-standing tradition. An exception is found in the expression *à tort et à travers* [a tɔɪr e a travɛɪr].

The foregoing rules exhaust all the cases in which linking can be declared compulsory. Many of the cases that remain to be discussed present problems that might be solved diversely even by Frenchmen of undoubted culture. It would, therefore, seem very desirable, in examining these cases, to cite the practice of particular individuals. This has been rendered to some extent possible by the publication of phonetic texts. In the following pages appeal will be made more particularly to the *Parlers parisiens* of Professor Eduard Koschwitz (Elwert, Marburg, 3rd ed 1898), and the *Chrestomathie française* of Jean Passy and Adolphe Rambeau (Henry Holt & Co., New York; 2nd ed. 1901). The former work is an attempt to record the different pronunciations of a number of educated Frenchmen. Each specimen of prose or verse is not only read by its author (de Bornier, Coppée, A. Daudet, Leconte de Lisle, Gaston Paris, Ernest Renan, Sully-Prudhomme, Zola, etc.), or declaimed by a well-known actor (Silvain, Got, etc.), but is reread by several other 'individus instruits et bien élevés,' the variant pronunciations taking the form of footnotes. Save in the case of the first specimen (a fragment from Alphonse Daudet's *Tartarin de Tarascon*), in which the pronunciations of thirteen readers are recorded, these secondary 'subjects' are in each instance M l'abbé Rousselot, the experimental phonetician of the Collège de France, professor at the Institut Catholique de Paris, Professor Ritter of Geneva; M. Omer Jacob, licencié-ès-lettres, of Paris, and M. Bleton, licencié-ès-lettres, of Lyons. In a task of such delicacy as this work implies, there is always the risk of error on the part of the recorder, but this risk is reduced to a minimum in the matter of liaison. The book may, therefore, be consulted on this point without hesitation. But it cannot be taken as a guide to the use of liaison in conversation: the specimens, though of varied character, are all literary, and were read or declaimed 'according to what is called the rules of art.' Its peculiar value lies rather in the fact that it helps in determining the maximum number of liaisons permissible in reading.

In the *Chrestomathie* the authors have recorded their own pronunciations, normalized 'on certain points where it was considered at variance with that of the majority.' This work, therefore, has value as the result of collaboration[1]: it does not merely represent the opinion of a single individual. At the same time it contains a few passages of a colloquial character in which the style of conversation is reproduced. What strikes one most in it is the very slight difference in point of treatment between these familiar extracts and the passages of a literary character. In the reading of prose passages more or less comparable to those of the *Parlers parisiens*, MM. Jean Passy and Rambeau often sanction and even recommend negligences which belong rather to familiar intercourse.[2] These negligences extend to the

---

[1] His original collaborator, Jean Passy, having died shortly after the appearance of the first edition, M. Rambeau (now professor at the University of Berlin) was assisted by Prof. Paul Passy in the preparation of the second edition. As its readings differ little from those of the first, we may conclude that they have threefold approval.

[2] They anticipate this charge: 'Nous nous attendons à ce qu'on nous reproche une prononciation vulgaire: c'est un grief assez général contre les phonétistes' (Intro. xliv). Their answer is as follows: 'Il existe une opération psychologique dont le rôle est considérable dans tout ce qui touche au langage, qui consiste à substituer inconsciemment dans notre esprit la forme pleine, lente et normale d'un mot à sa forme occasionnelle, modifiée considérablement dans la phrase par l'assimilation, l'élision ou la rapidité du discours.' This is an interesting observation and perfectly true; but it applies only to more or less rapid utterance. If the ear has time to detect the absence or abnor-

domain of liaison.   The authors certainly cannot be charged with excessive and pedantic linking.   And just for this reason the *Chrestomathie* will form a useful pendant to the work of Koschwitz in studying cases in which linking is more or less a matter of taste.   These cases may be summarized, together with those in which linking is avoided, as follows :

(i) Between a noun and an adjective following.

If the noun is in the singular, linking never takes place in conversation and is scarcely ever permissible in the reading of prose : *un déjeuner interminable* [œ̃ deʒœne ɛ'tɛrminabl], *accident imprévu* [aksidɑ̃ ɛ'prevy], *coup imprévu* [ku˴ ɛ'prevy], *un objet extraordinaire* [œ̃n ɔbʒɛ ɛkstraɔrdinɛɪr], *un perroquet empaillé* [œ̃ pɛrɔkɛ ɑ̃'pɑ'je], *marchand ambulant* [marʃɑ̃ ɑ̃'bylɑ̃], *chat échaudé* [ʃa eʃo'de], *escroc habile* [ɛskro abil], *une paix honorable* [yn pɛ ɔnɔrabl], *avis important* [avi ɛ'pɔrtɑ̃].   Should the noun end in a nasal, the consonant

mality of a sound, instead of unconsciously filling up the lacuna or normalizing the peculiarity, it is simply shocked by such absence or abnormality.   The only way to make some of the readings in the *Chrestomathie* pass muster is to increase the rapidity of utterance beyond what is good and reasonable.   Hence, in introducing the *Chrestomathie* to the student, we must warn him that the authors have adopted the lax pronunciations of familiar conversation.   We have no hesitation in adding that these pronunciations should not be adopted in reading.   'La conversation,' says Ernest Legouvé on a classical page [page 76] of his *Art de la Lecture*, 'admet et même demande une certaine négligence dans la prononciation, un laisser-aller dans le débit, des incorrections volontaires qui sont une grâce quand on cause, et qui seraient un défaut quand on lit.   Causer comme on lit ressemblerait à du pédantisme ; lire comme on cause serait souvent de la vulgarité. . . . Il y a sans doute dans la causerie un naturel, une vérité d'inflexions, une grâce de débit, qu'il est utile de faire passer dans la lecture ; mais il ne faut lui emprunter que ses qualités et rester à la fois vrai et correct.' These over-careless pronunciations adopted in the *Chrestomathie*, which are to be avoided by the student, can be summarized under several heads and will be referred to in due course.   The student should then have little difficulty in correcting the transcripts.

is never sounded even in reading: *lien intime* [ljɛ̃ ɛ'tim],
souverain absolu [suvrɛ̃ apsɔly], *punition injuste* [pynisjɔ̃
ɛ'ʒyst].

The linking of a noun in the singular with a following
adjective being thus rarely permissible and never obligatory,
the student will do well to avoid it in all cases. This
recommendation may even be extended to the recitation
of verse, though a final [t] may occasionally be carried over
with good effect. The linking of a singular noun and
adjective is consistently avoided by the authors of the
Chrestomathie, even in poetic extracts, *e.g. nuit éternelle*
[nɥi etɛrnɛl] (p. 183, l. 22).

With regard to the linking of a plural noun and its
adjective there is a great variety of practice. MM. Rousselot
and Laclotte declare the liaison customary,[1] but it is not
always made in the readings recorded by Koschwitz. Professor Paul Passy seldom sounds the [z]: thus in *Le
Français parlé* (Reisland, Leipzig; 5th ed. 1902) liaison
is avoided in *raisons historiques* (p. 80), *femmes élégantes*
(p. 56), *races inférieures* (p. 86), *nationalités étrangères* (p. 72),
and many other instances, but made in *le nom des peuples
avancés* (p. 94). In the prose passages transcribed in the
Chrestomathie the liaison is either not made (*e.g.* in *amas de
pièces inertes* (p. 61), *efforts énergiques* (p. 59), *forces opposées*
(p. 71), *forces humaines* (p. 91), *batteries immobiles* (p. 105),
rues adjacentes (p. 115), *tréteaux improvisés* (p. 119), *par-
dessus américains* (p. 119), *allures inquiétantes* (p. 123),
mouvements atmosphériques (p. 131)), or is indicated as
optional (*e.g.* in *relations étroites* (p. 59), *éléments essentiels*
(p. 75), *nobles héréditaires* (p. 91), *œuvres utiles* (p. 95),
titres incontestés (p. 101)).

On the other hand the plural [z] is not often heard in
conversation; while by common consent it seldom remains

---

[1] *Précis de Prononciation française*, p. 181.

silent in the reading of serious verse. The linking of a plural noun and an adjective, when the latter follows the noun, is, therefore, primarily a matter of style. As it tends to impart to the phrase a certain formal and ceremonious tone, it is peculiarly consistent with the language of poetry, but generally out of place in everyday intercourse, while its use in the reading of prose depends upon the nature of the passage or of the idea expressed.

But such a case of linking may be justified by the style and yet be well avoided. This happens when the sounding of the [z] would be inharmonious or likely to obscure the sense. Ambiguities will be comparatively rare, but a too frequent repetition of the sibilants [s] and [z] would be a sufficient reason to abstain from sounding a normally mute [z]: e.g. in *pour des raisons historiques* (*Parl. par.* p. 53, l. 18) and in *ces monceaux affreux d'ossements* (*Parl. par.* p. 85, l. 16). Opinions may naturally differ in such cases; hence we find that one reader, M. Jacob, sounds the [z] in *pour des raisons historiques*, when five others, including Prof. Passy (*Le Fr. parl.* p. 81, l. 8), leave it mute, and that MM. Bleton and Ritter link in *monceaux affreux*, where the author of the passage, le Père Hyacinthe, and M. Jacob avoid the liaison.[1] Again, the linking of a plural noun and following adjective may be avoided, because it would give rise to an inharmonious group of consonants. Many Frenchmen consider [rz] cacophonous and would hesitate, on this ground alone, to link in such expressions as *efforts énergiques*, *allures inquiétantes*. It is probably to avoid the group [lz] that Zola and Bleton do not link in *chapelles absidales* (*Parl. par.* p. 15, l. 2), where three other readers sound the [z].

Finally, if the adjective is connected with the verb rather

---

[1] M. Rousselot did not sound the [z] in the first of the above two examples, and Koschwitz is not sure that he sounded it in the second.

than with the noun, or if there is an ellipse between the noun and the adjective, linking must not take place : *pour rendre les peuples heureux* [pur rɑ̃'drə le pœpl œrø] ; *les terriers sont vides, les nids abandonnés* [le tɛrje sɔ̃ vid, le ni abɑ̃'dɔne]. The latter expression occurs in the *Parlers parisiens* (p. 3, l. 14), and the *Français parlé* (p. 13, ll. 8 and 9), and the latent [z] in *nids* is naturally not sounded by any of the fourteen readers.[1]

(ii) Between a noun-subject and its predicate.

The noun-subject is linked to its predicate only in very elevated style. This liaison is avoided in every instance, both in prose and in verse, by the authors of the *Chrestomathie* : *e.g.* in *les ennemis ont changé* (p. 73, l. 23), *les Grecs avaient déjà trouvé*, etc. (p. 77, l. 7), *tous les cœurs étaient contents* (p. 175, l. 32). Even in the loftiest passages of the *Parlers parisiens* the readers never all agree in sounding the final consonant : one out of five links in *Les deux voleurs_étaient crucifiés à ses côtés* (p. 59, l. 17) ; three out of five link noun and predicate in *Ses enfants_ont commencé à douter d'elle* (p. 73, l. 1), and *Un mouchoir dont les bouts_égouttaient* (p. 23, l. 18), as also in the lines *La nuit_autour de moi Descendait* (p. 113, l. 21), *De voix et de parfums le bois_est enchanté* (p. 125, l. 19) ; only one fails to sound the [z] in *Ses disciples_avaient fui* (p. 61, l. 4).

The final mute consonant of a proper noun is never sounded in any circumstances : *Paris était un camp* [pa'ri etɛt ɶ̃ kɑ̃], *Armand est arrivé* [armɑ̃ ɛt arive], *Edmond About est un romancier de talent* [edmɔ̃ abu ɛt ɶ̃ rɔmɑ̃'sje d talɑ̃].

(iii) Between two verbs.[2]

[1] Compare the reading of the line : *Ses petits, affamés, courent sur le rivage*, Part II. Chap. I. p. 71.

[2] The question of liaison is the same whether the first verb is followed immediately by the second, which of course is always an infinitive, or by *à*, *en* or *y* belonging to the latter.

Linking is here often neglected in familiar conversation
in such expressions as *je veux aller, tu peux aller, tu dois
écrire, il faut expliquer, il fallait en convenir.* Hence in the
colloquial phrase, *Il faut être fou pour prendre un bain par
ce temps-là!* (*Chrest.* p. 27, ll 34, 35), MM. Jean Passy and
Rambeau do not sound the latent [t] in *faut.* In more
careful speech the final [t] would be heard in such con-
nections, and, as the linking of [t] is here neither ceremonious nor affected, the learner may perhaps be advised
to make this liaison pretty freely, provided always that a
harsh group of consonants does not result.

It follows *a fortiori* that the liaison should generally be
made in the reading of all but colloquial passages. When
it is avoided by the authors of the *Chrestomathie*, its suppression may usually be explained on grounds of euphony :
e.g. in *concour(t) à détruire* (p. 63, l. 9), *concouren(t) à
donner* (p. 81, l. 6), *se fassen(t) entendre* (p. 89, l. 11). It
is made by them unconditionally in *Un pur mécanisme, qui
peut_être ingénieux* (p. 61, l. 7); *Ses pairs font_entendre une
voix toujours écoutée* (p. 79, l. 36); *Il faut_aimer notre vie
nationale* (p. 87, l. 18); *Elle allait_apercevoir le Caire* (p. 107,
l. 9); *Quand ils voulaient_enlever une position* (p. 107, l. 39);
Le plus étrange tohu-bohu qu'on pût_imaginer (p. 115, l. 30) ;
and considered optional in *Elle (l'eau) devait_être bien
chaude* (p. 9, l. 18); *Il le fait_entrer* (p. 15, l. 4); *Il en
vient_à demander,* etc. (p. 19, l. 9); *L'autre voulait_aller se
promener* (p. 27, l. 19); *Il se met_à faire sa correspondance*
(p. 27, l. 18); *Il peut_y avoir concorde entre' les gouvernants
et les gouvernés* (p. 97, l. 26); *Les brins de renseignements
qu'ils pouvaient_attraper* (p. 123, ll. 24, 25); *Il n'était personne . . . qui ne se fût fait_inscrire* (p. 113, l. 35). The
indication that the liaison is optional in these and similar
cases must be understood in the sense that the pronunciation would not cease to be French if the liaison were

neglected. It cannot be taken to mean that both readings
are equally good. On the contrary, only a careless reader
would fail to link in such cases. For proof of this we
need only refer to the *Parlers parisiens*, where the readers,
with almost complete unanimity, sound the final [t] of
the first of two successive verbs. It is sounded by all
thirteen in *Celui qui est en tête se met_à crier bien fort*,
etc. (p. 5, l. 7), though in his transcription of the same
passage Professor Paul Passy does not link (*Le Français
parlé*, p. 13, l. 20); by all five save M. Rousselot in
Le mari et la femme firent_arrêter l'omnibus (p. 31, l. 1),
and in *Il se préparait_à prendre ses grades* (p. 35, l. 7); by
all without exception in *Ce qu'il faut_entendre par ce mot*
(p. 45, l. 9), *On arriverait_à couvrir toute la France d'une
étoile*, etc. (p. 51, l. 9), *On offrit_à boire aux patients un vin
fortement aromatisé* (p. 59, l. 2).

Even the [z] liaison is usual in reading in such combinations as *Je veux_examiner* (*Chrest.* p. 59, l. 29), *Ce
que nous aurons_à faire* (*ib.* p. 59, l. 25), *Quand nous
revenons_écouter ce langage naïf* (*ib.* p. 89, l. 1), *Je vais_y
renoncer* (*ib.* p. 53, l. 13). It is, however, well avoided by
Passy-Rambeau in *Jamais je n'ai mieux appri(s) à connaître
. . . le caractère de la bourgeoisie parisienne* (p. 113, l. 36),
and in *Un petit nombre d'esprits accoutumé(s) à ne pas
limiter leurs réflexions* (p. 59, l. 7). The [z] of a past
participle is rarely sounded, and in the former case it would
certainly be cacophonous after the liaison of *mieux* with
appris. But four out of five readers sound the [z], although
it involves a repetition of the sound, in *J'ai bien lu dans les
Écritures que vous aimez_à prendre la faiblesse et le néant
pour vos instruments dans ce monde* (*Parl. par.* p. 75, l. 2).

Here, as elsewhere, the latent [r] of the infinitive in *-er* is
not readily carried over to the following syllable: *e.g.* in
Il ne peut se refuse(r) à admettre, etc. (*Chrest.* p. 67, l. 27).

The [r] liaison is avoided by Passy-Rambeau here and in every other case, even in verse. Nor does any of the five readers sound the [r] in *Elle semblait s'attache(r) à voir*, etc. (*Parl. par.* p. 27, l. 9). But three out of five link in *Il ne put se décider_à voir*, etc. (p. 85, l. 20).

(iv) Between a verb other than *être* and an adverb, or vice versa.

This case is closely akin to the one last discussed. Though neglected often enough in a free and easy type of conversation, the [t] liaison is by no means unusual in other circumstances. Hence the [t] will sometimes be heard and sometimes remain mute in such expressions as *Cela se fait ainsi*, *Il y en avait assez*, *Il en fallait encore*.

Its use becomes much more general in reading, though subject always to considerations of sense and euphony. Koschwitz's readers agree in avoiding the [t] liaison between verb and adverb only in two cases : *Les bonnes habitudes . . . auxquelles il avait été brusquemen(t) arraché* (p. 25, l. 17), *Et, profondémen(t) uni à son père, il commença*, etc. (p. 63, l. 12). In the former the [t] is left silent after the two [t]'s in *avait été*. With the second we may compare the following example from the *Chrestomathie* : *Cette force . . . qui maintient obstinément unis les groupes que tout concourt à détruire* (p. 63, l. 9). While the final [t] of *maintient* is left mute, the linking of *obstinément* and *unis* is here given as optional. Other instances where the liaison of verb and adverb is indicated as optional by Passy-Rambeau, and may be regarded by the student as advisable, are *Il y avait_une fois un petit oiseau* (p. 5, l. 1), *Il fallait_encore* (p. 9, l. 26), *Tous deux ne parlaient_encore français qu'à coup de dictionnaire* (p. 27, l. 22), *Il se met_en colère* (p. 29, l. 6), *Cette ancienne poésie française que nous avons si complètement_oubliée* (p. 59, ll. 4, 5), *Une telle société peut être gravement_atteinte* (p. 61, l. 14), *Il faut aussi qu'elle soit aimée* (p. 65, l. 6), *Cette nationalité allemande elle-même, qui paraît_actuellement si puissante* (p. 67, l. 32), *Elle découvrit_enfin . . . les hauts minarets* (p. 107, l. 11), *Cette police se compliquait_alors d'une foule de détails* (p. 121, l. 4).[1]

The liaison is made unconditional by the same authors occasionally in the prose passages, very frequently in verse: *e.g.* in *Si l'on peut_ainsi dire* (p. 57, l. 13), *Plusieurs . . . attendaient_encore* (p. 75, l. 33), *Il y avait_encore* (p. 85, l. 33), *Un Frédéric II. . . . un Napoléon . . . y suffiraient_à peine* (p. 93, l. 5), *Bonaparte fit_aussitôt ses dispositions* (p. 107, ll. 24, 25), *Qui venait_après* (p. 111, l. 9), *La bataille nous avait_à peine coûté une centaine de morts* (p. 113, l. 8). Where, however, the verb or adverb already ends in a sounded consonant, the authors of the *Chrestomathie*, in the reading of prose, usually carry this consonant over, leaving the latent final mute: *e.g.* in *Ils appellen(t) encore* (p. 89, l. 31), *Ils le peuven(t) encore* (p. 99, l. 35), *Les Allemands envisagen(t) autrement les choses* (p. 83, l. 16), *Nos braves soldats . . . les attendiren(t) avec calme* (p. 109, ll. 41, 42), *La forme . . . dont s'enveloppen(t) ici toutes les douleurs* (p. 119, l. 31), *Celles-ci les reçuren(t) avec fermeté* (p. 111, l. 31).

The [z] liaison is made more sparingly, especially in conversation. But the evidence of the *Chrestomathie* is here at variance with that of the *Parlers parisiens.* MM. Jean Passy and Rambeau seem generally to avoid linking the [z] in prose: *e.g.* in *Une société dont les membres ne sont maintenu(s) ensemble que par la force* (p. 61, l. 1), *On m'avait mi(s) en sentinelle* (p. 117, l, 16), *Nos braves soldats, devenu(s) aussi froids qu'ils avaient été fougueux jadis* (p. 109, l. 41), *Bon et Menou . . . arrivé(s) à une certaine distance, firent halte* (p. 111, l. 22). They give the liaison as optional, however, in *Ce qu'elle a parfois_été* (p. 73, l. 10). In verse

[1] See also *op. cit.* p. 93, l. 33 and p. 113, l. 36.

LINKING 95

they frequently sound the [z]: *e.g.* in *Attends_un peu, nous finirons_ensemble* (p. 167, l. 27), *Nous fuyons_en silence* (p. 173, l. 33). But in verse and prose alike they never sound the final mute consonant of *toujours*: *Une voix toujours écoutée* (p. 79, l. 37), *Il y avait toujours été* (p. 127, l. 8), *Il n'est pas toujours aisé de dormir sur de la paille* (p. 117, ll. 39, 40), *Toujours intact aux yeux du monde* (p. 225, l. 23).

On the other hand, Koschwitz's readers agree in avoiding the [z] liaison between verb and adverb only in the sentence *Les deux voleurs étaient crucifié(s) à ses côtés* (p. 59, l. 17 ; cf. p. 61, l. 22), and this instance is of doubtful validity, because the word *crucifiés* might end a sound-group. Elsewhere, even in prose, there is nearly always a majority in favour of the liaison : *e.g.* in *Que d'étroites allées obscures entrevues_au vol* (p. 23, l. 2), *L'homme assis_en face d'elle* (p. 29, l. 22), *Les faits relatés_au jour le jour* (p. 37, l. 12), *Assis_au pied de la croix* (p. 59, l. 19), *Mais nos cœurs, brisés_en mainte aventure* (p. 135, l. 18). The majority is uncertain in the phrase *Vous discernerez_à peine le sens de quelques mots* (p. 47, l. 10).

The effect of the [z] liaison between verb and adverb in conversation is well illustrated by a story told by Ernest Legouvé, in his *Art de la Lecture*, in the following words : 'Un jour, dans une pièce de Mme de Girardin, *La joie fait peur*, la jeune actrice chargée du rôle de l'ingénue dit, en parlant de fleurs qu'elle avait plantées avec son frère : "Nous les avions plantées-ensemble," en faisant sentir l's. Mme de Girardin bondit sur sa chaise. "Pas d's! pas d's!" s'écria-t-elle. "Planté ensemble. Vous n'avez pas le droit de faire de pareilles liaisons à votre âge ! Je me moque de la grammaire ! Il n'y a qu'une règle pour les ingénues, c'est d'être ingénues ! Cette affreuse s vous vieillirait de dix ans ! Elle ferait de vous une Armande au lieu d'une Henriette ! Oh ! l'affreuse s !"'

The [r] of the infinitive in *-er* is never linked to a following adverb in conversation, and may often remain silent
in the reading of prose. In the *Parlers parisiens* four
readers sound it in *Il ne voyait pas un tableau . . . sans
noter_aussitôt son impression* (p. 37, l. 18); M. Rousselot
alone, here as generally elsewhere, does not link the infinitive. MM. Jean Passy and Rambeau seem regularly to
avoid this liaison, even in verse: *e.g.* in *tombe(r) à genoux*
(p. 43, l. 14), *reste(r) en arrière* (p. 107, l. 41), *Je venais
d'entre(r) en ménage* (p. 175, l. 18), *J'entends frappe(r) à la
porte* (p. 177, l. 8).

(v) Between a verb other than *être* and an adjective or
adjectival expression.

With the linking of a verb and an adverb we may compare that of a verb and an adjective closely connected
with each other. In conversation the liaison is frequently
disregarded, especially if the consonant is [z]. MM. Jean
Passy and Rambeau consequently transcribe *Vous me semblez
arriéré* (p. 127, l. 14), [vu m sɑ̃'ble arjɛ're], without the [z].
The consonant is more often carried over in reading: *e.g.*
in *Le désordre devint_extrême* (*Chrest.* p. 111, l. 33), *Ce sol
que l'on croyait_inébranlable* (p. 87, l. 4), *Les racines vivaces
par lesquelles elle s'y tient_encore attachée* (p. 87, l. 33). The
same authors, however, do not link verb and adjective in
Il se voi(t) assailli par trois hommes de mauvaise mine
(p. 39, l. 2). But they do not link verb and adverb in *On
voi(t) à l'est l'horizon qui blanchit doucement* (p. 119, l. 1).

(vi) Between a verb and its object, direct or indirect.

This liaison is probably less common than that of verb
and adverb. In easy conversation it is generally neglected,
and even careful speakers as a rule link verb and object
only where they form a short and indissoluble sound-group:
*e.g. Il avait_une canne, Il lui faut_une plume, Il se fait_un
devoir*, etc.

The *Chrestomathie* and the *Parlers parisiens* are again at variance   MM. Jean Passy and Rambeau reduce the number of liaisons to a minimum, making no more than would be made in a tolerably careful style of conversation.   In their prose transcriptions this liaison is made unconditionally in but few cases: *e g.* in *On fit_invasion* (p. 123, l. 11), *Ne prenant_aucune part à la vie* . . (p 69, l 13), *Il avait_une lettre de recommandation* (p 25, l. 34), *Il donna dans le russe . . . et se fit_une âme d'oiseau de mer* (p 129, l. 13), *Il avait_une manière de dire le steppe* . . (p. 129, l. 23)   It is occasionally considered optional, as in *Qui faisaient_un petit voyage* (p 27, l. 15), *Quels liens étroits rattachent_à nous . . . cette ancienne poésie* (p. 59, l. 2); but more often neglected altogether: *e g.* in *À qui il montrai(t) un fruit* (p. 19, l. 10), *Ce n'est pas lui qui manquerai(t) à ce devoir* (p. 129, l. 31), *On les conduisai(t) au poste le plus voisin* (p. 121, l. 16), *Une populace qui se livrai(t) à tous les excès* (p. 113, l. 16), *Quelques-uns jouaien(t) au bouchon* (p. 117, l 5), *Il ser(t) à quelque chose* (p. 129, l. 35).

Koschwitz's readers, it is true, are not often unanimously in favour of the liaison, but it is made almost always by a very large majority   Thus the liaison is made by a majority of thirteen to one in *Et toute la bande fait_un crochet*[1] (p 5, l. 9), by a majority of four to one in *Elle n'avait_aucune science* (p. 13, l. 6), *En levant_un regard* (p 29, l. 4), *Elle s'offrit_aux regards* (p. 29, l. 19), *Il y ajoutait_une page nouvelle* (p 37, l. 8), *Un soldat . . . la mit_au bout d'un roseau* (p. 59, l. 16), *Les mots . . . qu'elles apprennent_à leurs enfants*[2] (p. 49, l. 1).   In the last four cases the dissentient is M. Rousselot.   The majority is somewhat smaller (ten to three and three to two) in favour of the liaison in *Et*

---

[1] In his transcription of the same passage in *Le Français parlé*, Prof Paul Passy does not link · p. 13, l 22.

[2] Prof. Passy does not link: *Le Français parlé*, p. 75, l. 19.

commencent̮un déjeuner interminable[1] (p. 7, l. 12), and in
Il en a fait̮amende honorable (p. 81, l. 6). But the link
is made by all without exception in *Il eut̮une agonie de
désespoir* (p. 63, l. 4), *La position . . . du corps, laquelle
entraînait̮un trouble affreux dans la circulation* (p. 63, l. 19),
Selon qu'il plaît̮à la fortune (p. 99, l. 11).

The foregoing examples illustrate only the liaison of [t].
A [z] is linked somewhat less readily in prose. None of
Koschwitz's readers sound the final [z] of the verb in the
following two cases : *Elle a permi(s) à mon savant confrère*,
etc. (p. 51, l. 12), *Ces mots n'ont de sens qu'appliqué(s) à la
production littéraire* (p. 53, l. 15). The expression *Je di(s)
'aux environs'* (p. 47, l. 4), in which none of the readers
link, is not an example in point, because neither linking nor
elision takes place before a quotation. On the other hand
a majority make the liaison in *Allez̮aux environs* (p. 47, l. 3),
Représentons-nous les parlers populaires livrés̮à eux-mêmes
(p. 49, l. 5), *Ses cris suprêmes de douleur tournés̮en odieux
jeux de mots* (p. 61, l. 13), *Sur son chapeau le mari avait
mis̮un mouchoir* (p. 23, l. 18). Here again, in prose, the
liaison is usually avoided by the authors of the *Chrestomathie* : *e.g.* in *La France romane . . . a pri(s) à son compte
l'idéal qu'il avait conçu* (p. 71, l. 39), *Quelques négociants
français . . . furent envoyé(s) à Bonaparte* (p. 113, l. 22),
Donne(z) à ces hommes une consigne (p. 101, l. 24). It is
recorded as optional in *Prêtons̮une oreille attentive* (p. 89,
l. 4). In verse it is made much more frequently. Here
even MM. Passy and Rambeau do not hesitate to sound
the [z] : *e.g.* in *Formez̮une sainte alliance* (p. 163, l. 8), *Sur
le passé jetez̮un voile épais* (p. 165, l. 7), *Je dis̮à cette nuit :
Sois plus lente* (p. 185, l. 19).

The [r] liaison between verb and object is not heard in
conversation, and is made more reluctantly than that of [z]

---

[1] Prof. Passy does not link : *Le Français parlé*, p. 15, l. 17.

in reading. It is regularly avoided by the authors of the *Chrestomathie*: *e.g.* in *Mieux vaut vise(r) un idéal moins élevé* (p. 19, l. 27), *Quand ils voulaient enleve(r) une position* (p. 107, l. 39). Of six readers one alone sounds the [r] in *formuler une loi* (*Parl. par.* p. 51, l. 13; *Le Fr. parlé*, p. 79, l. 5). But four out of five, the dissident being in each case M. Rousselot, make the liaison in *exprimer‿une chose* (p. 41, l. 3), *porter‿à l'autel* (p. 73, l. 21), *manquer‿à son instinct* (p. 91, l. 3), *retrouver‿un ami* (p. 113, l. 2), the last example alone being from verse.

(vii) Between an adverb and the object of the verb.

The adverb very often forms a sound-group, either by itself or with the verb, so that a pause intervenes between adverb and object. Linking is then precluded. But even when adverb and object may be combined in the same group the adverb does not cease to be more closely related to the verb than to the object, and it is, therefore, rarely linked with the latter. In the *Parlers parisiens* none of the readers make the liaison in *La France a depuis longtemp(s) une seule langue officielle* (p. 45, l. 2), and seven out of thirteen avoid it in *Le Rapide a passé depuis longtemp(s) à l'état de superstition locale* (p. 7, l. 2). Professor Paul Passy transcribes the same sentences without liaison (*Le Français parlé*, p. 73, l. 5 and p. 15, l. 6). Yet MM. Passy and Rousselot both link in the expression *C'est bien‿autre chose, si on essaye . . . de tracer une ligne de démarcation*[1] (*Parl. par.* p. 55, l. 4; *Fr. parlé*, p. 81, l. 15), where the majority of the readers pronounce [bjɛ̃ oːtrə ʃoːz], without sounding the [n]. Similarly the phrase *Il y avait bien une source dans le bois* is read by the authors of the *Chrestomathie* (p. 5, l. 8) without the liaison. Add to this that the readers of the *Parlers parisiens* never all agree in linking adverb and

---

[1] It should be observed that *bien* is not here an adverb qualifying the adjective *autre*; but is equivalent to 'no doubt,' 'it is true.'

object, that, indeed, the majority are generally against the liaison, and it will be clear that the student's wisest course is to avoid it.

Even in verse this liaison is rarely made unless the adverbial expression happens to follow the object, in which case it is usually optional. All Koschwitz's readers save Rousselot link in *Et depuis qu'on a mis ses piliers_à l'épreuve, Il apparaît plus stable* (p. 145, l. 20); while the authors of the *Chrestomathie* transcribe with an optional liaison of the [z] in *trônes, Ce boulet invincible Qui fracassa vingt trônes à la fois* (p. 171, ll. 31, 32), and with an optional liaison of the [t] in *tout, Que ce soit elle . . . Qui, bijoux, diamants, rubans . . . Des bras de vos enfants et du sein de vos femmes Arrache tout à pleines mains!* (p. 203, ll. 25-30). It is, however, introduced unconditionally between *moments* and *encore* in the line *Mais je demande en vain quelques moments encore* (p. 185, l. 17).

(viii) Between two adverbs or adverbial expressions.

Liaison between adverbs other than those enumerated in rule (vi) for obligatory liaisons is usually restricted to more or less elevated style. The readers of the *Parlers parisiens* are never all in favour of this liaison. It is true that a majority link in the following : *Ils étaient tous deux scrupuleusement_en noir* (p. 25, l. 19), *De nouvelles croyances . . . qui bientôt_aussi ne seraient plus que des cadavres* (p. 39, l. 13), *Comme on se l'imagine souvent_encore* (p. 53, l. 5), *Il en est parfois_autrement* (p. 53, l. 6). But on the other hand the majority read without linking *Ils s'allongent tranquillemen(t) à l'ombre d'un puits* (p. 7, l. 9), *Parlé aujourd'hui à peu prè(s) exclusivement* (p. 45, l. 6), *Quelques-uns, vaguemen(t) au courant de ses idées* (p. 61, l. 20); while all avoid the liaison in *Parlé au moins concurremmen(t) avec le patois* (p. 45, l. 7).

The authors of the *Chrestomathie* avoid it in *Disons-le franchemen(t) aussi* (p. 73, l. 10), *À peu prè(s) en même temps*

(p. 127, l. 27) and make it optional in *La conscience nationale . . . s'est incarnée plus naïvement_encore dans Jeanne
d'Arc* (p. 83, l. 41), and in the line *Tous n'y sont point assis
également_à l'aise* (p. 203, l. 10). An interesting example is
found, at page 85, line 6, of the *Chrestomathie*, in the phrase
*Cependant quelques esprits . . . se demandaient . . . si cette
sécurité était bien entièrement justifiée.* Here, although *bien*
modifies the verb and not the following adverb, the liaison is
given as optional. (Cf. Rule (vii).)

(ix) Between an adverb and an adjective ; or between an
adjective or adverb and its complement.

The relation between adverb and adjective being, as a
rule, closer than that between two adverbs, this liaison is
naturally more usual. It is employed by most of the
readers in *Des langues absolument_étrangères (Parl. par.*
p. 47, l. 13), by all in *Un vin fortement_aromatisé* (p. 59,
l. 3). The authors of the *Chrestomathie* link optionally in
Une grande vie nationale est essentiellement_organique (p. 61,
l. 10), unconditionally in *Ces procédés naïvement_atroces*
(p. 75, ll. 5, 6), *La vie vraiment_active et intellectuelle* (p. 81,
l. 40), *Il était admirablement_affirmatif de la nécessité de ne
rien affirmer* (p. 127, l. 2). In conversation this liaison is
usually neglected. Hence in the familiar expression *Ces
beaux raisins muscats . . . sont diablement appétissants aussi
(Parl. par.* p. 5, l. 2 ; *Fr. parlé* p. 13, l. 14), seven out of
fourteen avoid sounding the [t] of *diablement* even in
reading.

The adverb *toujours* is never linked by the authors of the
Chrestomathie ; they always carry the [r] over : *e.g.* in *Une
voix toujours écoutée* (p. 79, l. 37), *Il n'est pas toujours
aisé de dormir sur de la paille* (p. 117, l. 39). The [z] is,
however, very frequently sounded by other readers.

The nasal is never sounded in *enfin* : see *Parl. par.*
p. 59, l. 1 and the *Chrestomathie* p. 107, l. 11.

The question of liaison between an adjective or adverb and its complement is not one that often arises. In *bon à rien* and *prêt à partir* linking is usual even in conversation. All Koschwitz's readers save Rousselot link in *Impuissant à agir* (p. 35, l. 15). Similarly, in *Conformément à vos désirs*, the [t] would usually be sounded.

The [z] liaison is, however, avoided in the *Chrestomathie* in the line *Tous ils sont prêt(s) à nous fêter encore* (p. 167, l. 3).

The adverb *non* is not usually linked: *Ces deux forces opposées cherchaient à se limiter, à se balancer, non à se détruire* (*Chrest.* p. 71, l. 8). The transcription [nɔ̃ a ş detrɥiːr], without the [n] liaison, certainly represents the better practice.

(x) Between an adverb or adverbial expression preceding the subject and the subject.

An adverb in this position often must and nearly always may be treated as a distinct sound-group. It is, therefore, not surprising to find that the liaison is invariably avoided by the authors of the *Chrestomathie* in the transcription of the prose passages: *e.g.* in *Trois foi(s) il se pâme de douleur* (p. 79, l. 31), *Si depuis longtemp(s) ils avaient cette place* (p. 91 l. 6), *Commen(t) il s'appelle?*[1] (p. 131, l. 40), *Quelque-foi(s) on quitte la tente* (p. 117, l. 41). Similarly in verse they read without linking *Longtemp(s) aucun ne l'a cru* (p. 177, l. 33), *Alor(s) il se soulève* (p. 191, l. 33), *C'est pour renaître ailleurs qu'ici-ba(s) on succombe* (p. 213, l. 23). The liaison is, however, indicated as optional in *Parfois_il sommeillait* (p. 149, l. 23), *Jamais_aucune main n'avait passé sur elle* (p. 215, l. 5).

Examples from the *Parlers parisiens* in which all the readers concur in avoiding the liaison are *De temps en temp(s) elle relevait la tête* (p. 27, l. 5) and *Cette foi(s) elle abaissa ses*

[1] Cf. *Comment allez-vous?* in which the [t] is regularly sounded.

mains (p. 29, l. 18). Professor Ritter alone sounds the [t] in *Dans une heure où malheureusemen(t) elle divise et passionne* (p. 81, l. 22).

With the short adverbs *puis, plus, moins,* liaison may be heard even in conversation, though it cannot be considered usual. The liaisons are optional in *Mais plus_il se démenait, plus_il faisait de bruit, plus_il criait, et plus le garçon se gardait d'ouvrir* (*Chrest.* p. 29, ll. 7, 8). *Puis* may even be linked in spite of a comma : thus Zola, Ritter and Jacob sound the [z] in *Puïs, elle se sentait soulevée* (*Parl. par.* p. 13, l. 12). But if there is an inversion, linking does not take place quite so readily : it is avoided by the authors of the *Chrestomathie* in the following line from Victor Hugo's *Feuilles d'automne* : *Et pui(s) à votre fête il compare en son âme Son foyer* . . . (p. 203, ll. 1, 2).

(xi) Between a direct and an indirect object.

The available authorities seem to be unanimous in avoiding a liaison of this kind. The two objects usually belong to different sound-groups. In the sentence *On offrit à boire aux patient(s) un vin fortement aromatisé* (*Parl. par.* p. 59, l. 3), none of readers sound the [z]. Similarly, the authors of the *Chrestomathie* do not link the two objects in the following examples, both of which are taken from verse : *Ceux qui ne savaient pas la ruse* . . . *S'étonnaient de voir que Martin Chassât les lion(s) au moulin* (p. 153, l. 6), and *Dieu mit ces degré(s) aux fortunes humaines* (p. 203, l. 7).

(xii) Between any part of speech and the conjunction *et* or *ou*.

Where, as is often the case, the conjunction begins a fresh sound-group, there can, of course, be no question of liaison. But it no less frequently connects two words or expressions which may form a single group, and then linking becomes possible.

We may clear the ground at the outset, by observing that

the linking of a noun or adjective in the singular with either
of these conjunctions never takes place in conversation
(save in those consecrated expressions coming under rule
(x) for obligatory liaisons), is very seldom permissible in
the reading of prose, and not common in poetry. Thus
there must be no liaison in *un rat ou une souris* [œ̃ ra u yn
suri], *un chat et un chien* [œ̃ ʃa e œ̃ ʃjɛ̃], *le repos et la paix*
[lə rəpo e la pɛ], *le corps et le sang* [lə kɔːr e lə sɑ̃], *un
terrain plat et uni* [œ̃ tɛˈrɛ̃ pla e yni], *un couloir étroit et
sombre* [œ̃ kulwaːr etrwɑ e sɔ̃ːbr], *mon éminent et précieux ami*
[mɔ̃n eminɑ̃ e presjøz ami].   Hence none of Koschwitz's
readers sounds the [t] of *brillant* in *C'est le plus brillant et
le plus vaste génie de son siècle* (p. 83, l. 6), or the [n] of *bon*
in *Il ne lisait pas un livre, bon ou mauvais* (p. 37, l. 15), or
the [t] of *bouillant* in the line *D'avoir le sang bouillant et
l'âme un peu mutine* (p. 100, l. 13).   So too in the
Chrestomathie there is no liaison of adjective and conjunction in *Le corbeau, honteu(x) et confus* (p. 145, l. 20), *Un pur
mécanisme qui peut être ingénieu(x) et puissant* (p. 61, l. 7),
and in *Ce sont des faits d'un tout autre ordre, bien plus
délica(t) et plus élevé* (p. 59, l. 40).   Only in two instances are
singular adjectives linked with a conjunction in the *Parlers
parisiens*.   The first of these occurs in the prose passage
from the *Origine du déisme*: one of the readers sounds the
[z] of *doux* in *Le jeune homme doux et simple, aux mains
meurtries et gonflées*[1] (p. 85, l. 13).   The other example
is found in the extract from the *Fille de Roland*: M. Ritter
sounds the [k] of *long* in the line *Ou plutôt de ce long et dur
pèlerinage* (p. 111, l. 3), while all the other readers avoid the
liaison.   In his transcription of the fable *La Cigale et la
Fourmi*, M. Rousselot sounds the [t] in *Nuit‿et jour*
(*Précis de Pron. fr.* p. 199); and the [z] is often heard in

[1] The other readers are credited with the pronunciation [dus]; but
this is surely a misprint.

the line *Le corbeau, honteux_et confus*, already quoted, from
another of La Fontaine's fables.

A second class of cases which must be treated as exceptions comprises combinations of numerals with *et* and *ou*.
In *vingt et un* the [t] of *vingt* is always sounded. In
combinations such as *deux ou trois, trois ou quatre, trois et
quart* the liaison is optional even in conversation. It is
made by all the thirteen readers in *À deux_ou trois lieues de
la ville* (*Parl. par.* p. 7, l. 7), by twelve in *Deux_ou trois
enragés* (p. 5, l. 17), by all five in *On pouvait vivre trois_ou
quatre jours* (p. 63, l. 16). Prof. Paul Passy, however,
who has transcribed the first two of these examples in *Le
Français parlé* (p. 15, ll. 12 and 3), does not sound the [z].
The liaison is avoided by the authors of the *Chrestomathie*
in *deux ou trois fois* (p. 139, l. 42), and is given as optional
in *deux ou trois détails* (p. 95, l. 22).

The linking of plural nouns, of plural adjectives, of pronouns, verbs and adverbs with *et* and *ou* is comparable in
effect and frequency to the linking of a plural noun with a
following adjective. In daily intercourse it would generally
be heavy and pedantic. Hence in familiar expressions
such as *des tas et des tas* it is never heard even in reading.
Compare *des gens et des gens* (*Parl. par.* p. 21, l. 7) where
it is avoided by all the readers. Some speakers, however,
use it in expressions of time, such as *trois heures et demie*
[trwɑz œːrz e dmi], instead of the more usual [trwɑz œːr e
dmi]. But its proper sphere is poetry and the loftier kinds
of prose. A large number of expressions of the kind in
question occur in the prose passages transcribed in the
Chrestomathie and, save in the case of numerals, the liaison
is always avoided : *e.g.* in *Par d'obscure(s) et sanglantes révo-
lutions* (p. 57, l. 16), *Ces relations étroite(s) et sacrées* (p. 59,
l. 41), *Exception(s) et faveurs* (p. 91, l. 34), *Quelques travaux,
conçu(s) et exécutés avec l'ignorance turque* (p. 105, l. 26), *Tout*

cela émeu(t) et charme (p. 117, l. 29), *Une honnête famille cousan(t) ou lisant sous la lampe fidèle* (p. 121, l. 40), *Nous n'en savons pas plus, vou(s) et moi* (p. 129, l. 21). The linking of *émeut et charme* would create a confusion between the verbs and the nouns *émeute et charme* and must, therefore, be avoided. On the other hand, liaisons of this kind are not rare in the *Parlers parisiens*. A majority of the readers, for instance, link in the following cases : *Comprenant que ces vieilles pierres aimaient et pensaient comme elle* (p. 13, l. 5), *Chargés de clochetons, d'aiguilles et de pinacles* (p. 13, l. 18), *L'abside entière s'éveillait et grondait* (p. 15, l. 19), *Les sons, les mots et les formes* (p. 49, l. 1), *Les cadavres préparés et piqués par la main du même collectionneur* (p. 39, l. 13), *Aux mains meurtries et gonflées* (p. 85, l. 13). In two of these six examples, M. Rousselot is the only dissident, in three others he is one of two. The two liaisons in the expression *Les pernicieux et insensés systèmes des sophistes et des athées* (p. 83, l. 7) are made by all the readers.[1] But only one out of five links in *Deux vaillants et conscientieux explorateurs* (p. 55, l. 5), *Ses affaires trempées et frippées* (p. 25, l. 15); and none makes the liaison in *Les arcs-boutant(s) et les contreforts* (p. 15, l. 12), *Dont les effets fuyaien(t) et revenaient de page en page* (p. 39, l. 21), *Ses attaque(s) et ses sarcasmes* (p. 83, l. 15), *Ces allées si verte(s) et si riantes* (p. 85, l. 8). In the second and last of these six examples linking would give the idea too ponderous an expression, while in the first and the fifth the liaison is to be avoided for mere reasons of euphony.

Passing to verse the scale turns quite definitely in favour of the liaison. In most instances the link is made by all or almost all the readers of the *Parlers parisiens*. In the following instances all agree : *Je les reconnus trop, ces pics tristes et sombres* (p. 111, l. 10), *Et les champs et les mers* v

---

[1] Koschwitz is not sure that Rousselot sounded the [z] of *pernicieux*.

viennent tour à tour Se teindre d'une aurore éternelle et mouvante (p. 145, ll. 1, 2), *Avec le sol natal ils émergent_ou plongent* (p. 145, l 4)   All but M. Rousselot link adjective, noun or verb with the following conjunction in *Des voiles . changeants_et fidèles* (p. 129, l. 5), *De voix_et de parfums le bois est enchanté* (p. 125, l 19), *Les autres dans la nuit s'enfoncent_et s'allongent* (p. 145, l 6)   In their verse extracts MM Jean Passy and Rambeau usually mark this liaison as optional : *e.g.* in *L'hiver . . . Désole nos toits_et nos champs* (p 157, l 12), *Vassaux_et vilains* (p. 159, l. 22), *Et suivent de leurs yeux languissants_et superbes Le rêve intérieur* (p 219, ll. 27, 28), *Musculeux_et gonflés, L'Enfant sacré les tient* (p. 223, ll. 13, 14), *Lisant bien_ou mal ses immondes papiers* (p. 227, l. 25).   But even in verse, if the word already ends in a sounded consonant, the authors of the *Chrestomathie* usually carry this consonant over without resuscitating the latent final : *e.g.* in *Leurs amour(s) et leurs chants* (p. 157, l. 14), *Vous, page(s) et varlets* (p 161, l 29), *Nous maudissons ses fer(s) et ses bourreaux* (p. 171, l. 26).

(xiii) Between a conjunction and the word by which it is followed.

The question of liaison can present itself only with regard to the conjunctions *quand* and *mais*   In *et* the *t* is never linked; and all the other conjunctions end in a vowel or a sounded consonant   The linking of *quand*, as we have seen, may be considered obligatory.   Hence *mais* alone remains to be discussed.   In easy conversation the [z] in *mais* more often than not remains silent even when the conjunction forms a stress-group with a word or words that follow : *e.g. Mais enfin* [mε ɑ̃fɛ̃].[1]

In the reading of elevated prose and in the recitation of verse its treatment generally depends upon the nature of the contrast that it introduces.   If the contrast is striking,

[1] In *Mais oui* liaison is prohibited.

or if the reader wishes to give it peculiar force, *mais* forms
a sound-group in itself. The pitch of the voice is then
usually raised in uttering the conjunction, which is at the
same time more or less stressed. *Mais* is treated in this
manner by the authors of the *Chrestomathie* in the following
connection: *On y grelottait, sous la vaste capote du soldat,
pris de froid jusqu'à la moelle des os. Mais à cette époque,
c'était un plaisir* (p. 117, ll. 12-14). The *Parlers parisiens*
furnish an instructive example in a passage from Alphonse
Daudet's *Tartarin de Tarascon*: *Elles sont cependant bien
tentantes ces jolies colinettes tarasconnaises, . . . et ces beaux
raisins muscats gonflés de sucre qui s'échelonnent au bord du
Rhône, sont diablement appétissants aussi! Oui, mais il y a
Tarascon derrière, et dans le petit monde du poil et de la
plume, Tarascon est très mal noté* (p. 3, ll. 15, 16; p. 5,
ll. 1-4). Daudet himself and five other readers heighten
the contrast by pausing after *mais*, and avoiding the liaison.
Seven others carry the [z] over. Professor Paul Passy
makes a sound-group out of the words *mais il y a Tarascon
derrière*, which he transcribes with the very familiar pronunciation [me j a taraskɔ̃ dɛrjɛːr] (*Fr. parl.* p. 13, ll. 14, 15).
While fusing *mais* into a longer group he still does not
sound the [z]. The treatment of the conjunction in such
cases, therefore, depends upon the reader's conception and
interpretation of the passage.

Where the contrast is not sufficiently abrupt and surprising to justify this reinforcement of the conjunction, it forms
a group with whatever words may follow. The liaison then
becomes a matter of style. It will often be neglected in
passages of a colloquial character, more rarely, however, in
verse and elevated prose. Optional liaisons in the *Chrestomathie* are found in *Cette époque . . . se rattache . . . à la
personne et au règne de Charlemagne, mais_elle transforme ces
souvenirs* (p. 71, l. 31), *On constata bien la continuité de la*

vie nationale . . . mais_on ne chercha pas à discerner, etc.
(p. 83, l 8), *Son office n'est pas une sinécure comme leur rang ; mais_il comporte des inconvénients aussi graves* (p. 91, l. 14). The [z] is sounded in *La Renaissance n'y fut pas une révolution subite, mais_un mouvement continu* (p 83, l. 4), *Le corbeau . . . Jura . . . mais_un peu tard*, etc. (p. 145, l. 21), but not in *L'opposition des nations les unes aux autres est nécessaire pour qu'elles apprennent, non seulement à apprécier les autres, mai(s) à se comprendre elles-mêmes* (p. 65, l 29), nor in *Roland s'y refuse, par fierté personnelle d'abord et par orgueil de famille, mai(s) aussi par honneur national* (p. 77, l. 33) Koschwitz's readers never all agree in neglecting or avoiding this liaison, nor do they often all concur in making it. They all link, however, in *Mais_il s'engage à n'abandonner pas le dessein*, etc. (p. 70, l 3), *Ils n'osent pas se dire Anglais, mais_il se font Bourguignons* (p 73, l. 2), *Elle ne regardait alors aucune des personnes présentes, mais_entièrement retournée vers la vitre, elle semblait*, etc. (p 27, l. 8), *Il affirme, à sa manière, il est vrai, mais_enfin il affirme* (p. 81, l 17) But M. Rousselot dissents in *Non seulement dans les faits relatés au jour le jour, mais_avec tous les sentiments furtifs*, etc. (p. 37, l. 12), and in *Mais_il est des nations que Dieu aime* (p 69, l 14). An interesting example is found at page 47, line 1 : *Mais, au fur et à mesure qu'on s'éloigne de la capitale*, etc. Here all the readers save M. Rousselot link, in spite of the comma. Professor Passy transcribes the same sentence with a pause after *mais* and, therefore, like M. Rousselot, does not sound the [z] (*Fr. parlé*, p. 73, l. 22)

(xiv) Between a relative pronoun other than *dont* (which must always be linked) and the following word.

The question of liaison arises only in connection with the plurals *auxquels, auxquelles, lesquels, lesquelles*. The linking of these pronouns is confined to lofty style, and

rarely takes place even there. It is never made by the
authors of the *Chrestomathie*.   All five of Koschwitz's
readers avoid it in *Des langues . . . dans lesquelle(s) aucun
mot semblable . . . ne frappera votre oreille* (p. 47, l. 13),
and in *Les exécuteurs, auxquel(s) on abandonnait . . . les
menues dépouilles des suppliciés* (p. 59, l. 18): nor does
Professor Passy sound the [z] in his version of the former
phrase (*Fr. parlé*, p. 75, l. 10).   Three out of five readers
link relative and personal pronoun in *Il regrettait alors les
bonnes habitudes . . . auxquelles_il avait été brusquement
arraché* (p. 25, l. 17), but even here MM. Rousselot and
Jacob dissent.

(xv) Between the parts of compound locutions.

In plural compound nouns of a fixed form like *des guets-
apens, des arcs-en-ciel, des crocs-en-jambe, des chars-à-banc,
des pots-à-eau*, the [z] is not sounded: [de gɛt apɑ̃] [dez
ark ɑ̃ sjɛl] [de krɔk ɑ̃ ʒɑ̃ːb] [de ʃaːr a bɑ̃] [de pɔt a o].   But
in new forms created on the same model the determining
words have an adjectival force, and liaison may take place
as between a noun and an adjective (Rule (i)).   Thus in
the *Parlers parisiens* all the readers link in *fenêtres_à
plein cintre* (p. 13, l. 10), *des hommes_en blouse* (p. 21,
l. 11),[1] and all but MM. Rousselot and Jacob sound the
[z] of *noirs* in *Ces pins noirs_aux gigantesques ombres* (p. 111,
l. 11).   But in reading the long compound *Ses mains aux
veines saillantes et violettes, aux ongles cassés* (p. 25, l. 13),
all five pause after *mains* and avoid the liaison.

The combinations *les uns aux autres, les unes aux autres*
are best read [lez œ̃ oz oːtr] [lez yn oz oːtr]: for examples,
see the *Chrestomathie*, p. 101, l. 9, and p. 65, l. 16.   MM. J.
Passy and Rambeau further avoid the liaison in *les tournées
aux tournées* (p. 115, l. 36) where the [z] might well be

---

[1] M. Rousselot appears to have neglected the liaison in a second and
more rapid reading.

sounded as it is by three out of five readers in *de sommets
en sommets* (*Parl. par.* p. 115, l. 19). Similarly, *d'un bout
à l'autre* is transcribed in the *Chrestomathie* (p. 117, l. 3)
without liaison, while the [t] is sounded in the same expression by all five of Koschwitz's readers at page 55, line 16
of the *Parlers parisiens*, and by Professor Paul Passy at
page 83, line 1 of *Le Français parlé*.

This long array of rules and suggestions leaves a wide
field to choice. Linking is, after all, a kind of art. Judgment and taste must be exercised. And that they may be
exercised to good purpose these faculties need training. It
is inevitable that the learner should make many faults and
be often in doubt before he acquires, as a kind of special
instinct, the feeling that will enable him to satisfy all
requirements. This means careful study; but it is by no
means an unattainable ideal. And the student may be
encouraged by a knowledge of the fact that in a considerable
percentage of the cases that will come under his notice,
when he begins to read more or less widely, the opinions of
qualified Frenchmen as to the propriety of liaison would be
divided. In such cases he can hardly make a really bad
choice. But it is only in virtue of a real feeling for the
language, which also involves a certain degree of education
generally, that he will be able to detect these cases with
some assurance when he meets them. While being aware
of their existence he must, therefore, hesitate to exaggerate
their prevalence.

In training his taste and judgment beyond the range of
rule, any one or more of three courses may be adopted.
He may, in the first place, appeal to a well-qualified teacher.
The latter will have no easy task. Whether he be a
Frenchman, or of the student's own nationality, he will need
not only to have the gift of taste, but to have devoted
special study to the subject before he can give soundly

undogmatic advice. If the ordinary educated Frenchman is
consulted in a case of difficulty, he is almost sure to insist
on the link being made, not necessarily because he would
make it himself, but because he has been constantly warned
in his early school-days not to be careless in this matter, and
has not closely observed his own practice, or that of his
fellow-countrymen. In a similar way ask an educated
Englishman whether it is right to sound a final *r*, *e.g.* in
fire, *fare*, *more*, and he will very probably answer in the
affirmative, though, as a matter of fact, no [r] is heard in
the standard English pronunciation of such words. In
seeking advice it is, therefore, necessary to remember that
the school, and particularly the primary school, has been
the home of liaison in France. It is pleasing to note that
on this point teaching tends to become less conservative.

A second course, of great value, is the reading of texts in
phonetic script. Such texts are, unfortunately, not very
numerous. The most valuable for the study of liaison are
the *Parlers parisiens* of E. Koschwitz, and the *Chrestomathie française* of Jean Passy and A. Rambeau, from
which most of the examples in the present chapter have
been taken. To these may be added *Le Français parlé* of
Professor Paul Passy. The latter author, having adopted
the pronunciation of familiar speech, is, like the authors
of the *Chrestomathie*, very sparing with his liaisons. In
neither of the latter two works does the omission of a
liaison necessarily imply that its use in reading would be
improper.[1]

---

[1] The reading of phonetic texts is to be strongly recommended, not
only in connection with the subject of this chapter, but for French
pronunciation generally. Koschwitz's work, in addition to the
possibility of errors in the record, has the disadvantage of being written
in a rather complicated system of phonetic notation of the author's own
devising, and of recording provincial pronunciations as well as Parisian.
The *Chrestomathie* and the *Français parlé* are both transcripts of the

If the student is able to adopt the third course, and pass some time in France, he will need to choose or make his occasions for hearing with discrimination, he will need to gain admittance into the right kind of society and, therewithal, to have considerable powers of observation, and a keen and quick ear   The materials are not rapidly collected without much effort, and the right deductions cannot be made without some insight.   It will be of incalculable advantage to him to have first made a close study of French phonetics

authors' own pronunciation, and employ the system of the International Phonetic Association.

Other texts in international phonetic script are P. Passy's *Premier livre de lecture*, 4ᵉ éd Paris, 1899 ; *Deuxième livre de lecture*, 2ᵉ éd Paris, 1899 ; *Histoires pour enfants*, Paris, 1896-9 ; *Versions populaires du Nouveau Testament*, Paris, 1893-6 ; *Choix de lectures*, Köthen, 1904 , Ch Halter's *Histoire de France* ; V. Partington's *French Songs and Poems*, London, 1903 ; Felix Franke's *Phrases de tous les jours* (8th ed. Leipzig, Reisland, 1900).   The Association publishes a journal ' *Le Maître Phonétique*,' edited by Professor Paul Passy (Bourg-la-Reine, Seine).   The articles, in various languages, of which French, English and German predominate, are printed in phonetic type

CHAPTER III

ELISION

In certain positions in a sound-group certain sounds which are normally heard when the syllable in which they occur is pronounced in isolation drop away or suffer elision. The phenomenon is recognized to some extent by the traditional rules of grammar. We write *l'homme* for *le homme*, *j'ai* for *je ai*, *quelqu'un* for *quelque un*, *presqu'île* for *presque-île*, *entr'acte* for *entre-acte*, *l'âme* for *la âme*, *s'il est* for *si il est*, *ç'aurait été* for *ça aurait été* or *ce aurait été*.[1]

A. Elision of [ə] in single syllables.

The only vowel-sound, however, that regularly undergoes elision in this way is the so-called *e* mute : [ə]. A right treatment of the syllables in which this letter occurs is one of the chief marks of a good French pronunciation. It is essentially based on euphony tempered by the need to avoid obscurity, and can generally be set forth in the form of rules, but as, outside a certain range, the demands of euphony are variously interpreted, the elision or non-elision of [ə] may become a matter of feeling and taste.

In discussing this subject it is necessary to distinguish

[1] Strangely enough the elided letters in *s'il est*, *ç'aurait été* are usually sounded in speaking, though not in reading : [si il ɛ] [sa ɔrɛt ete] instead of [sil ɛ] [s ɔrɛt ete].

three positions in the sound-group: (1) the initial syllable,
(ii) the final syllable, and (iii) interior syllables.

(i) *An* [ə] *in the initial syllable of a sound-group.*

In the first syllable of a sound-group the [ə] is not elided.
Hence, when words of which the first syllable contains an [ə]
are named individually, and thus form sound-groups in
themselves, or when they introduce a larger sound-group, the
[ə] must be given its full value *venir* [vəniːr], *tenir* [təniːr],
lever [ləve], *demander* [dəmɑ̃·de], *ceci* [səsi], *cerise* [səriːz],
cheval [ʃəval], *serein* [sərɛ̃], *semelle* [səmɛl], *semaine* [səmɛn],
fenêtre [fənɛːtr], *dessus* [dəsy], *relief* [rəljɛf], *remise* [rəmiːz],
renard [rənaːr], *repas* [rəpɑ].

The only real exceptions are *pelote* [plɔt] and its kindred,
peluche [plyʃ] and its derivatives, *pelure* [plyːr] and *pelouse*
[pluːz] And of these *pelure* may be pronounced with [ə]:
[pəlyːr].

The rule applies to the monosyllables containing [ə]:
ce lac [sə lak], *le sel* [lə sɛl], *se plaire* [sə plɛːr], *te ranger*
[tə rɑ̃ːʒe], *je dis* [ʒə di], *me souvenir* [mə suvniːr], *ne pas
croire* [nə pɑ krwaːr], *de rire* [də riːr], *que voulez-vous* [kə
vule vu].

In free and easy conversation certain liberties are
frequently taken: *ce n'est pas* may become [snɛpɑ], *ce qui
nous manque* [ski nu mɑ̃ːk], *ce que tu dis* [skə ty di], *je l'ai
dit* [ʒle di], *je te dis* [ʒ̊tədi], *je crois* [ʒ̊krwɑ], *je peux dire*
[ʒ̊pø diːr], *je vous assure* [ʒvuz asyːr], *le maître* [lmɛːtr],
de temps en temps [d̥tɑ̃z ɑ̃ tɑ̃] [tɑ̃z ɑ̃ tɑ̃], *venez* [vne], *deviner*
[dvine], *relève* [rlɛːv], *secoue* [sku].   These and analogous
elisions are common, and may be imitated by the fluent
speaker.   They should not, however, be generally practised
by the student.

Thus, if we except *pelouse, peluche, pelote* and their
derivatives, we arrive at this simple result: In the first
syllable of a sound-group, that is, at the beginning of every

sentence and after every pause, the [ə] may always and
generally must be retained.

(ii) *An* [ə] *in the last syllable of a sound-group.*

In this position the [ə] is regularly elided. Hence the
last '*e*' is not sounded in the following expressions: *il faut
le prendre* [il fo l prɑ̃:dr], *il est sur la table* [il ɛ syr la tabl],
la mer est calme [la mɛːr ɛ kalm], *devant la fenêtre* [dəvɑ̃ la
fnɛːtr], *ils parlent* [il parl], *ils parlaient* [il parlɛ], *les voiles se
gonflent* [le vwal sə gɔ̃:fl], *c'est un dogme* [sɛt œ̃ dɔgm], *voilà
un prisme* [vwala œ̃ prism], *une forte somme* [yn fɔrtə sɔm],
une robe élégante [yn rɔb elegɑ̃:t], *dans la rue* [dɑ̃ la ry].
Expressions like *croyez-le*, *le mot je* are only apparent exceptions; under the stress of the tonic accent the vowel [ə]
becomes either [œ] or [ø]: [krwɑje lø] [lə mo ʒø]. When
que is immediately followed by a parenthesis it may end a
sound-group: it is then treated similarly and becomes [kø]
or [kœ].

The rule for the elision of the last [ə] in a sound-group is
subject to certain optional or occasional exceptions. Thus,
in deliberate speech, the [ə] in question may be pronounced
lightly when it follows a group of two or more consonants.
It is, therefore, not incorrect to sound the final [ə] in *il faut
le prendre*, *il est sur la table*, *c'est un prisme*. Again, any
mute [ə] may be resuscitated when words are set to music:
vie may become [viə], *j'aime* [ʒɛːmə]. Finally, if it were
necessary to distinguish pairs of masculine and feminine
words such as *donné* and *donnée*, *ami* and *amie*, the pronunciation of which is normally identical, the final [ə] of the
feminine might be sounded.

(iii) *An* [ə] *in an interior syllable of a sound-group.*

It is usually said that [ə] in an interior syllable is elided
unless its loss would give rise to a group of three consonants
which cannot be readily pronounced together. This statement undoubtedly embodies the main principle, but it is a

quite inadequate guide for the English-speaking student. The latter, producing the French sounds perhaps imperfectly, and being thoroughly accustomed to heavy groups of consonants in his own language, is apt to form wrong ideas as to the consonants that cannot be 'readily pronounced together' in French. To meet this difficulty the easy group has been defined as one in which the last of the three consonants is a liquid or a semi-vowel, that is, one of the sounds [r] [l] [w] [ɥ] [j]. Unfortunately the rule loses in accuracy what it thus gains in definiteness: in its amended form it covers many cases where elision is not permissible, and fails to include many others in which elision regularly takes place. Though the subject presents no great difficulties, it is not simple enough to be treated in a general formula.

The defects of the rule above-mentioned might be made good by framing rules to meet the exceptions. For practical purposes, however, it will be expedient to approach the subject in a simpler manner. The student need scarcely ever adopt the unnatural and tedious practice of looking on to see what consonants follow the vowel. When an [ə] stands between consonants its loss or survival, if it be not merely a matter of rhythm, depends upon the preceding sounds. The elision of [ə] in the body of a sound-group may, therefore, be considered under the following heads :

(a) When the [ə] follows or precedes a vowel.
(b) When it follows a single consonant.
(c) When it follows two or more consonants.

(a) *When the* [ə] *follows or precedes a vowel.*

In these positions the [ə] is dropped, even in verse : *flageolet* [flaʒɔlɛ], *geai* [ʒe], *louerai* [lure], *jouerai* [ʒure], *prierai* [prire], *fierai* [fire], *lierai* [lire], *oublierai* [ublire], *entre eux* [ɑ̃'tr ø], *quelque animal* [kɛlk animal], *pauvre homme* [po'vr ɔm].

An [ə] preceding a vowel survives exceptionally :

1. Where an 'h aspirate' intervenes in spelling : *e.g. le héros* [lə ero], *le hublot* [lə yblo], *je hais* [ʒə ɛ].

2. In certain cases where the vowel is a semi-vowel : *e.g. le oui et le non* [lə wi e l nɔ̃].[1]

3. In *le* and *de* before a quotation or the name of a letter or figure : *e.g. le 'a'* [lə a], *le 'e'* [lə e], *le un* [lə œ̃], *le onze* [lə ɔ̃z]. Elision, however, may take place before the name of a letter : *l''a'* [la], *l''e'* [le].

4. In the pronoun-object after an imperative, the [ə] usually changing to [œ] or [ø] : *e.g. donnez-le aux pauvres* [dɔne lø o po'vr].

(*b*) *When the* [ə] *follows a single consonant-sound.*

An [ə] following a single consonant-sound in the body of a sound-group is regularly elided. In applying this rule care must be taken not to confound 'consonant-sound' with 'consonant-sign.' Thus the [ə] in *commandement* follows the single consonant-sound [d], the *n* merely serving to show that the preceding vowel is nasalized : [kɔmɑ̃'dmɑ̃] ; the *ch* in *acheter* indicates the single sound [ʃ], hence we elide the [ə] : [aʃte] ; the *pp* in *rappeler* stands for a simple [p], and we say [raple]. Double consonant-signs nearly always represent a single sound.[2]

This rule is subject to certain compulsory and certain optional exceptions which will be mentioned in connection with each class of examples.

1. Examples where the [ə] occurs in a monosyllable :

N'est-ce pas ? [nɛs pɑ] ; *ai-je dit* [ɛ'ʒ di] ; *qui se dit* [ki s di] ; *loin de la maison* [lwɛ̃ d la me'zɔ̃] ; *tout le monde* [tu l mɔ̃d] ; *peu de chose* [pø d ʃoːz] ; *il faut le dire* [il fo l diːr]; *on doit le croire* [ɔ̃ dwa l krwɑːr]; *et ainsi de suite* [e ɛ̃ˈsi d̬ sɥit]; *le grec et le latin* [lə grɛk e l latɛ̃].

An obligatory exception is found in the pronoun *le* after an imperative : *notez-le bien* [nɔte lə bjɛ̃] or [nɔte lø bjɛ̃].

In deliberate speech, particularly in reading, the [ə] of a monosyllable may be sounded. The *Parlers parisiens* of Koschwitz furnish us with some interesting and instructive illustrations. This work, unfortunately, cannot be consulted at large on the question of elision ; first, because in such a delicate matter the risk of error in the record is too great,[1] and, secondly, because the pronunciation of some of the readers is emphatically provincial. But in one instance neither of these objections holds good. The pronunciation of Gaston Paris,[2] who, though born at Avenay, lived at Paris from his earliest infancy, would be universally accepted as a model. And as the transcript of the passage he read was examined and approved by him [3] it is sure to represent his pronunciation faithfully. This passage, moreover, being a good average specimen of literary prose, neither familiar nor very elevated in style, is peculiarly adapted for the study of elision. We may, therefore, cite the readings of Gaston Paris with confidence. At the same time we may compare them with those of Professor Paul Passy, who had previously published in *Le Français parlé*, a phonetic transcript of the same passage.[4]

This comparison as regards the elision of the ' *e* mute ' in monosyllables gives the following results :

Gaston Paris sounds and M. Passy elides the italicised ' *e* mute ' in the expressions : Le dialecte de Paris et de l'Ile de France ; allez aux environs de Valenciennes ; on a généralement adopté le français d'école ; un langage fort

---

[1] See Linking, p. 85.   [2] Pronounce [pɑˈris].
[3] See *Parlers parisiens*, Intro. xxviii, and pp. 43-55.
[4] *Le Français parlé*, pp. 72-86.

différent de celui que nous parlons et fort différent de celui qu'on parle dans chacun des autres ; du côté d'Avignon, . . . ou de Pau ; vous le savez ; faisant abstraction pour un moment de l'extension artificielle du parler de Paris ; nous aurons le tableau d'une immense bigarrure ; nous verrons des sons . . . couvrir une certaine région et ne pas pénétrer dans une autre ; mais le fait qui ressort . . . c'est que toutes ces variantes de phonétique, . . . et de vocabulaire n'empêchent pas une unité fondamentale, et que d'un bout de la France à l'autre, etc.; celui de la commune voisine ; son voisin de droite et son voisin de gauche ; une étoile dont on pourrait de même relier les rayons ; cette loi, c'est que dans une masse linguistique de même origine comme la nôtre, il n'y a réellement pas de dialectes ; il n'y a que des traits linguistiques ; avec le parler de chacun des quatre endroits ; une certaine étendue de terrain ; ou de plusieurs autres traits ; il suit de là que tout le travail qu'on a dépensé, etc.; ces mots n'ont de sens qu'appliqués à la production ; embarrassé de ranger ; et que d'un bout à l'autre, etc.

Both Gaston Paris and M. Passy elide the [ə] in the following instances : Entre la langue nationale et le parler populaire ; laissant de côté ; dans le territoire restant ; l'extension artificielle du parler de Paris ; dans tout le midi ; dans tout le nord ; dans tout le centre ; d'un bout de la France à l'autre ; un villageois qui ne saurait que le patois de sa commune ; avec un peu plus de difficulté ; et ainsi de suite ; comme on se l'imagine ; tout le travail qu'on a dépensé ; dans l'ensemble des parlers de la France ; des dialectes et ce qu'on a appelé des 'sous-dialectes' ; dès le moyen-âge ; entre le français et le provençal ; avaient plus de faveur que les autres ; entre le provençal et le français ; cette étrange frontière qui de l'ouest à l'est couperait la France.

In only one case does M. Passy sound the [ə] of a

monosyllable which Gaston Paris elides : ces trois coins de
métal étranger qui encadrent notre carte linguistique.   Here
M Passy apparently reads the words ' de métal étranger ' as
a distinct sound-group.
   The readings of Gaston Paris and M. Paul Passy thus
present a striking contrast as regards the elision of the [ə]
after a single consonant-sound in monosyllables : the one
dispenses with the [ə] in almost every case, the other more
often than not retains it.   This difference proceeds from a
difference in the style of diction.   M. Passy, like the authors
of the *Chrestomathie*, adopts in his version the pronunciations of familiar conversation, while the diction of Gaston
Paris is leisurely and ' correct.'   The contrast is referred to
by Koschwitz, in his prefatory note to the specimen, in
these words   ' M. G Paris et M Joret, qui assistait à
l'audition, trouvaient également que M. Passy avait donné
à son texte figuré un caractère par trop familier. . . .   M.
Paris qui, même dans la conversation, prononce avec une
rare correction, ne s'est permis, dans la lecture, presque
aucune des négligences du parler parisien : les *e* sourds
ne disparaissaient chez lui que bien à propos, etc.'
   The propriety of the elisions made by Gaston Paris is
more easily felt than explained.   They are such as do not
rob the phrase of its leisurely and dignified march.   It
is instructive to observe that while another careful reader
might well elide the [ə] more frequently than Paris, few
would retain it where it was dropped by him.   Elision
should take place even in deliberate diction when the
monosyllable forms part of a familiar expression such as
*ainsi de suite, tout de suite, tout le monde, peu de chose, jeu
de mots, dans le monde, ·tout le travail, cela se dit, qui ne
sait pas, n'est-ce pas ? ai-je dit*   It may also be noted
that of all the monosyllables *ne* is the one in which the
[ə] is most regularly elided, and *que* the one in which

it is most often retained. This is not the result of hazard, but has its reason in the respective functions of the two words. *Ne* is generally accompanied by *pas*, and that the idea of negation resides rather in the latter particle is shown by the fact that the *ne* is often entirely suppressed in conversation, and that even when it is retained the accent nearly always falls upon the *pas*. *Que*, on the other hand, as conjunction or as relative pronoun, indicates the relation between two sentences, and the elision of the [ə], involving as a rule their combination in a single sound-group, renders the transition from one to the other peculiarly abrupt. Gaston Paris does not elide the [ə] of *que* in a single instance. M. Passy himself retains it in the expression : *Un endroit où il n'entendrait plus que très péniblement l'idiome local.* In *ne . . . que* the *que* is very often preserved intact even in conversation.

2. Examples where the [ə] occurs in the initial syllable of a word :

Mon cheval [mɔ̃ ʃval], *la gelée* [la ʒle], *les leçons* [le lsɔ̃], *la religion* [la rliʒjɔ̃], *la Renaissance* [la rnɛsɑ̃ːs], *un secret* [œ̃ skrɛ], *dans lequel* [dɑ̃ lkɛl], *sans retour* [sɑ̃ rtuːr], *à genoux* [a ʒnu], *en revanche* [ɑ̃ rvɑ̃ːʃ], *la semaine* [la smɛn], *il s'y refuse* [il si rfyːz], *il est reçu* [il ɛ rsy], *nous regardons* [nu rgardɔ̃], *s'en retourner* [sɑ̃ rturne], *nous avons reconnu* [nuz avɔ̃ rkɔny], *vous avez repris* [vuz ave rpri], *vous venez* [vu vne], *nous tenons* [nu tnɔ̃], *vous menez* [vu mne], *nous devons* [nu dvɔ̃], *dix degrés* [di dgre], *nous serons* [nu srɔ̃], *vous ferez* [vu fre].

This [ə] survives exceptionally :

(a) Before the endings ' consonant + ions [jɔ̃] ' and ' consonant + iez [je] ' : *nous venions* [nu vənjɔ̃], *vous veniez* [vu vənje] ; *nous tenions* [nu tənjɔ̃], *vous teniez* [vu tənje] ; *nous menions* [nu mənjɔ̃], *vous meniez* [vu mənje] ; *nous devions* [nu dəvjɔ̃], *vous deviez* [vu dəvje] ; *nous serions* [nu sərjɔ̃], *vous seriez* [vu sərje] ; *nous faisions* [nu fəzjɔ̃], *vous faisiez* [vu fəzje], *nous ferions* [nu fərjɔ̃], *vous feriez* [vu fərje] ; *nous peltons* [nu pəljɔ̃], *vous peltez* [vu pəlje] ; *à relter* [a rəlje].

(β) In a few words which would otherwise lose their identity or become obscure : *un benêt* [œ̃ bənɛ], *la bedaine* [la bədɛn], *un bedeau* [œ̃ bədo], *la besace* [la bəzas], *les besicles* [le bəzikl], *au dehors* [o dəɔːr], *un denter* [œ̃ dənje], *la femelle* [la fəmɛl], *un levrter* [œ̃ ləvrie], *la pelade* [la pəlad], *il est penaud* [il ɛ pəno], *tl est tenace* [il ɛ tənas], *peser* [pəze] in all its parts and all its derivatives.

The [ə] in an initial syllable after a single consonant in the body of a sound-group may, like the [ə] of a mono-syllable, be retained in deliberate speech. A comparison of the pronunciations of Gaston Paris and M. Paul Passy in this respect, in the passage above referred to, gives the following result : Passy elides the [ə] in every case but one, Paris retains it in every case but two. Paris sounds and Passy elides the [ə] in the following · La France a depuis longtemps une seule langue officielle ; langue qui représente notre nationalité ; on relève des différences ; vous recon-naîtrez, nous remarquerons ; le fait qui ressort ; loi qui doit renouveler toutes les méthodes ; on doit reconnaître ; traits qui lui seront communs avec le parler. Both elide the [ə] in : Au fur et à mesure ; Il nous sera possible. Both retain it in   En faisant une vaste chaîne.

The contrast between the methods of Gaston Paris and Paul Passy is, therefore, no less marked in the treatment of initial [ə] syllables than in that of monosyllables ; and it is again Passy's method that is followed in the *Chrestomathie.* The comments made on the treatment of monosyllables apply *mutatis mutandis* in the present case. Only a halting delivery would retain the 'mute *e*'s' in conversation, whereas in reading they may very frequently be preserved. It may be noted that, if Koschwitz's record

is to be trusted, the other four readers never all agreed in
sounding the [ə] where it had been elided by M. Passy.

3. Examples where the [ə] stands in an inner syllable
of a word:

Complètement [kɔ̃'plɛtmɑ̃], *doucement* [dusmɑ̃], *seulement*
[sœlmɑ̃], *rarement* [ru'rmɑ̃], *gravement* [gra'vmɑ̃], *maintenant*
[mɛ̃'tnɑ̃], *enseignement* [ɑ̃'sɛɲmɑ̃], *effronterie* [ɛfrɔ̃'tri],
boulangerie [bulɑ̃'ʒri], *sellerie* [sɛlri], *honnêteté* [ɔnɛtte],
sainteté [sɛ̃'tte], *acheter* [a'ʃte], *achèterai* [a'ʃɛtre], *atteler* [atle],
accueillerai [akœjre], *soutenir* [sutniːr], *soutenez* [sutne],
soutenu [sutny], *contenir* [kɔ̃'tniːr], *maintenir* [mɛ̃'tniːr],
convenir [kɔ̃'vniːr], *provenir* [prɔvniːr], *prévenir* [prevniːr],
amener [amne], *développer* [devlɔpe], *échapperons* [eʃaprɔ̃],
trouvera [truvra], *tirerai* [ti'rre], *comparerez* [kɔ̃'parre],
arriveras [arivra], *différeront* [diferrɔ̃].

The [ə] in this position must, however, be sounded:

(α) Before the verbal endings 'consonant + ions [jɔ̃]' and
'consonant + iez [je]': *nous convenions* [nu kɔ̃'vənjɔ̃], *vous
conveniez* [vu kɔ̃'vənje]; *nous prévenions* [nu prevənjɔ̃], *vous
préveniez* [vu prevənje]; *nous amenions* [nuz amənjɔ̃], *vous
ameniez* [vuz amənje]; *nous soutenions* [nu sutənjɔ̃], *vous
souteniez* [vu sutənje]; *nous appelions* [nuz apəljɔ̃], *vous
appeliez* [vuz apəlje]; *nous donnerions* [nu dɔnərjɔ̃], *vous
donneriez* [vu dɔnərje]; *nous trouverions* [nu truvərjɔ̃], *vous
trouveriez* [vu truvərje][1]; *nous accueillerions* [nuz akœjərjɔ̃],
vous accueilleriez [vuz akœjərje].

This class of exceptions includes a few nouns in *-lier*: *e.g.*
atelier [atəlje], *râtelier* [rɑtəlje], *bachelier* [baʃəlje], *chapelier*
[ʃapəlje]. Cf. *cabaretier* [kabartje], and *savetier* [saɣtje].

(β) In all parts of the verbs *concevoir* [kɔ̃'səvwaːr], *décevoir*
[desəvwaːr], *recevoir* [rəsəvwaːr]. If the [ə] were elided

[1] In these persons of the Conditional of verbs of the First Conjugation the [ə] is sometimes elided: the ending then changes to [iɔ̃] [ie],
e.g. [truvriɔ̃] [truvrie].

here regressive vocalization [1] would take place, and the identity of the words would be imperilled. The pronunciation with elision, *e.g.* [kɔ'ṣvwaːr], is nevertheless occasionally heard in conversation.

The optional exceptions to the elision of an inner [ə] are few : the [ə] may be resuscitated only in verbs, particularly compound verbal forms in which it is the root vowel of the simple verb : *e.g.* in *maintenir* and other compounds of *tenir* ; in *convenir* and other compounds of *venir* ; in *amener* and other compounds of *mener*.

Elsewhere the suppression of the inner [ə] after a single consonant may be regarded as obligatory on all occasions. Pronunciations such as [kɔ'plɛtəmɑ̃] [dusəmɑ̃] [sœləmɑ̃] are as distinctly dialectal as the Scotch [wɔrəld] for [wɐːld] *world*.

4. Examples where the [ə] occurs at the end of a word :

Toute la terre [tut la tɛːr], *mille deux cents* [mil dø sɑ̃], *une lumière rouge* [yn lymjɛ'r ruːʒ], *elles fondent en larmes* [ɛl fɔ̃ːdt ɑ̃ larm], *ils peuvent en appeler* [il pœyt ɑ̃n aple].

In this position the [ə] is elided on all occasions and without exception. Thus in *l'ardente croix* (*Chrest.* p. 179, l. 29) the [ə] should not be sounded, even in verse, although it counts in the measure, and although its elision creates a group of four consonants : [lardɑ̃ːt krwɑ].

(*c*) *When the* [ə] *follows two or more consonant-sounds.*

An [ə] following a group of consonants in the interior of a sound-group is generally required as a supporting-vowel (voyelle d'appui) and must be given its full value whatever may be the nature of the consonant by which it is followed.

1. This rule is without exception when the two consonants belong to different words : *par ce moyen* [par sə mwajɛ̃], *l'art de lire* [la'r də liːr], *pour se sauver* [pur sə so've], *pour secourir* [pur səkuriːr], *pour te dire* [pur tə diːr],

---
[1] See Assimilation, p. 152.

il nous sert de guide [il nu sɛ'r də gid], *pour venir* [pur
vəniːr], *pour lever* [pur ləve], *peur de rien* [pœ'r də rjɛ̃].
Exceptions do occur occasionally in rapid familiar speech,
trop de cerises, for example, being pronounced [trɔḍ sriːz],
une petite [yn ptit], *je le ferai* [ʒəl fre], *il ne sera pas*
[in sra pɑ], *elles seront* [ɛl srɔ̃]. The student, however, is
recommended not to adopt such abbreviations, but to read
[trɔḍ səriːz] [yn pətit] [ʒəl fəre] [il nə sra pɑ] [ɛl sərɔ̃].

Hence we may make the helpful generalization that the
[ə] of a monosyllable and the [ə] in an initial syllable are
never elided when the preceding word ends with a consonant-sound.

2. The rule is again without exception when the consonants form an initial group : *en Bretagne* [ɑ̃ brətaɲ], *la
bretelle* [la brətɛl], *vous prenez* [vu prəne], *en prenant* [ɑ̃
prənɑ̃], *la première* [la prəmjɛːr].

3. On the other hand, elision of the [ə] after a group
of consonants takes place very commonly, in conversation,
in the Future and Conditional tenses of verbs of the First
Conjugation, save (α) where the [r] of the termination is
followed by [j], that is, in *-erions, -eriez* ; (β) where the
group preceding the [ə] ends in [r] or [l].

Examples : *je garderai* [ʒə gardəre] [ʒə gardre], *tu resteras*
[tu rɛstəra] [tu rɛstra], *il forcera* [il fɔrsəra] [il fɔrsra], *nous
observerons* [nuz ɔpsɛrvərɔ̃] [nuz ɔpsɛrvrɔ̃], *vous remarquerez*
[vu rəmarkəre] [vu rmarkre], *ils accepteront* [ilz aksɛptərɔ̃]
[ilz aksɛptrɔ̃], *je marcherais* [ʒə marʃərɛ] [ʒə marʃrɛ], *tu
porterais* [ty pɔrtərɛ] [ty pɔrtrɛ], *il verserait* [il vɛrsərɛ] [il
vɛrsrɛ], *ils formeraient* [il fɔrmərɛ] [il fɔrmrɛ].

The shorter forms are adopted in the *Chrestomathie*, but
it is perhaps preferable not to make the elision in reading.
Two examples of the kind in question occur in the passage
read for Koschwitz by the late Gaston Paris and transcribed
independently by M. Paul Passy : *Vous discernerez (Parl.*

par. p. 47, l. 10 ; *Fr. parl.* p. 75, l. 7) ; *Nous remarquerons*
(*Parl. par.* p. 49, l. 11 ; *Fr. parl.* p. 77, l. 5). Paris sounds
the [ə] in both : [vu disɛrnəre] [nu rəmarkərɔ̃] ; Passy elides
it in both : [vu disɛrnre] [nu rmarkrɔ̃].

In *Nous parlerons* (*Parl. par.* p. 49, l. 2 ; *Fr. parl.*
p. 75, l. 21) and *Il rencontrerait* (*Parl. par.* p. 51, l. 4 ;
Fr. parl. p. 77, l. 21), where the groups end in [l] and [r],
the [ə] is naturally retained by both. Similarly, even in
conversation, we must sound the [ə] in *Nous garderions*
[nu gardərjɔ̃], *vous resteriez* [vu rɛstərje], *nous forcerions* [nu
fɔrsərjɔ̃], *vous observeriez* [vuz ɔpsɛrvərje].

Allowance being thus made for the verbal forms in which
elision may take place in conversation, we may say that the
[ə] after a group of consonants in the body of a word must
always be sounded. Examples : *abstenir* [apstəniːr], *obtenir*
[ɔptəniːr], *apercevoir.* [apɛrsəvwaːr], *entrevoir* [ɑ̃'trəvwaːr],
entreprendre [ɑ̃'trəprɑ̃ːdr], *autrement* [o'trəmɑ̃], *opiniâtreté*
[ɔpinjɑ'trəte], *contresens* [kɔ̃'trəsɑ̃ːs], *fourberie* [furbəri],
Charlemagne [ʃarləmaɲ], *appartement* [apartəmɑ̃], *appartenir*
[apartəniːr], *parvenir* [parvəniːr], *parvenu* [parvəny], *parlement*
[parləmɑ̃], *lestement* [lɛstəmɑ̃], *véritablement* [veritabləmɑ̃],
brusquement [bryskəmɑ̃], *parchemin* [parʃəmɛ̃], *exactement*
[egzaktəmɑ̃], *justement* [ʒystəmɑ̃], *gouvernement* [guvɛrnəmɑ̃],
morseler [mɔrsəle], *marmelade* [marməlad].

4. If the [ə] stands at the end of a word after a group
of consonant-sounds its treatment depends (α) upon the
nature of the consonants by which it is preceded, (β) upon
the rhythm of the sound-group, and (γ) upon the style of
language.

(α) If the group of consonants ends in [k], [r] or [l], and
is not [rk] or [rl], the [ə] is sounded : *quelque temps* [kɛlkə
tɑ̃], *quelque chose* [kɛlkə ʃoːz], *quelques représentations* [kɛlkə
rəprezɑ̃'ta'sjɔ̃], *presque parfait* [prɛskə parfɛ], *jusque-là*
[ʒyskə la], *lorsque vous viendrez* [lɔrskə vu vjɛ̃'dre], *votre*

128   FRENCH PHONETICS

visite [vɔtrə vizit], *une autre méthode* [yn o'trə metɔd], *par ordre de mérite* [par ɔrdrə də merit], *il entre dans la salle* [il ɑ̃'trə dɑ̃ la sal], *ses propres mots* [se prɔprə mo]; *un cercle plus étendu* [œ̃ sɛrklə plyz etɑ̃'dy], *la table des matières* [la tablə de matjɛːr].

When the [e] is sounded after a group of consonants at the end of a word care must be taken not to exaggerate the value of the syllable. It should be pronounced very lightly, and often becomes scarcely audible. In this way some maintain that the [ə] may be elided after a group ending in [r]. Even Gaston Paris approves of the notation [rəkɔnɛːtr le limit] = *reconnaître les limites* (*Parl. par.* p. 53, l. 3). (See Elision of Consonants, pp. 141 ff.)

(β) The retention of the [ə] at the end of a word, but in the body of a sound-group, is often required by the rhythm of the phrase which demands that, wherever possible, there shall not be a succession of heavy beats. A syllable ending in a group of consonants necessarily bears either a tonic or a secondary accent; hence if the [ə] were elided after a group of consonants at the end of a word, that word would end with a secondary or principal accent, and if the next syllable bore a tonic accent we should have two accents in succession. This sequence is not unknown in French, but the order 'secondary + weak + strong,' which would be obtained by sounding the [ə], is preferred.[1] Accordingly if the syllable that follows the [ə] is accented the [ə] is preserved. The [ə] syllable, which is lightly pronounced, thus forms a kind of buffer between two heavy accented syllables. Examples: *Il se porte bien* [il sə pɔrtə bjɛ̃], *j'en reste là* [ʒɑ̃ rɛstə la], *il n'existe pas* [il negzistə pɑ], *ne le cherche pas* [nəl ʃɛrʃə pɑ], *n'importe qui* [nɛ̃'pɔrtə ki], *artiste-peintre* [artistə pɛ̃ːtr], *George Sand* [ʒɔrʒə sɑ̃], *Charles Douze* [ʃarlə duːz], *porte-clefs* [pɔrtə kle], *porte-cartes* [pɔrtə

[1] See Chap. VI. p. 165.

kart], *porte-queue* [pɔrtə kø], *porte-plume* [pɔrtə plym], *garde-fou* [gardə fu], *garde-robe* [gardə rɔb], *garde-chasse* [gardə ʃas], *garde-meubles* [gardə mœbl], *garde-crotte* [gardə krɔt], *il tourne bride* [il turnə brid], *barbe grise* [barbə griːz], *barbe blanche* [barbə blɑ̃ːʃ], *barbe-bleue* [barbə blø], *volte-face* [vɔltə fas].

Exceptions are heard only in rapid and careless speech: *e.g. tourne-toi* [turn twa], *il ne le cherche pas* [in lə ʃerʃ pɑ], *il se porte bien* [is pɔrṭ bjɛ̃].

(γ) Should rhythm alone not forbid elision, the treatment of the medial [ə] at the end of a word, after a group of consonants, becomes generally a matter of style. As in the case of liaison, however, much depends upon the nature of the words: the closer the relation between the word ending in [ə] and the one by which it is followed, the more often the [ə] survives.

We have seen that when an adjective is followed by its noun the relation of the two words is so close that liaison always takes place between them: similarly, if the adjective should end in a group of consonants + [ə] and the noun begin with a consonant the [ə] should not be dropped. Examples: *Ses justes limites* [se ʒystə limit] (*Chrest.* p. 65, l. 19); *de fortes racines* [də fɔrtə rasin] (*Chrest.* p. 87, l. 34); *le superbe soleil d'automne* [lə sypɛrbə sɔlɛ'j dɔtɔn] (*Chrest.* p. 117, l. 9); *la vaste capote du soldat* [la vastə kapɔṭ dy sɔlda] (*Chrest.* p. 117, l. 12); *une vaste tapisserie* [yn vastə tapisri] (*Parl. par.* p. 55, l. 17; *Fr. parl.* p. 83, l. 2); *une vaste chaîne de gens* [yn vastə ʃɛ'n də ʒɑ̃] (*Parl. par.* p. 51, l. 7; *Fr. parl.* p. 77, l. 25); *de tristes pensées* [də tristə pɑ̃'se], *une lourde voiture* [yn lurdə vwatyːr], *une exacte connaissance* [yn egzaktə kɔnɛsɑ̃ːs].

Adjective and noun are no longer so intimately related to each other when their order is reversed; and in this position elision becomes more common, just as linking becomes more rare. In reading with deliberation, however, the [ə] is still

heard pretty frequently between noun and adjective, particularly if the expression belongs to elevated style.   Thus
the authors of the *Chrestomathie*, whose elisions are as
numerous as their liaisons are few, sound the [ə] in *le
scepticisme transcendental* [lə sɛptisismə trɑ̃'sɑ̃'dɑ̃'tal] (p. 125,
l. 35); *le dilettantisme raffiné* [lə dilɛ*t*tɑ̃'tismə rafine]¹ (p. 125,
l. 36) ; *sous une forme concrète* [suz yn formə kɔ̃'krɛt] (p. 71,
l. 4); *la force brutale* [la forsə brytal] (p. 75, l. 16); *l'organisme
primitif* [lɔrganismə primitif] (p. 85, l. 36); *ces haltes gran-
dioses* [se altə grɑ̃'djoːz] (p. 57, l. 18) ; and mark the elision
as optional in *cette force mystérieuse* [sɛt forsə misterjøːz]¹
(p. 63, l. 6) ; *la force centrale* [la forsə sɑ̃'tral] (p. 61, l. 4) ;
des sources diverses [de sursə divɛrs] (p. 63, l. 11) ; *la garde
nationale* [la gardə nasjɔnal] (p. 113, l. 35) ; as in the following expressions in which the noun is followed by a genitive
or a relative clause : *le terme de sa course* [lə tɛrmə də sa
kurs] (p. 57, l. 19) ; *la courbe du siècle* [la kurbə dy sjɛkl]
(p. 123, l. 35) ; *l'organisme d'une nation* [lɔrganismə dyn
nɑ'sjɔ̃] (p. 63, l. 31) ; *le mécanisme d'un empire* [lə mekanismə
dœ̃n ɑ̃'piːr] (p. 63, l. 32) ; *le contraste qui existe souvent* [lə
kɔ̃'trastə ki egzistə suvɑ̃] (p. 19, l. 24).   But they choose to
elide the [ə] in *portes cochères* [port kɔʃɛɪr] (p. 137, l. 14) ;
la marche naturelle de ce cours [la marʃ natyrɛl də s kuːr]
(p. 57, l. 9) ; *une corde secrète* [yn kɔrd̪ səkrɛt] (p. 67, l. 6) ;
une sorte de substitution [yn sɔrt̪ də sypstitysjɔ̃] (p. 71, l. 37) ;
une des formes toutes particulières [yn de form tut partikyljɛːr]
(p. 77, l. 2).   Gaston Paris and M. Paul Passy both elide in
notre carte linguistique [nɔtrə kart lɛ̃'gɥistik] (*Parl. par.* p. 47,
l. 18 ; *Fr. parl.* p. 75, l. 16) ; but after the necessary survival of the [ə] in *notre* the [ə] in *carte* must, for rhythmic
reasons, drop away, much in the same way as a liaison is
omitted to avoid the repetition of a sound.   In another

¹ The italicized phonetic sign is used in the *Chrestomathie* to indicate
an optional sound.

example which occurs in the same passage, viz. *les recueils de textes français et provençaux* (*Parl. par.* p. 55, l. 3; *Fr. parl.* p. 81, l. 14), they adopt diverse courses.

The group [kt], which is more clearly articulated than in English, nearly always requires the supporting-vowel in this position : *acte deux* [aktə dø], *acte religieux* [aktə rəliʒjø].

Nouns, adjectives and verbs are almost the only kinds of words in which the ending 'group of consonants + [ə]' is found ; hence the only other positions in which the question of elision is likely to arise are (i) between subject and predicate, and (ii) between verb and object or adverb.

In the former case elision will be the rule, *e.g.* in *La carte m'est parvenue* [la kart mɛ parvəny], *La porte reste ouverte* [la pɔrt rɛst uvɛrt]. Both G. Paris and P. Passy elide in *Le même verbe se prononce*, etc. [lə mɛ'm vɛrb sə prɔnɔ̃ːs] (*Parl. par.* p. 49, l. 11 ; *Fr. parl.* p. 77, l. 6). Nor in any one of the five readings did Koschwitz hear the [ə] in *Le christianisme l'avait enrichi* [lə kristjanism lavɛt ɑ̃'riʃi] (p. 79, l. 5). Between a verb and the word that follows the [ə] is frequently heard in the reading of elevated prose, but more usually dropped in conversation. G. Paris sounds and M. Passy elides the [ə] in *Le paysan parle comme le Parisien* (*Parl. par.* p. 45, l. 16 ; *Fr. parl.* p. 73, l. 22) ; *Les parlers populaires se perdent les uns dans les autres* (*Parl. par.* p. 49, l. 21 ; *Fr. parl.* p. 77, l. 17). They both elide in *Différent de celui qu'on parle dans chacun des autres* (*Parl. par.* p. 47, l. 8 ; *Fr. parl.* p. 75, l. 4). The authors of the *Chrestomathie* regard elision as optional in *Elle se manifeste par l'amour* (p. 63, l. 31), and in *Le perpétuel devenir dont parlent les philosophes* (p. 123, l. 33), but drop the [ə] unconditionally in *Elle transforme ces souvenirs* (p. 71, l. 31) and in *Il comporte des inconvénients* (p. 91, l. 14).

Compound nouns formed by the junction of a verb and a noun (and not coming under 4 (β)) have a more or less

familiar ring, and are generally heard without the [ə] :
garde-malade [gard malad], *garde-magasin* [gard magazɛ̃],
porte-bonheur [pɔrt bɔnœːr], *porte-manteau* [pɔrt mɑ̃'to], *porte-
monnaie* [pɔrt mɔnɛ], *porte-parole* [pɔrt parɔl], *porte-flambeau*
[pɔrt flɑ̃'bo].

Finally, in the locutions *de sorte que*, *parce que*, *à force de*,
n'importe quel the [ə] is suppressed or retained according
to the occasion. It should usually be retained in reading.

B. Elision of [ə] in series of syllables.

The foregoing rules meet the case of a single [ə] syllable
in all positions. But we frequently get a series of [ə]
syllables in unbroken succession, sometimes as many as
eight, very commonly two or three. What happens in such
cases ? It will be found that if the rules are applied every
alternate syllable may be elided (save where the series ends
with a word beginning with two consonants and [ə], *e.g.*
nous ne le prenons pas). Thus, in *C'est que je ne le veux
pas*, the first [ə] drops after a single consonant-sound : *c'est
que* = [sɛ k]. The [ə] in *je* is then preceded by two consonants and is retained : *c'est que je* = [sɛ k ʒə]. The third
[ə], in *ne*, consequently follows a single consonant and is
elided : *c'est que je ne* = [sɛ k ʒə n]. The fourth [ə], in *le*,
follows two consonants and is preserved. Hence the complete group is pronounced [sɛ k ʒə n lə vø pɑ]. Again, if we
apply the rules to the phrase *Il faudra que je le tienne*,
it will be read [il fodra k ʒə l tjɛn]. These readings, both
of which are perfectly good, show that an application of
the rules to such cases means a more or less violent
reduction in the length of the phrase : in the first, half
the particular syllables are elided ; in the second, two-
thirds. Such extreme abbreviations are compatible only
with rapid familiar utterance. Hence the following conclusion : The rules for the elision of [ə] may be strictly

and universally applied to series of syllables only in quick,
colloquial speech From this we may further infer that
although in deliberate speech no elision is ever made that
would break the rules, the [ə] is sometimes preserved when
the rules would have sanctioned its elision

I. *Series of two* [ə] *syllables.*

(*a*) Certain very common pairs of [ə] syllables must
always be treated in the same way. When a word which
ends with a single consonant-sound plus [ə] is immediately
followed by an [ə] syllable of any kind (*i.e.* a monosyllable
or the first syllable of a longer word), the first is invariably
elided and the second invariably sounded. This is so
because, by the rule for the elision of [ə] after a single consonant-sound (Rule A (iii) (*b*) 4, p. 125), the [ə] is invariably
dropped, in those circumstances, at the end of a word ;
the second [ə] being then always preceded by two sounded
consonants, must be preserved.

Examples *Une petite rivière* [yn pətit rivjɛːr], *il arrive
demain* [il ariˈv dəmɛ̃], *elle se lève* [ɛl sə lɛːv].

(*b*) We may next take pairs like those in *faibles ressources*,
les membres de ma famille, where the first [ə] must be
sounded (Rule A (iii) (*c*) 4 (α), p 127). In deliberate
and careful speech the second [ə] will usually be sounded as
well as the first : [fɛblə rəsurs] [le mɑ̃ˈbrə də ma famiːj]
Both Paris and Passy retain the second [ə] in *un certain
nombre de traits* [œ̃ sɛrtɛ̃ nɔ̃ˈbrə də trɛ] (*Parl. par.* p. 51,
l. 21 ; *Fr. parlé,* p. 79, l. 15) On other occasions we may
drop the second [ə] and say [fɛblə rsurs] [le mɑ̃ˈbrə d ma
famiːj]. Paris and Passy both drop it in *l'opposition entre
le provençal et le français* [lɔpozisjɔ̃ ɑ̃ˈtrə l prɔvɑ̃ˈsal ɛ l
frɑ̃ˈsɛ] (*Parl. par* p 53, l 20 ; *Fr. parl.* p. 81, l. 11),
though three of the other four of Koschwitz's readers appear
to have sounded the [ə] here too. In hasty familiar intercourse a third method of treating such pairs of [ə] syllables

is usually adopted : the first [ə] is dropped and carries with
it the preceding [r] or [l] : [le mɑ̃·b də ma famiːj] [œ̃ sɛrtɛ̃
nɔ̃·b də trɛ].[1]

(c) In pairs of the kind found in *de sorte que, à force
de, les formes de la vie*, the elision or non-elision of the
first [ə] becomes a matter of style (Rule A (iii) (c) 4 (γ)
p. 129), but, whatever its fate may be, the second [ə]
is always sounded. On a ceremonious occasion one will
say [də sɔrtə kə] [a fɔrsə də] [le fɔrmə də la vi], but in
ordinary circumstances [də sɔrt kə] [a fɔrs də] [le fɔrm də
la vi].

(d) We may next consider cases in which a monosyllable
is followed by a longer word beginning with an [ə] syllable :
*le regard, se lever, te demander, je relève, de tenir, de redire,
tu me reçois, ne reconnaissez-vous pas ?*

Supposing the first [ə] has to be retained (and it has to be
when it begins a sound-group and when the preceding word
ends with a sounded consonant (Rules A (i) p. 115, and A
(iii) (c) 1, p. 125)), the second is dropped more or less
regularly in conversation, but is frequently retained in reading : *pour le regarder* [pur lə rgarde] [pur lə rəgarde]; *pour
se lever* [pur sə lve] [pur sə ləve]; *pour te demander* [pur tə
dmɑ̃·de] [pur tə dəmɑ̃·de]; *je refuse* [ʒə rfyːz] [ʒə rəfyːz];
ne reconnaissez-vous pas [nə rkɔnɛse vu pɑ] [nə rəkɔnɛse vu
pɑ]. Where the initial syllable of the second word is one
of those which are saved by a group of consonants, or
exceptionally retained as a mark of identity (Rules A (iii)
(c) 2, p. 126 ; A (iii) (b) 2, p. 122), both [ə] syllables must
be sounded : *avec le premier* [avɛk lə prəmje], *pour le peser*
[pur lə pəze].

Suppose next that the monosyllable in a pair of [ə]
syllables of the kind under discussion follows a vowel, as in
à le regarder, en se levant, qui me demande, si je refuse. The

[1] For the elision of consonants see pp. 141 ff.

first [ə] being preceded by a single consonant is now liable
to be elided (Rule A (iii) (*b*) 1, p. 118). A comparison of
the forms [a l rəgarde] and [a lə rgarde], [ɑ̃ s ləvɑ̃] and [ɑ̃ sə
lvɑ̃], [ki m dəmɑ̃ːd] and [ki mə dmɑ̃ːd], [si ʒ rəfyːz] and
[si ʒə rfyːz] shows that the second pronunciation, in which
elision is delayed till the second syllable, has a more
deliberate rhythm. By a strict application of the rules
(A (iii) (*b*) 1 and (*c*) 1, pp. 118, 125), the first syllable
would be elided and the second retained : this course is
sometimes followed in rapid familiar speech. But delayed
elision—retention of the first and elision of the second
syllable—is generally preferable. A special case, however,
must be made of pairs beginning with *ne : nous ne devons
pas, vous ne refusez pas.* With these the normal rules are
strictly applied even in careful speech : [nu n dəvɔ̃ pɑ]
[vu n rəfyˈze pɑ]. In ordinary circumstances the negative is
felt to be sufficiently emphasized by the second particle. In
very deliberate diction both syllables may be sounded : [a
lə rəgarde] [ɑ̃ sə ləvɑ̃] [ki mə dəmɑ̃ːd] [si ʒə rəfyːz] [nu nə
dəvɔ̃ pɑ].

(*e*) The only other case in which series of two [ə]
syllables in separate words are found is when two [ə] monosyllables follow each other in immediate succession : *je me
souviens, il me le dit, de me battre, je le vois, je ne crois pas,
ce ne sont pas mes livres.*

If the first [ə] is necessarily sounded (and it must not
be elided if it begins a sound-group or follows two consonants : Rules A (i) p. 115 and A (iii) (*c*) 1, p. 125) the
second is dropped regularly in conversation, frequently even
in careful speech : [ʒə m suvjɛ̃] [il mə l di] [də m batr] [ʒə
l vwa] [ʒə n krwɑ pɑ] [sə n sɔ̃ pɑ me liːvr]. A deliberate
reader, however, will occasionally retain both : [ʒə mə suvjɛ̃]
[il mə lə di].

The pair *ce que* forms an exception to the general rule

for pairs of [ə] monosyllables; the second syllable being invariably sounded: *par ce que* [par sə kə], *pour ce que* [pur sə kə]. Save in these two locutions, *ce que* after a consonant or at the head of a phrase is not seldom pronounced [skə] in quick, familiar speech, notwithstanding the general rules: *Ce que vous dites* [skə vu dit] instead of the more correct [sə kə vu dit].

When pairs of monosyllables are preceded by a vowel, 'delayed elision' is generally more appropriate in deliberate speech, and even both syllables may occasionally be retained: *Il faut que je fasse* will be pronounced [il fo k ʒə fas][1] or [il fo kə ʒ fas], *Quand je me souviens* [kɑ̃ ʒ mə suvjɛ̃] or [kɑ̃ ʒə m suvjɛ̃], *Qui me le dit* [ki m lə di] or [ki mə l di] according to the occasion. Gaston Paris sounds both [ə]'s in *Excepter de ce jugement*: [ɛksɛpte də sə ʒy'ʒmɑ̃] (*Parl. par.* p. 53, l. 12); M. Passy elides the second: [ɛksɛpte də ṣ ʒy'ʒmɑ̃] (*Fr. parl.* p. 81, l. 1). Koschwitz records that three readers elided the first [ə] and sounded the second: [ɛksɛpte d̩ sə ʒy'ʒmɑ̃]. Delayed elision may be regarded as the rule when *ne* is the second of the pair: *Si ce ne sont pas mes livres* [si sə n sɔ̃ pɑ me liːvr]. In *Si ce que vous me dites*, on the other hand, one must say [si s kə] or [si sə kə].

(*f*) Finally we may have pairs of [ə] syllables in one and the same word: *e.g.* in *rejeter, mousqueterie.*

When both of such syllables occur in the interior of a word the ordinary rules (A (iii) (*b*) 3 and (*c*) 3, pp. 124, 126) are applied: *mousqueterie* [muskətri], *parqueterie* [parkətri], *marqueterie* [markətri]. In these and similar words, however, the first [ə] frequently becomes [ɛ]: [muskɛtri] [parkɛtri] [markɛtri]. In *papeterie* both [ə]'s may be elided in spite of the rules: [paptri] or [papɛtri]: in *échevelé* and *ensevelir* elision is usually delayed: [eʃəvle], [ɑ̃'səvliːr].

[1] The pronunciation [i fo k ʒə fas] is not uncommon in careless speech. On elision of consonants see p. 141.

More common are words of which the first two syllables contain an [ə]. When such a word begins a sound-group or follows a consonant the first [ə] necessarily survives (Rules A (i) p. 115 and A (iii) (*c*) 1, p. 125): the second is dropped regularly in conversation and very often even in reading. Examples: *redemander* [rədmɑ̃'de], *devenir* [dəvni:r], *revenir* [rəvni:r], *retenir* [rətni:r], *relever* [rəlve], *rejeter* [rəʒte], *ressemer* [rəsme] and kindred nouns and adjectives, such as *revenu* [rəvny], *retenu* [rətny], *relevage* [rəlva:ʒ], *rejeton* [rəʒtɔ̃].[1]

On the other hand, the verbs *redevoir, repeser, recevoir, refaisant,* in all parts in which these two syllables occur, generally retain the second [ə] under pain of losing their identity : [rədəvwa:r] [rəpəze] [rəsəvwa:r] [rəfəzɑ̃]. Kindred nouns and adjectives, however, having but one form, run no such risk and, therefore, drop the second [ə]: *redevance* [rədvɑ̃:s], *redevancier* [rədvɑ̃'sje], *receveur* [rəsvœ:r], *recevable* [rəsvabl].

But how are words beginning with two [ə] syllables treated when they follow a vowel-sound and the elision of the first [ə] becomes possible (Rule A (iii) (*b*) 2, p. 122)? All the nouns and adjectives belonging to this class have a fixed form and remain intact, that is, they retain their first syllable and lose the second : *un rejeton* [œ̃ rəʒtɔ̃], *des revenus* [de rəvny], *être en retenu* [ɛ'tr ɑ̃ rətny], *un receveur* [œ̃ rəsvœ:r]. Those verbs which cannot lose the second syllable without forfeiting their individuality may drop the first in couversation : *il voulait recevoir* [il vulɛ rsəvwa:r], *en refaisant* [ɑ̃ rfəzɑ̃], *nous repesons* [nu rpəzɔ̃]. Finally, verbs which when isolated drop the second syllable generally retain the same form even when, being preceded by a vowel, the first

---

[1] Those parts of the verbs in which the second [ə] is followed by the ending ' consonant + -ions ' or ' consonant + -iez ' form exceptions (Rule A (iii) (*b*) 3, p. 124) : *devenions* [dəvəniɔ̃], *releviez* [rələvje].

could be elided : *je l'ai redemandé* [ʒə le rədmɑ̃'de], *en rejetant* [ɑ̃ rəʒtɑ̃], *nous relevons* [nu rəlvɔ̃]. In hasty, careless speech these forms are occasionally disturbed : *en revenant* being pronounced [ɑ̃ rvənɑ̃] in place of the more correct [ɑ̃ rəvnɑ̃], *vous retenez* [vu rtəne] in place of [vu rətne].

II. *Series of three* [ə] *syllables.*

These are governed by the same principles as series of two, and may be treated more summarily. It will be found that two can never be elided in succession.

(*a*) When the first of a series of three is necessarily elided by the general rules, the remaining two are treated precisely in the same way as a pair of which the first must be sounded. *La marche naturelle de ce cours* (*Chrest.* p. 57, l. 9) is transcribed [la marʃ natyrɛl də s kuːr] in accordance with the first part of I. (*e*) in which the treatment of two mono-syllables of which the first must survive is explained. But the suppression of the third [ə] is not obligatory. Similarly *Je jure de le faire* is usually pronounced [ʒə ʒy'r də l fɛːr].

In pursuance of the first part of I. (*d*), the third of the series will again, as a rule, be elided in *La tempête le secoue* [la tɑ̃'pɛt lə sku], *Il décide de remonter* [il desid də rmɔ̃'te]. We arrive at the same result, under the first part of I. (*f*), in such series as those in *Il désire revenir* [il deziˑr rəvniːr] and *Une redevance* [yn rədvɑ̃ːs].

(*b*) When the first of a series of three [ə] syllables is necessarily sounded, the remaining two are governed by the rules for pairs of which the first is liable to elision. In a very few cases the trio belong to the first three syllables of a word formed by the addition of the iterative particle *re* to a word beginning with two [ə] syllables ; the word retains its previous ordinary form (I. (*f*)), that is, the second [ə] of the three, though now preceded by a single consonant, is not elided : *redevenir* [rədəvniːr]. *Ressemeler* [rəsəmle] and its noun *ressemelage* [rəsəmlaːʒ] are treated ın the same way, although they exist only in the compound forms. As a consequence of this rule all three syllables survıve ın the parts *redevenıons* [rədəvənjõ], *redeveniez* [rədəvənje]. Three such syllables never occur ın the interior of a word.

Contre le secret in deliberate speech is pronounced [kõ'trə lə skrɛ] with delayed elision in pursuance of the second part of I. (*d*). In hastier speech we may say [kõ'trə l səkrɛ].

Pour se relever ıs usually read [pur sə rəlve] (I. (*f*), *ad fin.*), *pour te le reprendre* [pur tə lə rprɑ̃ːdr] (I. (*d*), *ad fin.*), *pour que je le fasse* [pur kə ʒə l fas] (I. (*e*), *ad fin*).

(*c*) Where the second of the series of three [ə] syllables must be pronounced, as in *de sorte que le soir*, etc., the third ıs frequently elided : [də sɔrt kə l swaːr] or [də sɔrtə kə l swaːr]. An example is found in the passage read for Koschwitz by the late Gaston Paris : *De telle sorte que le parler d'un endroit contiendra*, etc. (*Parl. par.* p. 51, l 19) Here Parıs reads [sɔrtə kə lə parle], preserving all three '*e* mutes' ; but M. Passy elides the first and the third : [sɔrt kə l parle] (*Fr parl.* p. 79, l. 12).

(*d*) Where the first of a serıes of three [ə] syllables might be elided, delayed elision is the rule in deliberate speech, as in the case of pairs (I. (*d*) and I. (*e*) *ad fin.*). The first of the three then surviving, two courses become possible in the treatment of the remaining pair. We may let them follow the ordinary rules and elıde the first : *Il faut que je le fasse* [ıl fo kə ʒ lə fas] ; or we may again delay the elision and drop the third : [il fo kə ʒə l fas]. The rhythm of the latter reading, in which elision is doubly delayed, is the more reposeful. Hence while ın quick, familiar speech the first and the third [ə]'s are elided : [il fo k ʒe l fas], ıt will be either the second or the third, and generally the third, that drops out in deliberate utterance. Further examples : *Il faudra que je le tienne* [ıl fodra k ʒə l tjɛn] [ıl fodra kə ʒ

lə tjɛn] [il fodra kə ʒə l tjɛn] ; *Le temps de te revoir* [lə tɑ̃ ḍ
tə rvwaːr] [lə tɑ̃ də t rəvwaːr] [lə tɑ̃ də tə rvwaːr] ; *Vous me
retenez* [vu m rətne] [vu mə rtəne] [vu mə rətne].

III. *Longer series of* [ə] *syllables.*

It is unnecessary to discuss in detail longer series of [ə]
syllables. They are comparatively rare, and will present no
difficulty to the student who is familiar with the treatment
of series of two and three. The same principles are applied.
The doubly-delayed elision, of which we have had examples
in series of three [ə] syllables, is rarely exceeded in longer
series, and two [ə] syllables cannot be dropped in succession
without breaking the rules : in other words, seldom more
than two [ə] syllables survive in succession, and two can
never perish in succession. The following are examples of
series ranging from four to eight syllables, with the pronunciations which should usually be adopted by the learner :
Je te le demande [ʒə tə l dəmɑ̃ːd], *Je ne le demande pas* [ʒe n
lə dmɑ̃ːd pɑ] or [ʒə nə l dəmɑ̃ːd pɑ], *Ce que je demande* [sə
kə ʒ dəmɑ̃ːd], *Je ne veux que ce que je vous ai dit* [ʒe n vø
kə s kə ʒ vuz e di] or [kə sə ḵ ʒə vuz e di], *Je te le redemande*
[ʒə tə l rədmɑ̃ːd], *Je ne te le redemande pas* [ʒə n tə l rədmɑ̃ːd
pɑ], *Est-ce que je ne te le redemande pas ?* [ɛs kə ʒə n tə l
rədmɑ̃ːd pɑ].

C. Elision of other Vowels.

Other vowels than [ə] are occasionally elided in vulgar
or overcareless speech : *voilà* is pronounced [vla] instead of
[vwala] ; *cet homme, cette année* [st ɔm] [st ane] instead of
[sɛt ɔm] [sɛt ane] ; *peut-être* [ptɛːt] instead of [pøtɛːtr] ;
and the semi-vowel is dropped in *puis* : [pi] for [pɥi]. But
such pronunciations should not be imitated by the student,
even in familiar intercourse. Less objectionable is the
elision of [a] in *extraordinaire* : [ɛkstrɔrdinɛːr] for [ɛkstra-
ɔrdinɛːr] ; it is very common in conversation, but more often

avoided in reading. *Août* is pronounced [au] [u] [ut].
Here the elision of the [a] is perhaps to be recommended ;
but in the verb *aoûter* the [a] is regularly sounded : [aute].
Caen is always [kɑ̃] ; *Saône* is always [soːn]. But *taon*,
faon, *paon* should be pronounced [tɑ̃] [fɑ̃] [pɑ̃].

D. Elision of Consonants.

The consonants that suffer elision are [r] [l] and [k]. The
liquids, [r] and [l], are dropped when they end a final group
of consonants, and they carry with them the supporting-
vowel [ə]. Thus *pauvre petit* [poˈvrə pəti] becomes [poˈy
pəti], *autre chose* [oˈtrə ʃoːz] becomes [oˈt ʃoːz], *maître d'hôtel*
[mɛˈtrə dɔtɛl] becomes [mɛˈt dɔtɛl], *il me semble que oui* [il
mə sɑ̃ˈblə kə wi] is reduced to [il mə sɑ̃ˈb̥ kə wi], [mə sɑ̃ˈb̥
k wi], *le peuple de Paris* [lə pœplə də paˈri] to [lə pœp̥ də
paˈri]. The elision of [r] and [l] is not confined to such
cases. The [r] is dropped in *parce que* [parsə kə], which then
becomes [paskə], and sometimes even when it stands alone
at the end of a word : *sur le dos* [syr lə do] is shortened
to [syl do], and words like *art* [aːr] and *soir* [swaːr] are
pronounced [aː] and [swaː]. The [l] is dropped in *il* when
followed by another consonant, and, if the next syllable
contains an [ə], elision takes place : *il me semble que oui*
[im sɑ̃ˈb̥ k wi], *il ne faut pas* [in fo pɑ], *il se moque* [is
mɔk], *il se bat* [iʂ ba]. The [l] again falls away from *quelque*
and its compounds, with the result that, a single consonant
alone remaining, elision of the following [ə] becomes
necessary : *quelquefois* is pronounced [kɛk fwa] instead of
[kɛlkə fwa], *quelque chose* [kɛk ʃoːz] instead of [kɛlkə ʃoːz],
quelqu'un [kɛkœ̃] instead of [kɛlkœ̃], *quelques-uns* [kɛgzœ̃]
instead of [kɛlkəzœ̃], *quelques jours* [kɛk̬ ʒuːr] instead of
[kɛlkə ʒuːr].

Elision of [k] occurs only in *Qu'est-ce que tu dis?* [kɛs kə
ty di] which becomes [kɛs ty di], and in the prefix *ex* when

followed by a consonant: *e.g. exprès* [ɛksprɛ] becomes [ɛsprɛ],
expliquer [ɛksplike] becomes [ɛsplike]. But no elision takes
place in words like *exagérer* [egzaʒere], *exotique* [egzɔtik], in
which the root of the word begins with a vowel.

The elision of [k] generally, that of [r] when it stands
alone, and that of [l] in *quelque* and cognate words are still
vulgarisms to be avoided by the student on all occasions.
But the [r] and [l] at the end of a final group, the [r] in
parce que and the [l] in *il* before a consonant are very
commonly, though as a rule unconsciously, dropped in
conversation, even by the educated. These abbreviations,
however, do not cease to be negligences of speech. The
learner will do well not to adopt them voluntarily, even in
familiar intercourse; they are tolerable only when the
delivery is so fluent that they escape notice. On the other
hand, not even the most fluent diction can make them
commendable in reading.[1] It was doubtless these licences
of speech that M. l'abbé Rousselot had in mind when he
wrote: ' Il y a des négligences qui passent inaperçues dans
une conversation rapide, mais qui choqueraient dans une
lecture lente ou une prononciation bien soignée. Nous
les déconseillerons aussi. Si l'étranger parle vite, et s'il les
reproduit à son insu par suite du seul mouvement organique,
il se trouve dans les mêmes conditions que le Français et
personne ne le remarquera. Mais si au contraire, et c'est
le cas le plus habituel, la prononciation est lente et quelque
peu embarrassée, l'étranger qui en émaille son discours est
tout à fait ridicule ' (*Précis de Pron. fr.* p. 12).

---

[1] It is to be regretted that the elision of [l] in *il* is so often made
in the *Chrestomathie.* However fluently the student may read, he is
recommended to pronounce the consonant. This will sometimes
necessitate the restoration of an [ə]: *il ne suffit pas* which is transcribed
[i n syfi pɑ] at page 65, line 40 should, for instance, be read [il nə
syfi pɑ].

E. Elision in Verse.

The reading of French verse presents special difficulties owing to the fact that the measure depends upon the number of syllables, and not upon the number of accents, in the line. If elisions were made as regularly as in conversation, verse would often enough be transformed into something very like prose. If, on the other hand, every [ə] were sounded, the language would sometimes cease to be French. It is, therefore, customary to dismiss the subject with two very vague, though very safe, recommendations: sound more of these syllables than in prose, but do not sound them all. This may be sufficient for the Frenchman, but for the English-speaking student, especially if he has not had the opportunity of hearing French verse well read, it amounts to little less than a challenge to read French verse correctly if he can. Such counsel wrongly postulates that the foreigner has the Frenchman's instinctive feeling for the propriety or impropriety of elision. It is true that much must always be left to personal taste, and that outside a certain range the taste of well-educated Frenchmen often dictates diverse courses in reading verse; but just for that reason one can give the English-speaking student guidance that will make it almost impossible for him to read verse in a way that would necessarily be condemned as incorrect in the matter of elision. An attempt to supply this guidance is made in the following suggestions:

I. In the first place, the really mute *e* may always be elided in verse. By the 'really mute *e*' is meant the *e* which is invariably elided in prose. This *e* can be easily recognized, it is found in four positions: (1) before a vowel, as in *l'astre échevelé* [lastr eʃəvle]; (ii) after a vowel, as in *ils fuient* [il fɥi], *ils étaient* [ilz etɛ]; (iii) at the end of a word after a single consonant-sound, as in *belle voix* [bɛl vwa], *l'ardente croix* [lardɑ̃t krwa], *chaque jour* [ʃak ʒuːr];

(iv) after a single consonant-sound in the interior of a word in which it is never heard in prose, *e.g. matelot* [matlo]; whereas *se relevant* may be read [sə rələvã].

When the *e* mute stands between consonants, as in the third and fourth positions, it counts in the measure, and some readers maintain that it must not be elided. Careful attention will, however, show that even these readers themselves do not as a rule pronounce the [ə]. They merely suggest its existence, either by lengthening the preceding consonant if it be a fricative, or by articulating it with a clear explosion if it be a stop.

II. Whenever [ə] must be heard in prose, it must be heard in verse. If we except Futures and Conditionals of verbs, and the position at the end of a word, the rule may be stated thus : In the interior of a sound-group, after any two or more sounded consonants, the [ə] must be pronounced. Examples : *tristement* [tristəmã], *fourberie* [furbəri], *marquetait* [markətɛ], *sur le trône* [syr lə troːn], *avec le printemps* [avɛk lə prɛ̃'tã].

Even in the Futures and Conditionals the [ə] after any two consonants may always be sounded in verse : *fermera* [fɛrməra], *bercera* [bɛrsəra].

Between words in a sound-group the [ə] after a group of consonants must always be heard if the last of the group is [r] or [l] (unless the group is [rl]) : *pauvre soldat* [poːvrə sɔlda], *noble fille* [nɔblə fiːj].

III. The only isolated [ə] syllables the elision of which depends upon taste and is not covered by the preceding definite rules are (i) the [ə] at the end of a word, after consonant-groups other than those ending in [r] or [l]; (ii) the [ə] of a monosyllable which follows a vowel ; and (iii) the [ə] in the first syllable of a longer word, when that word begins with a single consonant and follows a vowel-sound.

Those of the first class are nearly always sounded, and the

student will probably not offend good taste if he makes it a
rule to pronounce them on all occasions. He must, however, bear in mind that the end of a line is generally the
end of a sound-group and, therefore, not within the rule

For the treatment of *e* mutes of the second and third classes
(*i e.* in monosyllables and initial syllables) no mechanical
rule can be framed. They are certainly sounded more often
than not but one can seldom say that they must be
sounded. The monosyllable which most seldom undergoes
elision is *que*, and the student will probably do well not to
elide the [ə] in this word. Perhaps *de* and *ne* are the monosyllables which most readily lose their vowels, as in the lines :

C'est que si je cherchais du bout de mon épée . . . [sɛ kə si ʒə
    ʃɛrʃɛ dy bu d mɔn epe]   (*Parl. par.* p. 111, l 19) ;
Et moi, qu'avait brisé cet arrêt de la tombe . [e mwa,
    kavɛ bri'ze sɛt arɛ d la tɔ̃ːb]   (*ib.* p. 115, l. 21) ;
Un moment, je voulus au fond de ces retraites
M'ensevelir . . . [œ̃ mɔmã, ʒə vulyz o fɔ̃ d sɛ rətrɛt
    mã'səvəliːr]   (*ib.* p. 117, ll. 1, 2) ,
I as de pardon, jamais ? [pɑ d pardɔ̃, 'ʒamɛ]
                      (*ib.* p. 115, l. 18) ;
      La fleur
Qui ne s'est point épanouie [la flœːr ki n sɛ pwɛ̃'t epanwi]
               (*Chrest.* p. 197, ll. 1, 2).

IV. Series of [ə] syllables must be treated at least as
generously as in the most deliberate prose. Even three or
four may occasionally be heard in succession. Four out of
five of Koschwitz's readers are said to have sounded all four
e mutes in *Quand je me relevai* [kã ʒə mə rələve] (p. 115,
l. 23), and three out of five are said to have sounded all three
in *Je relevai la tête* [ʒə rələve la tɛːt] (p. 115, l. 9). On the
other hand, four out of five elided the second [ə] in *Mais
je me rappelai, mon père, vos avis* [mɛ ʒə m raple, mɔ̃ pɛːr,
voz avi] (p. 116, l. 3).

V. No other elisions should be made in serious verse.

CHAPTER IV

ASSIMILATION

ASSIMILATION may be described as the attraction of one speech-sound to another standing in its neighbourhood, whereby the attracted sound either acquires characteristics belonging to the other, or loses characteristics peculiar to itself. It is the complete assimilation of [d] to [t] that gave rise in Latin to the form *attendere* in place of the older *adtendere*, the partial assimilation of [n] to [p] that led to the substitution of *implicare* for the original *inplicare*. In such cases, and they might be multiplied by the score, the phenomenon has been sanctioned by orthography and is of interest from a historical point of view. But we have to note how it is manifested at the present day in spite of traditional spelling.

In French and English, consonants are more liable to assimilation than vowels, and assimilation between consonants consists, in its simplest and commonest form, in the addition or subtraction of the element that has been called *voice*. Thus the voiceless [s] of our word *serve* [sɐːv] becomes voiced [z] in *observe* [əbzɐːv] under the influence of the preceding voiced consonant [b]. The English final *s* is sounded [s] or [z] according as it follows a voiceless or a voiced consonant: compare *keeps* [kɹips], *picks* [pɪks], *bits* [bɪts] with *cabs* [kæbz], *pigs* [pɪgz], *bids* [bɪdz]. Similarly, the *d*, which is voiced in *flagged* [flægd], *stabbed* [stæbd], is reduced to its voiceless counterpart in *picked* [pɪkt], *tapped* [tæpt]. At the same time it is just as easy to quote instances in which no assimilation takes place · the voiceless [s] is preserved in *obsolete* [ɒbsəliit], *subsist* [sʌbsɪst]; the [d] remains voiced in *misdeal* [mɪsdiil] Assimilation of another kind takes place in the word *month*: the [n] immediately preceding [θ] is attracted by that sound away from its normal position; that is, instead of being articulated with the tip of the tongue against the upper front gums, it is produced with the tongue against the teeth. In the hasty pronunciation of *I can go* the [n] is attracted in the opposite direction by the [k] and the [g] and becomes [ŋ] · [aɪ kəŋ gɔo] [aɪ kŋ gɔo].

In French, assimilation always consists in the loss of voice (devocalization) or the acquisition of voice in its pure (vocalization) or nasalized form (nasalization) [1] It is constant and regular in its operation, admitting of no such variations and exceptions as are found in English. It takes place only between consonants, and only between consonants [2] that are in juxtaposition. [3] Its sphere of

[1] Assimilation of the kind that takes place in *month, ninth, I can go* is not absolutely unknown in French : *e.g. une petite*, in very familiar and hasty speech, may become [ymtit] But, while the English assimilations are so constant that they must be regarded as correct, the French are exceptional and perhaps vulgar A somewhat similar and regular case of assimilation is, however, found in the displacement of the explosives, particularly [k] and [g], in favour of the vowel of the syllable These changes have already been discussed in treating the individual sounds

[2] Exceptional cases of vowel assimilation are (i) the nasalization of a pure vowel under the influence of a following nasal consonant, as when *maman* [mamɑ̃] becomes [mɑ̃mɑ̃]; (ii) the occasional attraction of a back-vowel by a front-vowel, as when *joli* [ʒɔli] is pronounced [ʒœli] Such assimilations are not to be imitated.

[3] Phonetically, not necessarily in spelling . *e.g.* the [v] and [t] in *savetier* are in phonetic juxtaposition because the intervening *e* is an idle sign : [savtje].

influence is the sound-group, that is, both consonants need
not be in the same word, the final of one word being
subject to assimilation by the initial of the word following.
Assimilation as a rule increases in proportion with the
rapidity of utterance. It is less common in verse than
in familiar prose because elisions are there less frequent,
but even there it is perfectly good and proper in its place.
It can be avoided in very slow and very careful enunciation,
but in some cases its avoidance would be so unnatural
as to betray the foreigner ; and in others it would amount
to absolute mispronunciation.

The phenomenon may be considered, in accordance
with its results, under three heads : (i) Devocalization,
(ii) Vocalization, (iii) Nasalization.

(i) *Devocalization.*

A voiced consonant is devocalized when in producing
it the vocal chords do not vibrate, or vibrate less distinctly
or less continuously than in its normal articulation. Such
devocalization is due to the juxtaposition of a voiceless consonant, that is, one of the sounds [k] [t] [p] [f] [s] [ʃ]. It
may be called *regressive* when the influence proceeds from
the second consonant of the group to the first ; *progressive*
when it proceeds from the first to the second. In
French, regressive devocalization is much more usual than
progressive.

(a) *Regressive devocalization.*

Whenever a voiced consonant is followed immediately by
a voiceless one it is liable to be devocalized. A distinction,
however, must be drawn between the liquids and nasals,
[l] [r] [m] [n], on the one hand, and all the other vocalized
consonants, [b] [d] [g] [v] [ʒ] [z] [j],[1] on the other. The
liquids and nasals tend to resist devocalization ; with them

---

[1] The consonants [w] and [ɥ] are never followed by a consonant, and
therefore, cannot suffer regressive devocalization.

ıt is hardly ever complete. What usually happens is that
the vocal chords vıbrate a lıttle less dıstinctly than otherwise ; they seldom altogether cease to vıbrate while the
articulation is stıll in progress. It often needs a well-trained
ear to detect any change, and sometimes perhaps devocalization does not take place. The student wıll at all
events, be quite justified in neglecting the devocalizatıon of
these four sounds [l] [r] [m] [n], *e.g.* in *haletant* [altɑ̃], *force*
[fɔrs], *porte* [pɔrt], *arc* [ark], *hameçon* [amsɔ̃], *hanneton* [antɔ̃]

In all other cases, however, regressive devocalizatıon is
far from beıng a theoretıcal subtlety. In the body of a
word, and even between words ın set expressıons, it is often
so complete that the loss of voice carrıes wıth ıt a change ın
the method of artıculatıon, so that a *d* is pronounced pre-
cısely as [t], a *b* as [p] and so on. Examples · *obstacle*
[ɔpstakl], *observer* [ɔpsɛrve], *obscur* [ɔpskyːr], *subsıster*
[sypsıste],[1] *subtıl* [syptıl], *médecın* [mɛtsɛ̃] or [mɛd̥sɛ̃], *savetıer*
[saftje] [savtje], *chauve-souris* [ʃoˈfsuri] [ʃoˈv̥suri], *là-dessus*
[latsy] [lad̥sy], *roı de France* [rwɑ t frɑ̃s] [rwɑ d̥ frɑ̃s], *tout
de suite* [tutsɥit], *chemin de fer* [ʃəmɛ̃ d̥ fɛːr] [ʃəmɛ̃ t fɛːr], *je
croıs* [ʒ̊krwɑ] [ʃkrwɑ], *je te dıs* [ʒ̊tə di] [ʃtə dı] In careful
speech, the last two expressions would be pronounced · [ʒə
krwɑ] [ʒə t̥ di].

When the attractıng and attracted consonants belong to
dıfferent words the transformatıon, save in current expressıons of the kind already noted, is not always quite so
decided. Although the vocal chords may vıbrate very
faintly, or even cease to vibrate altogether, the consonant
remains as a rule distinguishable from ıts voıceless counterpart. It ıs still articulated as if it were goıng to be voiced,
that is, less energetıcally than where the transformation is
complete. Professor Paul Passy observes that *Je vıens de
parler* [ʒə vjɛ̃ d̥ parle] ıs · not equivalent to *Je vıens te parler*

---

[1] Perhaps more often pronounced [sybzıste]

[ʒə vjɛ̃ t parlə]. Examples of devocalization where the consonants belong to different words are: *Une vague tendance* [yn vaɡ̊ tɑ̃'dɑ̃ːs], *un étage plus haut* [œ̃n eta'ʒ̊ ply o], *étude continue* [etyd̥ kɔ̃'tiny], *onze timbres* [ɔ̃ːz̊ tɛ̃ːbr], *excuse factice* [ɛksky'z̊ faktis], *longue série* [lɔ̃ːɡ̊ seri], *globe solide* [glɔb̥ sɔlid], *grave forfait* [gra'v̥ fɔrfɛ]. When the two consonants are cognate sounds, *e.g.* [z] and [s] or [ʒ] and [ʃ], devocalization is often avoided more or less effectively in careful speech: *quinze sous* [kɛ̃ːz su].

Regressive devocalization is not one of the regular characteristics of English. It may occur, exceptionally, in words of minor import hastily uttered, *e.g. of* [ɒv]: *a cup of tea*, for example, is sometimes pronounced [ə kʌp əy tɹi] or even [ə kʌp əf tɹi]. But it is unknown between consonants in the body of a word. In this position, on the other hand, the phenomenon of regressive devocalization which characterizes French is sometimes absolutely reversed in English, that is, instead of the first consonant losing voice by assimilation to the second (regressive devocalization), the second acquires voice by assimilation to the first (progressive vocalization—see next section): cf. English *observe* [əbzɐːv] with French *observer* [ɔpsɛrve]. But contrasts of this kind are rare. In English both consonants usually resist assimilation: *obstacle* [ɒbstəkl̩], *obscure* [ɒbskjʊuə]. In one French word, *subsister* [sybziste] [sypsiste], progressive vocalization very commonly takes place.

(*b*) *Progressive devocalization.*

The only consonants that suffer devocalization under the influence of a preceding voiceless consonant are the liquids [l] [r], the nasals [m] [n], and the so-called semi-vowels [w] [ɥ] [j]. Progressive devocalization, moreover, takes place only when the attracted and attracting consonants belong to the same syllable. When they begin the syllable, devocalization is very seldom complete and never obligatory. The

phenomenon may, therefore, be neglected in such cases :
pois may be pronounced [pẘa] or [pwa], *puis* [pɥ̊i] or [pɥi],
tiens [tj̊ɛ̃] or [tjɛ̃], *pied* [pj̊e] or [pje], *plus* [pl̥y] or [ply],
près [pr̥ɛ] or [prɛ], *pneumonie* [pn̥ømɔni] or [pnømɔni].
The English-speaking student will be naturally inclined to
devocalize the semi-vowels in such combinations ; the
sounds analogous to [w] and [j] are regularly devocalized
in the same positions in his own language : cf. *few* [fjʊu]
and *view* [vjʊu], *queen* [kẘɪin] and *Gwendolin* [gwɛndəlɪn].
At the end of a sound-group, in French, [l] [r] and [m] [1]
are, as a rule, completely devocalized when preceded by a
voiceless consonant.   Hence, in the position in question,
peuple is pronounced [pœpl̥], *encre, ancre* [ɑ̃ɪkr̥], *maître*
[mɛɪtr̥], *prisme* [prism̥].   Groups ending in [r] and [l] cannot
close a syllable in any other position.   If they are followed
by another word in the same sound-group, they begin a new
syllable, and devocalization does not take place.   In *un
peuple fort intéressant* [œ̃ pœplə fɔrt ɛ̃'terɛsɑ̃], *encre noire*
[ɑ̃'krə nwaɪr], *maître d'études* [mɛ'trə detyd], where the
following word begins with a consonant, the [ə] survives.
In *peuple heureux* [pœpl œrø], *encre à écrire* [ɑ̃'kr a ekriɪr],
maître ou serviteur [mɛɪtr u sɛrvɪtœɪr], they are carried over
to form a syllable with the following vowel.

In hasty speech [l] [r] and [m] at the end of a sound
group may be devocalized even after a voiced consonant.
We have seen in the foregoing chapter on Elision, that there
is a tendency to simplify the groups in question by dropping
the final consonant.   But even where the consonant does
not fall away, the tendency may be shown in its loss of
voice.   Pronunciations like the following are not uncommon :
capable [kapabl̥], *il me semble* [ɪl mə sɑ̃ɪbl̥], *ordre* [ɔrdr̥],
sabre [saɪbr̥].   On the other hand, as we shall see in the

[1] The semi-vowels [w] [ɥ] [j] never occur in a group at the end of a
syllable, and [n] is not found in that position after a voiceless consonant.

following section, *sm* may be sounded [zm] : *fanatisme*
[fanatism̦] or [fanatizm].

In English [r] falls away altogether at the end of a
syllable, and, therefore, also at the end of a sound-group,
while [l] and [m] in this position, after another consonant,
are voiced and have syllabic value : *people* [pɹip-l], *prism*
[pɹiz-m], sometimes [pɹipəl] [pɹizəm].[1]   The English-speaking student must, therefore, be careful not to treat the
French [r] [l] or [m] in the same manner.

(ii) *Vocalization.*

Vocalization is the acquisition of voice by a normally
voiceless consonant under the influence of a contiguous
voiced consonant.   In French, vocalization is *always regressive*, that is, the influence always proceeds from the second
consonant to the first.   It is only logical that those voiced
consonants which are liable to progressive devocalization[2]
should not at the same time be capable of bringing about
the vocalization of a preceding voiceless consonant.   Hence
the only consonants that produce this effect are [b] [d] [g]
[v] [z] [ʒ]   All the voiceless consonants, without exception,
become more or less vocalized when followed by one of
these voiced ones : *j'étouffe d'émotion* [ʒetuʃ demosjɔ̃], *chaque
jour* [ʃak ʒuːr], *avec douceur* [avɛk dusœːr], *transvaser*
[trɑ̃'sva'ze], *anecdote* [anɛkdɔt], *le Cap de Bonne Espérance*
[lə kap̌ də bɔn ɛsperɑ̃ːs], *il échappe de ses gardes* [il eʃap̌ də
se gard], *ace de cœur* [aș də kœːr], *cette bouteille* [sɛṭ butɛːj],
je le cache bien [ʒə l kaʃ bjɛ̃], *bec de gaz* [bɛk̦ də gɑːz], *est-ce
bien ?* [ɛș bjɛ̃].   So characteristic of the language is this
phenomenon of regressive vocalization that a normally mute
consonant resuscitated in linking has assimilative power :
de vifs enthousiasmes [də vifz ɑ̃'tuzjasm̦], *les Juifs et les Turcs*
[le ʒɥifz e le tyrk].

[1] See Part II. Chap. I. p. 74.
[2] See p. 150.   [m] in the group [sm] is an exception.

Though the voiceless consonant is seldom quite transformed into its voiced counterpart by assimilation, the
vocalization is generally very clearly perceptible even in
careful speech. The voiceless consonant may be attacked
in the normal manner, but the vocal chords begin to vibrate
before the organs articulate the attracting consonant. The
English-speaking student will need to acquire a habit of
regressive vocalization, for vocalization by attraction is rare
in English. In *book-binder* [buk bəɪndə] and *fit better* [fɪt
bɛtə], for example, there is no assimilation of the [k] to the
[b] or of the [t] to the [b]. When it does occur in English
it is progressive: *e.g. figs* [fɪgz] instead of [fɪgs], and the
examples given at page 146.

Avoiding negligible details, we may sum up the essential
characteristics of vocalization and devocalization in French
as follows :

(i) The consonants [r] [l] [m] are subject to progressive
devocalization at the end of a sound group.

(ii) Assimilation in all other cases is regressive · it is
always the first consonant that is affected. If the order is
voiced + voiceless, the first loses voice; if *voiceless + voiced*,
the first acquires voice. Compare *obtenir* [ɔptəniːr] and
il cesse de nier [il sɛ'ş də nie].

(iii) *Nasalization.*

This kind of assimilation amounts to the substitution of a
nasal consonant for an explosive : [m] for [b], [n] for [d]
and [ŋ] for [g].[1] It takes place when the explosive is both
preceded by a nasal vowel and followed (*a*) by a nasal
consonant, or (*b*) a fellow-explosive. Examples : *de longue
main* [də lɔ̃'ŋ mɛ̃] instead of [də lɔ̃'g mɛ̃], *point de mire*
[pwɛ̃ n miːr] instead of [pwɛ̃ d miːr], *une tombe neuve* [yn
tɔ̃'m nœːv] instead of [yn tɔ̃'b nœːv], *vingt-deux* [vɛ̃n dø]

---

[1] This [ŋ] is the sound in our word *long* [lɒŋ]. It is found in French
only in cases of the kind mentioned in the text.

instead of [vɛ̃'t dø], *ne tombe pas* [nə tɔ̃'m pɑ] instead of
[nə tɔ̃'b̥ pɑ], *une longue guerre* [yn lɔ̃'ŋ gɛɪr] instead of
[yn lɔ̃'g gɛɪr].   Such assimilations are characteristic of
rather hasty speech, and are usually avoided more or less
effectively in reading.   They have no exact equivalents in
English.   Pronunciations such as [kɑɪŋ gɔɔ] for *can't go*
[kɑɪnt gɔɔ] [dɔɔm mɛɪk] for *don't make* [dɔɔnt mɛɪk] are
no doubt occasionally heard, but they belong to very
careless speech.

CHAPTER V

THE TRANSITION FROM ONE SOUND TO
ANOTHER—GLIDES

WHEN two successive sounds are formed with different organs, or with the same organs in the same place, the second sound may follow the first immediately; but when they require the same organs of speech in different positions there must clearly be a fraction of time, between the completion of the one and the commencement of the other, during which the organs are passing from the first to the second position, and neither of the two sounds is being articulated. One of two things must then happen : either glide-sounds are produced, or there is a momentary silence. In our word *print* [pɹɪnt], for example, the transition from the [p] to the [r] is immediate, because the tongue prepares to articulate the [ɹ] while the lips are producing the [p], and the transition from the [n] to the [t] is immediate, because the position of the tongue is the same for both sounds; but a glide must intervene between the [ɹ] and the [ɪ] and again between the [ɪ] and the [n] because these three sounds, [ɹ] [ɪ] [n], are produced with the tongue in three different positions. As a rule the transition is effected the same way in French as in English, by taking the shortest cut from the one sound to the other, and is so rapid that we are not conscious of any intermediate glide. Hence, if the English-

speaking student produces the right French sounds, he will,
as a matter of course, usually effect the right transitions.
His attention, however, must be directed to the following
cases :

(i) *Transition between identical consonants (double sounds).*

In English, double stops are pronounced with a single
explosion, *e.g.* the double [t] in *coat-tail* [kɔotteɪl], the
double [d] in *head-dress* [hɛddɹɛs], the double [k] in *book-
case* [bʊkkɛɪs]; but in careful speech a distinct gemination
of the sound is effected by lengthening the period during
which the organs are in contact, and by first momentarily
decreasing, and then, in passing to the second syllable,
slightly increasing the pressure.[1] Double continuants (*e.g.*
the [l] in *scaleless* [skɛɪlləs], *dully* [dʌlli], the [n] in *thin-
ness* [θɪnnəs], *unnerve* [ʌnnɐːv], the [s] in *house-surgeon*
[haʊssɐːdʒn̩], *misspell* [mɪsspɛl]), are treated in an analogous
manner : there is no actual break in the continuity of the
sound, but it is lengthened and slightly reinforced for the
second syllable.

Allowance being made for differences in the method of
production, we may say that double sounds undergo similar
treatment in French. Hence, the organs of speech do not
part between the twin-sounds in *sainteté* [sɛ̃'tte], *netteté*
[nɛtte], *honnêteté* [ɔnɛtte], *intimement* [ɛ̃'timmɑ̃], *extrêmement*
[ɛkstrɛmmɑ̃], *inné* [inne], *illettré* [illɛtre], *illimité* [illimite],
illogique [illɔʒik], *illisible* [illizibl]. In the same way there
is a weakening followed by a strengthening of the sound,
but no interruption, in articulating a double fricative, as in
the words *conseillions* [kɔ̃'sɛjjɔ̃], *serrurerie* [sɛryrri], *parerai*
[parre], *mourrons* [murrɔ̃], *croyions* [krwɑjjɔ̃].

But in spite of the similarity of treatment in the two
languages the double sound is perceptibly longer, the
gemination more clearly defined, in French than in English.

[1] Compare Syllabication, p. 73.

In producing such a sound in the foreign language it is helpful to remember that it belongs to two syllables, *e.g.* [ɔ-nɛt-te], [ɛks-trɛm-mɑ̃], and that it cannot be neglected in either. The tendency in less careful English is either to scamp the sound in the unaccented syllable, or to pronounce it in a way between the syllables without attaching it clearly to either instead of [dʌl-lɪ], we are apt to say [dʌ-l-ɪ] or even [dʌl-ɪ]; instead of [mɪs-spɛl], [mɪ-s-pɛl] or even [mɪ-spɛl]. In French, care must be taken to close the first syllable with the consonant, and to sustain the sound a perceptible fraction of time before passing to the second syllable : *croyons* [krwɑjɔ̃] must not be confounded with *croyions* [krwɑjjɔ̃], nor *parerai* [parre] with *parai* [pare].

In the body of words double sounds occur only (*a*) when two like sounds are brought together by the elision of an intervening [ə]; (*b*) in verbal forms *mourrons* [murrɔ̃], *courrai* [kurre], *accueillions*, [akœjjɔ̃], *empaillions* [ɑ̃pɑjjɔ̃]; (*c*) in a few words of learned origin beginning with *ill-*, *inn-* examples of which have been given above. It is true that a double sound is sometimes heard in a few other words such as *immortel*, *immense*, *grammaire*, *irruption*, *irréligion*, *annales*, *ascenseur*, *transsubstantiation*, *diffusion*, *syllepse*, but its use in these cases is not obligatory. Hence, in the vast majority of words, the double sign represents a single sound. This is also the case in English : *e.g.* *common* [kɒmən], *bitten* [bɪtn̩], *abbot* [æbət]. On the other hand, it happens very frequently that the same sound occurs in succession in two different words, as the final of the one and the initial of the other, and we have then a genuine double sound which has to be treated just as if it were contained in the body of a word. Thus *une grande dame* is pronounced [yn grɑ̃'d dam], *cette tête* [sɛt tɛːt], *combien cela coûte-t-il* [kɔ̃'bjɛ̃ sla kut til], *le même moment* [lə mɛ'm mɔmɑ̃], *comme moi* [kɔm

mwa], *nous ne nous voyons plus* [nu n nu vwajõ ply], *celle-là*
[sɛl la], *il l'a* [il la], *qui se sauve* [ki s soɪv], *faire relier*
[fɛ'r rəlje], *une lumière rouge* [yn lymjɛ'r ruːʒ], *avec calme*
[avɛk kalm].[1]

The above method of treating double sounds may be
regarded as the rule even in careful speech.   Nevertheless,
in the deliberate reading of formal and elevated passages,
the two sounds will at times be clearly separated.   The
effect is then very much the same as if a faint [ə] had been
intercalated.   In the transcripts of Professor Koschwitz we
even find the sign [ə] in some instances : two out of the
thirteen readers of the passage from A. Daudet's *Tartarin
de Tarascon* are, for example, credited with the pronunciation [sɛtə tɛːr] = *cette terre* (*Parl. par.* p. 4, l. 17).   The
sounding of a definite [ə] in such cases must none the
less be regarded as dialectal.   But pronunciations like
[setʰ tɛːr], [ɔnɛtʰte], in which a mere 'breathing' is heard,
consequent upon the separation of the organs after the first
explosive, cannot be considered incorrect.   It should be
noted, however, that this dissolution of double sounds
belongs above all to the diction of the stage, and that its
frequent recurrence, even in formal speech, would savour of
pedantry.

The English-speaker is perhaps inclined to treat double
sounds between words more carelessly than those which
occur in the body of a word.   If we examine our pronunciation, for instance, of the expressions *this song, immense
success, fit together, set to music, don't tell, feel limp, with the
stream, safe from harm, iron nail, same measure*, we find
that, unless we articulate with unusual deliberation, the
twin-sounds are often scarcely recognizable as such.   A
good reader would doubtless make a clear distinction

[1] *Je l'ai* is often pronounced [ʒə l le] : but the double sound is here
incorrect.   A single sign never stands for a double consonant.

between *with the stream* [wɪð ðə stɹiːm] and *with a stream* [wɪð ə stɹiːm], between *safe from* [seɪf fɹəm] and *say from* [seɪ fɹəm], but in conversation the difference is very minute   In French, double sounds are not usually treated so negligently.   It is true that the gemination of a double sound between words is not always as distinct in daily intercourse as it should be in reading, but it is rarely quite as imperfect as in English.   In both languages, moreover, the laxer pronunciation is permissible only as a result of fluent utterance.   The learner, while avoiding the opposite error of exaggeration, should consequently make it a rule to articulate French double sounds distinctly as such.

(ii) *Transition between voiceless and voiced or nasalized stops produced at the same place.*

We need only consider the following series: 1. Pairs of voiced and voiceless stops: [td] [dt] [pb] [bp] [kg] [gk]; 2. Combinations of the voiceless stops with the corresponding nasal consonants: [tn] [nt] [pm] [mp], 3. Combinations of the voiced stops with the corresponding nasals · [dn] [nd] [bm] [mb].   In none of the cases are the combined sounds identical in nature, yet, being formed with the same contact of the organs, the transition from the one to the other is effected essentially in the same way as that between pairs of like sounds: that is, without separating the organs   The process, however, is not quite so simple as that described in the foregoing section   With pairs of the first series there will naturally be regressive assimilation, *i.e.* the first consonant being attracted to the second will tend to lose voice if the second is voiceless, and to acquire voice if the second is voiced.[1]   If the assimilation is complete, these pairs will fall under the rules for double sounds; if only partial, the vocal chords will, as the case may be, begin or cease to vibrate during the transition.   Supposing then that the

[1] See Assimilation, pp 148, 152

second consonant is voiced, as in *miettes de pain* [mjɛt də
pɛ̃], and that partial assimilation takes place : the vocal
chords will begin to vibrate as nearly as possible with the
formation of the contact, the vibration at first more or less
faint, increasing gradually, so that the full-voiced sound is
heard before the explosion occurs. And this process will
be reversed in *assez de temps* [ase d̥ tɑ̃], where the second
consonant is voiceless. If, as in exceptional cases of the
kind referred to in the preceding section, there is an
explosion after the first of the two sounds, there will be
no assimilation : *vingt-deux* will then be pronounced
[vɛ̃'tʰ dø] instead of [vɛ̃'t dø] or [vɛ̃n dø].[1]

In combinations of the second series assimilation as a
rule does not take place, and the difference between the
two sounds is very clearly marked by the element of
nasalized voice which characterizes one of them, and ceases
or begins, as the case may be, in passing to the second
syllable : *développement* [devlɔpmɑ̃], *campement* [kɑ̃'pmɑ̃],
hanneton [antɔ̃]. Here again, however, in ceremonious
speech, the first sound may be sharply separated from the
second by bringing the organs apart. The sounds [t n] in
sa haute nature were pronounced separately by Renan in
reading for Koschwitz (*Parl. par.* p. 59, l. 7), but the
other four readers appear to have hyphenated the sounds
in the usual way.

In the third series both consonants are voiced, but the
one is nasalized and the other oral. The transition is here
effected by lowering or raising the velum according as the
nasal consonant follows or precedes the other. The same
thing happens in English (*e.g.* in *candour, symbol*). It
should be borne in mind that a nasal consonant-sign
followed by another consonant in the body of a French
word scarcely ever stands for a consonant-sound : *condo-*

[1] On the pronunciation [vɛ̃n dø], see p. 154.

léance is pronounced [kɔ̃'dɔleɑ̃ːs] not [kɔ̃ndɔleɑ̃ːs], *symbole* [sɛ̃'bɔl] not [sɛ̃mbɔl], *simple* [sɛ̃ːpl] not [sɛ̃mpl]   Where the second consonant is a nasal and the first is preceded by a nasal vowel, assimilation often takes place in hurried speech.[1]   This assimilation may be easily avoided, and cannot occur if there is an intermediate explosion.

(iii) *Transition between dissimilar stops*

In English, the first of two consecutive dissimilar explosives is seldom completely articulated, i e. the contact for the second is formed while the organs with which the first is produced are still in touch   Examples are found in the words *factor, captive, fig-tree, flagged, foot-path, bugbear.* In French, on the other hand, the first explosive is as a rule fully articulated in careful speech   *facteur* being pronounced [fakʰtœːr], *captif* [kapʰtif], *acte* [akʰtə], *arcs-boutants* [arkʰ butɑ̃], *arc de triomphe* [arkʰ də triɔ̃ːf], *parc de Montsouris* [parkʰ də mɔ̃'suri], *Bagdad* [bagⁿdad].   The explosion, however, should not be exaggerated, in some cases it is scarcely audible, and in easy conversation it often enough does not take place.   The transition from [p] to [t], for instance, is frequently effected as in English   But [k] and [g] should be carefully and fully articulated in the sequences [kt] and [gd] : if the explosion be here omitted, the effect in French ears is that of [tt] or [dd].

(iv) *Transition from a voiceless stop to a vowel.*

This transition has already been referred to in the description of the individual sounds [p] [t] [k], but it may here be summarized on account of its importance.   In English, the explosion is heard before the vocal chords vibrate for the vowel · *part* [pʰɑit], *teach* [tʰiitʃ], *cool* [kʰuul]   In French, no voiceless breathing must intervene between consonant and vowel   in other words, the vocal chords must begin to vibrate simultaneously with the separation of the organs.

[1] See Assimilation, p 153.

F.P.   L

With the English examples compare *pâte* [pɑːt], *tige* [tiːʒ], *coule* [kuːl]. The difference between the two systems lies in the management of the vocal chords, the state of which, with a little practice, can be distinctly felt. When the explosion takes place in English they are still relaxed as in breathing : in French, they are brought together when the organs form the contact for the consonant, and the instant the breath escapes they begin to vibrate. The glide is thus voiceless in English, whereas it is voiced in French.[1]

(v) *Transition between vowels.*

The French system is here in essential agreement with the English ; but the learner may perhaps be warned against introducing a glottal stop as the result of hesitation and exaggerated stress. This glottal stop is permissible between French vowels only when the second begins a quotation, or in expressions like the following, which is to be found at l. 4, p. 124 of the *Chrestomathie* : *Mais être ainsi, c'est être inconstant* [mɛ ʔɛːtr ɛ'si, s ɛt ɛːtr ɛ'kɔ̃stɑ̃]. The use of the glottal stop, if not obligatory here, is at least desirable. In all other cases, the passage from one vowel to another must not be jerky or rasping, but smooth and gradual, as in the English words *react, peony, poetic, hiatus.*

Successive vowels are found in the body of but few words : *e.g. chaos* [kao], *poème* [pɔɛm], *noël* [nɔɛl], *fléau* [fleo], *réel* [reɛl]. Most of the combinations of vowel-signs in the body of words stand for combinations of a consonant and vowel, as in *loin* [lwɛ̃], *rien* [rjɛ̃], *trois* [trwɑ], *puits* [pɥi], *fouet* [fwɛ], *mieux* [mjø] ; or for a single vowel-sound, as in *baie* [bɛ], *main* [mɛ̃], *trou* [tru], *beau* [bo]. In successive words, however, hiatus is very common : *e.g. tu as* [ty a], *il a oublié* [il a ublie], *j'ai osé* [ʒe o'ze], *avis important* [avi ɛ̃'pɔrtɑ̃].

Double vowels occur, though more rarely, both in the

[1] See pp. 44 ff.

body of words and between words : *e.g. créé* [kree], *alcool* [alkɔɔl], *coopération* [kɔɔpera'sjɔ̃], *je l'ai évité* [ʒə le evite], *les héros* [le ero], *au haut bout* [o o bu]. Passy observes that a vowel may occur as many as four times in succession, as in *Papa a à aller à Paris* [papa a a ale a pa'ri] But such combinations should be avoided, where possible, on grounds of euphony. The transition between double vowels is effected by a slight diminution and reinforcement of the sound (see Syllabication, p 73). The English-speaking student will have to guard against a tendency to overstress and diphthongize, *e.g.* to say [lei eiro] [kreiei | [ou ou bu]. This must be avoided by keeping the jaws and tongue rigidly in the one position.

When the second of two vowels (double or dissimilar) is accented, the hiatus is sometimes avoided by the inter-calation of a faint [h] : *créé* becomes [krehe], *fléau* [fleho], *réel* [rehɛl], *cent un* [sɑ̃ hœ̃] Such pronunciations must be regarded as exceptional. They are not to be recommended save in exclamations, like *aha* [ɑhɑ], *oho* [oho], in which the [h] is regularly heard.

On the other hand, no effort need be made to avoid the glide [j] which is often interposed, by a natural movement of the organs, between [i] and a following vowel. *Oublier* may be pronounced [ublie] or [ublije], *crier* [krie] or [krije] But the introduction of this glide after other vowels than [i], as in [kreje] for [kree] or [idejal] for [ideal], is vulgar.

In hasty speech the first of two vowels, if it is [i] [u] or [y], is often transformed into a consonant or semi-vowel. *Il y a* [il i a] becomes [il j a] [i j a] or even [j a], *tu as* [ty a] becomes [tɥa], *où est-il* [u ɛt il] becomes [wɛt il]

(vi) *Transition from a consonant to a vowel which belongs to another syllable.*

Examples, which are comparatively rare, are found in *cette haie, quelle haine, une harpe, une haie, elle hait, il hait,*

âme haute. Where, in cases of this kind, an '*e* mute' figures
after the consonant, it is often pronounced : [sɛtə ɛ] [kɛlə
ɛːn] [ynə arp] [ynə ɛ] [ɛlə ɛ] [ɑːmə oːt] ; the question under
consideration does not then arise. Again, the [h] may be
sounded, and we then have a simple transition between two
consonants : [sɛt hɛ] [kɛl hɛːn] [yn harp] [yn hɛ] [il hɛ]
[ɑːm hoːt]. But if neither of these courses be adopted, we
have in immediate succession a consonant and a vowel
which do not belong to the same syllable. In English we
often unconsciously link in such expressions as *an ass*
[ə-næs], *not at all* [nɒ-tə-tɒːl], *an aim* [ə-neɪm]. If we
carry this practice over into French in cases .of the kind
under discussion, and pronounce *il hait* as [i-lɛ], we shall
be understood to say *il est* or *il ait.* But even where no
such ambiguity would result, there must not be a suspicion
of linking. The problem thus presented is solved by
sounding an off-glide after the consonant, or even by attack-
ing the vowel with a faint glottal-stop and pronouncing
[il ʔɛ] [sɛt ʔɛ] [kɛl ʔɛːn], etc. In the same way we may
pronounce *an aim* [ən ʔɛɪm] when we wish to distinguish
it carefully from *a name* [ə neɪm]. Care must be taken not
to exaggerate the glottal-stop.

CHAPTER VI

ACCENTUATION

OF no less importance than the production of the right sounds is a right distribution of the accents, and nowhere does the French language differ more widely from English than in its accentuation. By accent is here meant the stress or degree of force with which a sound is uttered, considered quite apart from the musical pitch or melody of the phrase, a characteristic to which a later chapter will be devoted.

At the outset we must distinguish accent from emphasis. In English the difference is merely one of degree, emphasis there generally consisting in a reinforcement of the normal accent. If, for example, we wish to emphasize the expression *It's ridiculous* [ɪts ɹɪ'dɪkjʊləs], we simply increase the stress on the second and normally accented syllable of the adjective: [ɪts ɹɪ"dɪkjʊləs]. In French, on the other hand, the difference is often of a much more radical kind. In ordinary placid utterance the group *C'est ridicule* is accented on the last syllable: [sɛ ridi'kyl]; but if feeling be displayed, the stress shifts to the initial syllable of the adjective: [sɛ "ridikyl]. Emphasis thus disturbs the normal accent. This disturbance, which is very frequent, takes place in a more or less methodical manner admitting of definition. We shall, however, first direct attention to what may be

called the normal method of accentuation, meaning thereby
the accentuation of dispassionate, emotionless speech.

(i) *Normal accentuation.*

The rule may be expressed as follows : In the absence
of special emphasis, the principal accent is borne by the
last full syllable of the stress-group. It is important to
observe that the incidence of the accent is determined by
the division of the phrase into stress-groups.[1] To say that
each word is accented on the last syllable is not true of
connected speech ; it holds good for the isolated word
only because the word is then a sound-group and stress-
group in itself. In ordinary speech, the stress-group, as we
have seen in an earlier chapter, more often contains
several words, and may comprise the whole of a short
sentence. We may refer to the example that was used in
illustrating the division into stress- and sound-groups : *En
révoquant l'édit de Nantes Louis XIV porta un coup désastreux
au commerce de son pays, car les protestants s'expatrièrent en
foule et portèrent à l'étranger les secrets des arts et des industries
de France.* If this sentence were being dictated very slowly,
it might be divided and accented as follows : [ã revɔ'kã]
[ledi də 'nãːt] [lui ka'tɔrz] [pɔrta œ̃ ku dezas'trø] [o kɔ'mɛrs]
[də sõ pe'i] [kar le prɔtɛs'tã] [sɛkspatri'ɛir] [ã 'ful] [e pɔr'tɛir]
[a letrã'ʒe] [le sə'krɛ] [dez 'aːr] [e dez ɛ̃'dys'tri] [də 'frãːs].
Read in this manner, each group is at once a stress-group
and a sound-group. But, as we have seen, we may, and, in
ordinary circumstances, we should, combine two or more
stress-groups in each sound-group : *e.g.* [ã revɔ'kã ledi d "nãːt]
[lwi ka'tɔrz pɔrta œ̃ ku dezas"trø] [o kɔ'mɛrs də sõ pe"i] [kar le
prɔtɛs'tã sɛkspatri'ɛrt ã "ful] [e pɔr'tɛrt a letrã"ʒe] [le s'krɛ
dez 'aːr e dez ɛ̃'dys'tri ḍ "frãːs]. When several stress-groups
are thus combined in a single sound-group the final syllable
of all but the last is not quite so strongly accented as when

[1]See p. 72.

they formed sound-groups ; but it still bears a heavier stress than all the other syllables in the stress-group. This heavy beat on the last syllable of each stress-group is therefore called the *principal* or *tonic* accent

All the other syllables of the stress-group are said to be 'unstressed' or 'unaccented.' They follow each other with a more or less even march. Yet they are not all uttered with precisely the same gentle stress. A delicate analysis would reveal several degrees among unstressed syllables. But for practical purposes it is not necessary to distinguish more than two, which may be called *secondary* syllables and *weak* syllables.

To lay down rules for the distribution of secondary accents is impossible. Their incidence depends not only on the number of syllables in the group, but often on the nature of the words, and it may become a matter of style and taste. They have, however, a strong tendency to alternate with weak syllables in iambic or trochaic rhythm. In the group of three syllables the order will generally be secondary–weak–strong This is the case in the following groups *voulez-vous*, *montrez-moi*, *entrez donc : l'armée de France ; tu l'as dit, a-t-il dit, l'examen ; tableau noir, simplement ; l'Australie.* Four syllables will generally follow each other in the order weak–secondary–weak–strong : e.g. *le voulez-vous, montrez-le-moi, vous a-t-il dit ; répondit-elle ; l'armée d'Espagne ; le grand tableau, profondément ; la jalousie ; reconnaissance* Similarly a group of five will commonly begin with a secondary accent : *e.g. popularité, efficacité, générosité, nous apercevons.* This rhythmic alternation is, however, no more than a tendency. Two weak syllables in succession, or two secondary ones, and the series weak–secondary–strong are of frequent occurrence : *e.g. l'âge de mon frère* ['lɑ'ʒ də mɔ̃ "frɛ:r] ; *l'examinateur* [leg'zamina"tœ:r], *la nation* ['la 'nɑ"sjɔ̃] ; *le roi Jean*

['lə 'rwɑ "ʒɑ̃]; *mon frère Charles* ['mɔ̃ 'frɛ·r "ʃarl]; *civilisation*
['sivili 'za·"sjɔ̃]; *voulez-vous me dire* ['vule 'vu m "diːr].
A half-long vowel often enough attracts the secondary
accent : *e.g. mon bâton* [mɔ̃ 'bɑ· "tɔ̃]; *il courait* [il 'ku·"rɛ];
définitivement ['defini'ti·v"mɑ̃].

The rhythmic tendency which has been described is a
natural one, and it characterizes to some extent our own
language. It is more active in French, but must not be
exaggerated. The English-speaking student should rather
remember that the differences of stress in unaccented
syllables are much less marked in French than in English.
It is helpful to compare in this respect such pairs of English
and French words as *difficulty* [dɪfɪkʌltɪ] and *difficulté*
[difikylte], *opposition* [ɒpəzɪʃn̩] and *opposition* [ɔpozisjɔ̃],
particularity [pətɪkjʊlæɪɪtɪ] and *particularité* [partikylarite],
incomprehensible [ɪnkɒmpɹɪhɛnsəbl̩] and *incompréhensible*
[ɛ̃kɔ̃'preɑ̃'sibl]; and to observe closely, when occasion
offers, the Frenchman's pronunciation of English. It will
be found that the weak syllables are not so weak in French
as they are in English, and that the Frenchman who speaks
English imperfectly is very apt to give these syllables in our
language too much value. The near approach to uniformity
and balance between weak and secondary syllables is one of
the most striking features of French, and demands very
careful attention of the English-speaking student.

The principal accent, again, though stronger than the
secondary accents, is less heavy than the strong accent
in English. A stress-group composed of a half-long syllable
with a secondary accent followed by a short accented
syllable, such as we have in *beauté* ['bo·"te], *creuser*
['krø·"ze], seems often in untrained English ears to consist
of two equally stressed syllables, or even of a strong accent
followed by a secondary one. The accent which falls on
the last syllable of a sound-group containing several stress-

groups is, however, perceptibly stronger than all the other tonic accents. Hence, from the point of view of accent, the simple emotionless French sentence of several stress-groups produces the effect of a succession of almost uniform beats, punctuated from time to time by a slightly heavier one, and ending with the heaviest.

(ii) *Emphasis.*

The foregoing account of accent is true only of dispassionate speech where the mere placid utterance of the words conveys all the meaning intended But in everyday life such speech must be regarded as the exception, especially in the everyday life of the Frenchman, who is more emotional, or rather gives readier expression to his emotions, than the average Englishman. More commonly the speaker wishes to convince, to contradict or contrast, to show sorrow, indignation, surprise, delight, disgust, to call forth these feelings, to drive his meaning home For all these purposes he resorts to emphasis, laying special stress on the words to which he wishes to give a special value.

In emphasizing monosyllables the ordinary principles of accentuation may be modified in one of two ways : either a normally weak syllable may be stressed or a normally strong syllable may be made still stronger. Thus the weak negative in the simple statement *Ce n'est pas vrai* [sə nɛ pɑ 'vrɛ], may become stressed under the influence of emotion · [sə nɛ "pɑ 'vrɛ].· In the emphatic *C'est faux* [sɛ "fo], on the other hand, there is merely a reinforcement of a syllable already stressed in unemotional speech. Similar modifications result in English compare the phrase *I didn't say so* with the emphatic contradiction *I did "not say so ;* and the simple statement *It is false* with the energetic assertion *I say it's "false.* But certain monosyllables of which the English equivalents may be emphasized cannot always be so treated in French. If, for example, I wish to emphasize the pronoun-subject in *Je ne le crois pas*, I must add another form of the word and say *Moi je ne le crois pas*. To emphasize the pronoun-objects in *Qui t'a (vous a, lui a) donné cela?* I must say *Qui t'a (vous a, lui a) donné cela à toi (à vous, à lui* or *à elle)?* The particle *ne* is not often stressed, and in the familiar emphatic forms of such phrases as *Ce n'est pas vrai, Je ne sais pas*, it is usually omitted altogether: [sɛ pɑ vrɛ], [ʒ se pɑ] or [se pɑ]. With such reservations the treatment of monosyllables is essentially the same in both languages.

The French method of emphasizing polysyllables, on the other hand, is often widely divergent from the English. While we say *It's quite im″possible, It's ″absolutely in″credible, Most ri″diculous*, simply increasing the force of the ictus on the normally accented syllable, the French, instead of stressing the final syllable as in emotionless speech, shift the accent to an earlier syllable and say: *im″possible, ab″solument, in″croyable, ″ridicule*.

Emphatic accent does not vary with the position of the word; the same syllable is stressed whether the word stands at the end or in the body of a stress-group. In unemphatic speech, therefore, the word in question may not bear a strong accent at all, but as in the absence of emotion a strong accent always falls on the final syllable, such emphatic accentuation of a non-final syllable is commonly said to involve a displacement or shifting of the accent.

Although the syllable of emphatic stress is fixed for any particular word it varies from one word to another. In the examples given it will be observed that it is the first syllable of words beginning with a consonant, the second of words beginning with a vowel. There is a reason

for these variations. They depend upon the essential
nature of emphasis. The ordinary accent is rhythmic
and characteristic of the particular language, it is not
influenced by the meaning to be expressed, it controls
the cadence of the phrase as a whole. On the other
hand, it is of the essence of emphatic stress to single
out particular words and reinforce their significance. And
in French a word tends to become most striking by
being accented on the initial syllable   But if this syllable
begins with a vowel the laws of linking would often require
the carrying over to it of the final consonant of the
preceding word, and this new and unusual syllable being
emphatically stressed would not readily call up any particular
idea.[1]   Instead of casting added light upon the meaning
it would tend to obscure it.   Hence the origin of the
rule : The emphatic accent falls on the first syllable if
the word begins with a consonant, on the second if the
word begins with a vowel.   The reason given for the
rule is supported by the fact that words beginning with
' h aspirate ' are emphatically accented on the first syllable,
e g. *hurler, honteux* ; and that in positions where linking
is out of the question polysyllables beginning with a vowel
are capable of taking an accent on the initial syllable,
e.g. *"Impossible, mon cher, "impossible* [2]   Further, when
polysyllables which differ only in a normally unaccented
syllable are contrasted, that syllable takes the abnormal
stress even though it be an initial one beginning with
a vowel : *L'homme "propose, Dieu "dispose ; Qui "s'excuse,
"s'accuse ; L'œuvre de Shakespeare est "amorale , Il trouve
toujours ses "expressions trop faibles pour ses "impressions*

[1] This is not the case with monosyllables.   Nor does the rule
apply to them   Compare the very common emphatic English *Not
at all !* [nɒt ə "tʊ:l].

[2] This example is taken from Passy, *Sons du Français.*

It should be observed that no displacement of the accent occurs under the rule in the case of dissyllabic words beginning with a vowel. The emphatic forms of *énorme, affreux, absurde* are [e″nɔrm], [a″frø], [ap″syrd] with increased stress upon the final syllable. In all other cases the accent shifts. Dissyllables and polysyllables beginning with a consonant are stressed, under emotion, on the initial syllable : *beaucoup* [″boːku], *toujours* [″tuʒuːr], *jamais* [″ʒamɛ], *parfait* [″parfɛ], *terrible* [″tɛribl] [″tɛrribl], *splendide* [″splɑ̃ːdid], *crier* [″krie] ; *merveilleux* [″mɛrvɛjø], *prodigieusement* [″prɔdiʒjø′zmɑ̃], *ravissant* [″ravisɑ̃], *misérable* [″mizerabl]. Polysyllables beginning with a vowel usually have the second syllable stressed when uttered with feeling: *abominable* [a″bɔminabl], *énormément* [e″nɔrmemɑ̃], *extrêmement* [ɛks″trɛmmɑ̃], *assommant* [a″sɔmɑ̃], *épouvantable* [e″puvɑ̃′tabl], *ahuri* [a″yːri], *éhonté* [e″ɔ̃te]. Many of these words, and others which by their nature are generally used with considerable feeling, especially terms of abuse, are more often heard with displaced than with normal accent.

Emphatic accentuation of a non-final syllable is not invariably accompanied by a weakening of the normal stress. If the syllable to which the accent shifts is not felt to be sufficiently distinctive, if the essence of the word seems to lie more particularly in the final syllable, the latter may be given an equal value, and occasionally every syllable in a word is stressed in this way. Exceptional words of this kind are *élégant, délice, dévore.* When a final syllable containing a normally long vowel is weakened, the quantity of the vowel may be slightly reduced, but it never becomes quite short.

Finally, emphatic displacement of the accent may entail other modifications of normal conditions. There is a tendency to sustain the stressed syllable. A half-long vowel under abnormal stress may become long, even abnor-

mally long : *Au contraire, il y en avait beaucoup* [o 'kɔ̃ːtrɛɪr
il j ɑ̃n avɛ "boːku]   A short vowel is not usually lengthened,
but the need to lengthen the syllable is often met by
lengthening the initial consonant . *Il est assommant* [il ɛt
a"sːɔmɑ̃] ; *jamais* ["ʒːamɛ], *faux* ["fːo], *horrible* [ɔ"rːibl].[1]

Again, the emphatic syllable is very frequently, in fact
generally, uttered at a higher than the normal pitch (see
Chap. VIII p 185).   But perhaps the most remarkable
change occurs when a syllable which would normally be
elided is preserved to receive the abnormal accent, as in
the emphatic *la seconde* [la "sœgɔ̃ːd] in place of [la z'gɔ̃ːd].

The English-speaking student will do well to give particular heed to the purity of his vowel and to his syllabication,
according as the vowel under abnormal stress is long or
short.   The English habit of diphthongization is most
difficult to combat in the case of sustained vowels : to avoid
bad pronunciations such as [bouku] [pleɪzɪːr] the tongue
and lower jaw must be kept carefully in the one position.
As short vowels, on the other hand, do not occur in open
accented syllables in English, we are tempted to close such
syllables in French by annexing to them a consonant from
the following syllable, and special emphasis makes this
inclination specially hard to resist.   As a rule, thorough
and constant drilling alone will enable the English-speaking
student to avoid assimilating, for example, the emphatic
open syllables of *ridicule* ["rɪ–dɪ–kyl], *misérable* ["mɪ–ze–rabl],
ravissant ["ra–vi–sɑ̃], *impossible* [ɛ̃ˈ–"pɔ–sɪbl], *abominable*
[a–"bɔ–mɪ–nabl] to the emphatic closed syllables of our
words *ridicule* ["ɹɪd-ɪ-kjuul], *miserable* ["mɪz–ə–ɹəb–l],
ravishingly ["ɹæv–ɪʃ–ɪŋ–lɪ], *impossible* [ɪm–"pɔs–ɪb-l], *abominable* [ə–"bɔm-ɪn-əb-l].

[1] See the following chapter on the Quantity of Vowels and Consonants.

CHAPTER VII

QUANTITY

The duration of the individual sounds is necessarily increased or diminished with the rate of utterance, but the
relation between long and short sounds remains more or
less constant throughout such fluctuations. It is to these
relative differences that reference is made in speaking of
the quantity of vowels and consonants.

A. Vowels.

All the French vowels are subject to variation in point of
quantity. Of the many degrees that exist, it is unnecessary
to distinguish more than three: long, half-long, and short.
Accented vowels are either long or short; unaccented, half-
long or short, the lengthened vowel of an unstressed syllable
being naturally less sustained than that of a stressed one.
In phonetic script the long vowel is indicated by the sign
[ː] placed after the sign of quality, the half-long by ['], and
in the absence of either of these signs the vowel is short.
Thus in *haut* [o] the 'o' is short, in *hôte* [oːt] it is long, and
in *hauteur* [o'tœːr] half-long.

The length of the vowel is not always due to the operation
of phonetic principles. It serves in some cases merely to
distinguish words which are otherwise alike, and not seldom
varies with the speaker. It is, therefore, impossible to
formulate constant and exhaustive laws for vowel-quantity.

But the following rules will be found to cover the great majority of cases.

I. *In Normally Accented Syllables.*

(i) In a final open[1] syllable the vowel is short. This rule holds good even of the nasal vowels and of [o] and [ø], which are half-long or long in most other cases, and it overrides all the vagaries of traditional spelling. Examples: *fini* [fini], *finie* [fini], *souris* [suri], *dit* [di], *gît* [ʒi]; *dé* [de], *gai* [ge], *je l'ai* [ʒə le], *je sais* [ʒə se], *papier* [papje], *tuer* [tɥe]; *fait* [fɛ], *je vais* [ʒə vɛ], *baie* [bɛ], *prêt* [prɛ], *paraît* [parɛ]; *voilà* [vwala], *créa* [krea], *aimât* [ɛ'ma]; *amas* [ama], *pas* [pɑ], *bât* [bɑ], *droit* [drwɑ]; *beau* [bo], *dos* [do], *éclôt* [eklo], *plutôt* [plyto]; *fou* [fu], *boue* [bu], *bout* [bu], *goût* [gu]; *tribu* [triby], *tribut* [triby], *affût* [afy]; *peu* [pø], *peux* [pø], *lieu* [ljø], *lieue* [ljø]; *vin* [vɛ̃], *vain* [vɛ̃], *vingt* [vɛ̃], *qu'il vînt* [kil vɛ̃]; *sang* [sɑ̃], *cent* [sɑ̃]; *bon* [bɔ̃], *tronc* [trɔ̃]; *un* [œ̃], *jeun* [ʒœ̃].

This rule is a direct contradiction of the principle governing the quantity of vowels in the same position in English. We lengthen, and therefore usually diphthongize a final accented free vowel: *e.g. fee* [fiː], *delay* [dɪlɛɪ], *true* [tɹuu], *shah* [ʃɑː] [ʃɑɪə], *mow* [mɔo] [mɔu]. English-speaking students of French find great difficulty in combating this tendency. It is true that final French vowels in open syllables are not so short as short vowels in closed syllables, and that they may become half-long in deliberate speech, especially in the recitation of verse, but to convert them into long vowels is dialectal.

(ii) In a final closed syllable all the nasal vowels, [ɛ̃] [ɑ̃] [ɔ̃] [œ̃], and the oral vowels [o] and [ø] are invariably long. Examples: *mince* [mɛ̃ːs], *crainte* [krɛ̃ːt], *feindre* [fɛ̃ːdr], *vinrent* [vɛ̃ːr], *vente* [vɑ̃ːt], *France* [frɑ̃ːs], *monde* [mɔ̃ːd], *humble* [œ̃ːbl],

---

[1] An open syllable is one that ends with a vowel: see p. 73.

faute [foːt], *côte* [koːt], *neutre* [nøːtr]. Hence the short vowels of such masculine adjectives as *grand* [grɑ̃], *long* [lɔ̃], *faux* [fo], *gracieux* [grasjø] become long in the feminine : *grande* [grɑ̃ːd], *longue* [lɔ̃ːg], *fausse* [foːs], *gracieuse* [grasjøːz].

(iii) Any vowel is long in a final closed syllable, if the consonant closing the syllable is a voiced fricative other than [l], viz. [r] [v] [z] [ʒ] [j].[1] Examples : *pire* [piːr], *faire* [fɛːr], *poire* [pwaːr], *soir* [swaːr], *rare* [rɑːr], *mort* [mɔːr], *cour* [kuːr], *pur* [pyːr], *sœur* [sœːr], *rive* [riːv], *cave* [kaːv], *fleuve* [flœːv], *tige* [tiːʒ], *page* [paːʒ], *âge* [ɑːʒ], *loge* [lɔːʒ], *juge* [ʒyːʒ], *bise* [biːz], *aise* [ɛːz], *base* [bɑːz], *chose* [ʃoːz], *muse* [myːz], *fille* [fiːj], *soleil* [sɔlɛːj], *veille* [vɛːj], *taille* [tɑːj] [taːj], *feuille*, [fœːj]. This rule holds good of syllables ending with [vr] : *givre* [ʒiːvr], *livre* [liːvr], *lièvre* [ljɛːvr], *œuvre* [œːvr]. But if [r] is followed by another consonant the vowel is short : compare *père* [pɛːr] and *perte* [pɛrt], *char* [ʃaːr] and *charte* [ʃart], *court* [kuːr] and *courte* [kurt], *corps* [kɔːr] and *corse* [kɔrs].

(iv) In closed syllables, other than those specified in the preceding rule, [ɑ] is always long, except in the words *droite* [drwɑt], *adroite* [adrwɑt], *étroite* [etrwɑt], *froide* [frwɑd], *froisse* [frwɑs], *paroisse* [parwɑs]. Examples : *basse* [bɑːs], *casse* [kɑːs], *passe* [pɑːs], *flamme* [flɑːm] [flaːm], *fable* [fɑːbl], *sabre* [sɑːbr].

[i] [a] [ɔ] [u] [y] [œ] are short. Examples : *riche* [riʃ], *signe* [siɲ] ; *balle* [bal], *femme* [fam], *patte* [pat], *nappe* [nap] ; *bonne* [bɔn], *sol* [sɔl], *molle* [mɔl], *Rome* [rɔm] ; *boule* [bul], *groupe* [grup], *route* [rut], *souffre* [sufr] ; *mule* [myl], *commune* [kɔmyn], *sud* [syd] ; *meuble* [mœbl], *seul* [sœl].

This section of the rule is, however, subject to the follow-ing reservations :

(α) There is no unanimity of practice with regard to the quantity of the six vowels last-mentioned when the consonant

---

[1] Close *e* [e] does not occur in this position.

closing the syllable is a voiced explosive: [b] [d] [g].
Words like *fade*, *bague*, *vague*, *vide*, *figue* are often heard
with a long vowel.

(β) In the Greek and Latin endings -*os*, -*us*, usage wavers
between the long and the short vowel: *Minos* [minɔs] or
[minɔːs], *obus* [obys] or [obyːs], *crocus* [krɔkys] or [krɔkyːs].

(γ) *Tous*, *veule* have long vowels: [tuːs] [vœːl], and are
thus distinguished from *tousse* [tus], *veulent* [vœl]. The
lengthening of [u] before [l] is generally considered dialectal,
but the pronunciations *il coule* [il kuːl], *il roule* [il ruːl] are
Parisian.

(δ) A circumflex accent on a vowel in a closed syllable
generally indicates a long sound, as in *abîme* [abiːm], *boîte*
[bwaːt], *poêle* [pwɑːl] [pwaːl]. But the vowel is often
pronounced short in *île* [il], *gîte* [ʒit], *dîme* [dim], *dîne* [din],
flûte [flyt], *voûte* [vut], and in the endings -*âmes*, -*âtes* of the
past definite tense, *e.g.* *parlâmes* [paʀlam], *arrivâtes* [arivat].
Aumône is sometimes pronounced [oˈmɔn] instead of
[oˈmoːn].

The vowels [i] [u] [y] in this position demand special
attention. The close sounds [i] and [u] are never found in
short syllables in English, their place being taken by the
open sounds [ɪ] and [ʊ] which are unknown in French.
The learner may, therefore, be inclined to assimilate the
vowels in *mille* [mil] and *poule* [pul] to those in our words
mill [mɪl] and *pull* [pʊl], and by analogy to pronounce
the [y] in *hutte* [yt] like the open vowel in the German
word *Hütte* [hʏtə]. Care must be taken not to relax the
organs in shortening these sounds. Conversely, the [i] and
[u] being found only in long syllables in English, the learner
is apt to conclude, on hearing the short sounds correctly
pronounced, that they are long: *e.g.* that the vowels in
libre [libr] and *livre* [liːvr] are of the same quantity. Only
by constant observation and practice will the ear become

quick to detect the difference in length. A still more serious mistake is to substitute the English diphthongs [ɪi] and [ʊu] for the short French vowels : *e.g.* to assimilate *mille* and *poule* to our words *meal* [mɪil] and *pool* [pʊul].

[ɛ] is perhaps usually short, as in *sec* [sɛk], *sel* [sɛl], *faites* [fɛt], *mettre* [mɛtr], *lettre* [lɛtr], *belle* [bɛl]. But it is long :

(α) when written *ê*, *aî* : *tête* [tɛːt], *rêne* [rɛːn], *fête* [fɛːt], *faîte* [fɛːt], *chaîne* [ʃɛːn], *naître* [nɛːtr], *maître* [mɛːtr] ; *êtes* [ɛt] and *arrête* [arɛt] form exceptions ;

(β) in the endings *-ème, -aime, -ène, -eine, -ès, -aisse* : *thème* [tɛːm], *il aime* [il ɛːm], *il mène* [il mɛːn], *scène* [sɛːn], *reine* [rɛːn], *veine* [vɛːn], *pataquès* [patakɛːs], *caisse* [kɛːs] ; the numerals in *-ème* form exceptions : *deuxième* [døˈzjɛm] ;

(γ) in the words *aide* [ɛːd], *aigre* [ɛːgr], *cèdre* [sɛːdr], *gaine* [gɛːn], *haine* [ɛːn], *nègre* [nɛːgr], *poète* [pɔɛːt], *traite*, in the sense of trade [trɛːt], *il traite* [il trɛːt].

In a considerable number of words the quantity is not well defined. Thus usage varies between the long and the short vowel in *aigle, aile, cesse, cède, collègue, Grèce, graisse, laide, laine, mètre, presse, peine, saine, sème, vaine, zèle*.

Summary.—Exceptions apart (numerous only in the case of [ɛ]) we may sum up the rules for the quantity of accented vowels as follows :

(1) In an open syllable the vowel is always short.

(2) In a closed syllable the nasal vowels and [o] [ø] [ɑ] are long ; but all other vowels are short unless they are followed by a voiced fricative other than [l] or bear a circumflex accent.

II. *In Unaccented Syllables.*

(i) In a stress-group composed of several words, the final vowels of all words but the last are short if they would have been short under the accent, and usually half-long if they would have been long under the accent: *grand homme* [grɑ̃t ɔm], *grande œuvre* [grɑ̃'d œːvr], *dans la salle* [dɑ̃ la sal], *point d'appui* [pwɛ̃ dapɥi], *brave homme* [braˈv ɔm], *une chose à faire* [yn ʃoˈz a fɛːr]. The otherwise long vowel, however, may become short in unimportant words: *e.g. pour vous* [pur vu]. But a short vowel is not liable to be lengthened. Compare *une heureuse enfance* [yn œrøˈz ɑ̃ˈfɑ̃ːs], *qu'il rende un service* [kil rɑ̃ˈd œ̃ sɛrvis] with *un heureux enfant* [œ̃n œrøz ɑ̃ˈfɑ̃], *il rend un service* [il rɑ̃t œ̃ sɛrvis]. The vowels [ø] and [ɑ̃] remain short in the last two examples although the normally mute consonant following is sounded. Thus liaison does not affect the quantity of vowels.

(ii) In initial or medial syllables the nasal vowels and the oral vowels [ɑ], [o] and [ø] are regularly half-long: *bonté* [bɔ̃ˈte], *chanter* [ʃɑ̃ˈte], *maintenir* [mɛ̃ˈtniːr], *humblement* [œ̃ˈblɑmɑ̃], *beauté* [boˈte], *fausser* [foˈse], *creuser* [krøˈze], *bâtir* [bɑˈtiːr], *tailleur* [tɑˈjœːr].

(iii) Other vowels than those of rule (ii) are regularly short in an initial or medial syllable: *regarder* [rəgarde], *amertume* [amɛrtym], *murmure* [myrmyːr], *souvenir* [suvniːr], *feuilleter* [fœjte], *amateur* [amatœːr], *naissance* [nɛsɑ̃ːs], *dévouement* [devumɑ̃], *parallèle* [paralɛl], *courageux* [kuraʒø]. The vowels of this rule sometimes become half-long in penultimate syllables, but not elsewhere. Thus in adverbs, nouns, and adjectives formed from adjectives or nouns by the addition of a suffix (other than *eux*), the root generally preserves its identity sufficiently to be treated as a separate word under rule (i). Hence words like the following have a half-long vowel in the penultimate syllable: *incurable* [ɛ̃ˈkyˈrabl], *purement* [pyˈrmɑ̃], *pureté* [pyˈrte], *durement* [dyˈrmɑ̃], *vivement* [viˈvmɑ̃], *définitivement* [definitiˈvmɑ̃], *antérieurement* [ɑ̃ˈterjœˈrmɑ̃], *rougâtre* [ruˈʒɑːtr], *gravement* [gra'vmɑ̃]. Again, where, under the rules for accented syllables, a vowel is long in the singular present indicative of verbs, that vowel is nearly always half-long in all other parts of the verb in which it occurs in an open syllable as an unaccented vowel: compare *brise* [briːz] and *briser* [bri'ze], *trouve* [truːv] and *trouver* [tru've], *aime* [ɛːm] and *aimer* [ɛ'me], *laisse* [lɛːs] and *laisser* [lɛ'se], *dure* [dyːr] and *durer* [dy're], *dore* [dɔːr] and *dorer* [dɔ're], *tire* [tiːr] and *tirer* [ti're], *effleure* [ɛflœːr] and *effleurer* [ɛflœ're], *désire* [deziːr] and *désirer* [dezi're]. But if the vowel be followed by [j], it is usually pronounced short: *brille* [briːj] but *briller* often = [brije], *pille* [piːj] but *piller* often = [pije], *accueille* [akœːj] but *accueiller* [akœjiːr], *someille* [sɔmɛːj] but *sommeiller* [sɔmɛje].

A third class of exceptions consists of words, particularly disyllables, with open penultimate syllable. The vowel of this syllable is often lengthened if followed by a voiced fricative other than [j] or [l], viz. [v] [z] [ʒ] [r]: *périr* [pe'riːr], *parisien* [pari'zjɛ̃], *carré* [ka're], *curé* [ky're], *mari* [ma'ri], *Paris* [pa'ri], *maison* [me'zɔ̃], *raison* [rɛ'zɔ̃], *raisin* [re'zɛ̃], *déjà* [de'ʒa], *plaisir* [ple'ziːr], *paisible* [pɛ'zibl], *lisant* [li'zɑ̃]. But the vowel is perhaps no less frequently short in this position: *saurais* [sɔrɛ], *aurais* [ɔrɛ], *pouvait* [puvɛ], *savoir* [savwaːr], *oiseau* [wazo], *civil* [sivil], *hiver* [ivɛːr], *heureux* [œrø]. The length in many cases is by no means well defined.

III. *In Abnormally Accented Syllables.*

When the accent is disturbed by emphasis, and a non-final syllable becomes stressed, the vowel is lengthened if it was already half-long, but, as a rule, not otherwise. Hence the accented vowel, though not final, is long in the emphatic forms of *beaucoup* ["boːku], *durement* ["dyːrmɑ̃], *vivement* ["viːvmɑ̃], *plaisir* ["pleːziːr]; short in those of *impossible* [ɛ·"pɔsibl], *agaçant* [a"gasɑ̃], *jamais* ["ʒamɛ].   The vowel [ə] in such a case is generally changed to [ø] or [œ] : *il grelottait* [il grəlɔtɛ], with disturbed accent becomes [il "grœlɔtɛ] and when *second* [səgɔ̃] is contrasted with *premier* it is generally pronounced ["sœgɔ̃].

On the other hand, if the accent shifts to another final syllable, the vowel of that syllable is very frequently lengthened, even though it would have been short under a normal accent : *un gros village* with stress on the adjective becomes [œ̃ "groː vilaːʒ] ; an emphatic *tant mieux* is ["tɑ̃ː 'mjøː], *deux fois* ['døː fwa], *trois hommes* ['trwɑːz ɔm], *très bon* ['trɛː bɔ̃], *dix ans* ['diːz ɑ̃].

B. Consonants.

The lengthening of consonants in French, as in English, takes place only in accented syllables, and is governed in general by the laws which control the same phenomenon in our own language :

(i) A final consonant is lengthened after an accented *short* vowel.   Hence, when the words in question are accented, the [l] of *belle* [bɛlː] is longer than that of *bêle* [bɛːl], the [n] of *renne* [rɛnː] longer than that of *reine* [rɛːn], just as the [l] and [n] of the English words *bell* [bɛlː], *wren* [ɹɛnː] are longer than those of *bale* [bɛɪl], *rain* [ɹɛɪn].[1]

(ii) If an accented syllable is closed with two consonants, the first is lengthened when the second is voiced.   Compare *courbe* [kurːb] and *course* [kurs] or *courte* [kurt], *marge* [marːʒ] and *marche* [marʃ], *targue* [tarːg] and *marque* [mark], *Elbe* [ɛlːb] and *Alpe* [alp].   Similarly, in English we say *felled* [fɛlːd] and *felt* [fɛlt], *mend* [mɛnːd] and *meant* [mɛnt].

---

[1] Professor Passy's opinion that the difference in length is not so marked in French as in English (*Sons du Français*, p. 67) is perhaps open to question.

(iii) An initial consonant of a syllable bearing an abnormal stress is often lengthened, especially when the following vowel is short : *jamais* ["ʒːamɛ], *bourreau* ["bːuro], an emphatic *non !* [nːɔ̃]. *Mon cher ami*, with unusual stress on the adjective, may become [mɔ̃ ʃːɛr ami]. In English we more usually preserve the short consonant ; yet in emphatic but deliberate speech, the consonant is occasionally sustained : *e.g. very* is sometimes pronounced [vːɛɹɪ], *no* [nːou].

(iv) In elliptical expressions, such as *sais pas* for *je ne sais pas*, the initial consonant may be lengthened : [sːe pɑ].[1]

[1] On the subject of Quantity the student is recommended to study the very careful transcripts in the *Chrestomathie française*, par Jean Passy et Adolphe Rambeau (New York : Henry Holt & Co.).

CHAPTER VIII

PITCH

DIFFERENCES in stress are generally accompanied by differences in pitch ; in other words, the voice usually rises or drops in passing from a syllable of one degree to that of another. As long as the language is entirely emotionless and the accentuation what has been described as normal, these variations in pitch are more or less regular. They are controlled partly by the accentuation and partly by the meaning of the phrase, and may be reduced to the following rule : While the sense of the phrase is incomplete, an increase in stress implies a rise in pitch ; but the voice drops slightly in uttering an accented syllable that completes an idea. Thus, in the sentence *André Chénier périt sur l'échafaud* the voice is lowered for the final syllable. But if the idea as a whole were *André Chénier périt sur l'échafaud à l'âge de trente-deux ans*, it would be natural to raise the voice for the last syllable of *échafaud*, and if, on the contrary, the voice were lowered, the rest of the sentence would have the force of an afterthought.

The pitch of the English phrase might be described in the same terms. But the difference in the distribution of the accents carries with it a difference in musical effect and makes comparison misleading. Thus, even if the voice were raised at such a word as *gallows*, which is accented on the first syllable, there would still be a relative drop in passing to the second syllable. Most English words of more than one syllable having a weak final, this drop in pitch is characteristic of our language. But it is a direct contradiction of the French system, the last syllable being there uttered at a higher pitch than any other. His failure to observe this contrast is largely responsible for the English-speaking student's faulty intonation of French.

Again, although the voice drops at the end of a sentence in French, it does not, as a rule, drop so low as in English.[1] The difference is especially noticeable when the English sentence ends with a word of the kind just referred to, in which the final syllable is weak, because the voice drops still lower for this syllable than for the accented one. Some teachers of French have even found it advisable to inform their pupils that the pitch remains level or rises at the end of an affirmative sentence.

The marks of punctuation have much the same values in French as in English,[2] and parenthetical expressions are pitched in a lower key than the rest of the sentence. But the voice will sometimes drop at a colon or semi-colon when the sense has a certain completeness, while the pitch may be sustained or even raised at a full-stop when the speaker's idea is imperfectly expressed by the single phrase. The mark of interrogation being a sign of incompleteness regularly implies a raising of the voice, and as in modern French the direct construction is becoming more and more customary in interrogative clauses, there is often nothing

[1] In America the voice is raised at the end of an affirmative sentence. The same tendency is often observable in the pronunciation of the native-born Australian, but it is as yet less characteristic of the 'Australian accent' than the drawl. Nothing could differ more widely than the latter from the delivery of the Parisian.

[2] But see p. 71.

but this rise in pitch to distinguish a question from a statement.

While the sense is incomplete the voice is raised higher for an accented syllable than for a secondary one, higher for a secondary than for a weak syllable.   And as there is a closer approach to equilibrium in point of stress between the various syllables of a French sound-group, the weak syllables of French being rarely as weak as those of English,[1] it follows, first, that there is more monotony, more evenness of tone, in unemotional French than in unemotional English ; and secondly, that the general pitch of the French phrase is higher than that of the English.   This result is, of course, relative and unaffected by differences in the pitch of individual voices : the same voice speaking French and English will seem to have a higher pitch in French because there are fewer low notes in the French sentence.   It is interesting for the learner, if opportunity offers, to observe a French student speaking English : in his mouth our language has a higher pitch and produces a more monotonous effect.   Various causes contribute to bring about this result, but the overstressing of weak syllables is not the least important.

When we pass from the simple statement to speech that implies feeling—and speech generally implies feeling—the problem of pitch loses all its simplicity.   Except in more or less extreme cases, where notable stress is laid upon a word, emphasis is a subtle affair, and the learner of a foreign language devoting his attention to difficulties presented by the form of expression or the nature of the sounds is inclined to overlook the finer points of stress and pitch which give life to the phrase.   But even if the English-speaking student succeeds in reading and speaking French with such emphasis and variations of pitch as would

[1] See Accent, p. 168.

characterize, *mutatis mutandis*, an intelligent use of his own language, the problem is still far from being solved. The intonation, the melody of emphatic French is often far from being what would seem natural to the Englishman. Not that the difference is so often one in kind: on the contrary, the various feelings and emotions— surprise, delight, contempt, incredulity and the rest—are rendered, generally speaking, much in the same way in French as in English. The Frenchman's voice, that is, does not often rise where the Englishman's would drop, and conversely seldom drops where the Englishman's would rise; but it very often rises or drops much more abruptly, much more emphatically than the Englishman's. A modification of the tone, a raising or lowering of the pitch, often adds infinite force to a word or idea, gives it a significance which it would not otherwise possess; and the Frenchman takes advantage of this fact much more than the Englishman. The idea may, after all, be a trifling one, and may seem to the Englishman not to call for such a show of feeling: but the Frenchman does not leave his hearer to guess part of the meaning. With him, moreover, each phrase is treated as an artistic creation: to neglect the intonation would be comparable to the disregard of light and shade in a painting. It is, indeed, just another aspect of his craving after elegance and clearness that leads the Frenchman to put so much music into his phrase; and if the Englishman is to speak French quite as the Frenchman does, he must be prepared to 'come out of his shell' and to make the expression of his feeling strikingly clear by the same effective means.

Theory can here do very little. To indicate the varied changes that can be rung in upon the gamut of speech-sounds would be a herculean task. Moreover, it would be hazardous to lay down general rules beyond those which are instinctive to Englishman and Frenchman alike. The personality stands for much in this matter, and the differences are without end.   One might as well attempt an account of gesture, which, like pitch, often plays an important part in reinforcing the French vocabulary. Observation of the living idiom is in the last resort indispensable   We must be prepared to admit that there is a point at which precept fails, and that a language cannot be mastered through the medium of paper and ink.

INDEX

NOTE.—[ɒ] and [ɐ] follow *a*, [ð] follows *d*, [θ] follows *t*, [ɔ] follows *e*, [ɲ] and [ŋ] follow *n*, [ɹ] and [ʁ] follow *r*, [ʃ] follows *s*, [ʒ] follows *z*, [ʌ] follows *v*, [ɥ] follows *y*.

[ɑ], 2, 4, 10, 11, 14, 21, 22-23, 176, 179.
[ɑ̃], 1, 4, 36, 81, 175, 179.
[a], 4, 14, 20-22.
a, 20, 22.
à, 2.
â, 20, 22.
abnormal oral vowels, 27.
  ,,   stress—see *emphasis*.
  ,,   vowels, 10-11, 13, 27.
abnormally accented syllables, pitch of, 185-186.
abnormally accented syllables, quantity of vowels in, 180.
accent, principal or tonic, 7, 166-169.
accent, secondary, 12, 167-168.
  ,,   weak, 12, 167-168.
accented syllables, 165-173.
  ,,   ,,   pitch of, 183-187.
accented syllables, quantity of vowels in, 175-178.
accents, 2, 3, 177.
accentuation, 165-173.
Adam's apple, 43.

[æ], 4, 21, 22, 34, 35.
ai, 16, 19, 30.
aî, 178.
aie, 19.
aim, 1, 35.
ain, 1, 35.
ais, 16, 19.
ait, 19.
alphabet, phonetic, 3-6.
am, 1, 22, 36.
American pronunciation, 17, 25, 33, 65, 184.
-*âmes*, 2, 177.
an, 1, 36.
aon, 1, 36, 141.
août, aoûter, 141.
arrête, 178.
aspiration—see *breathing*.
assimilation, 146-154.
-*âtes*, 2, 177.
au, 23, 25.
aumône, 177.
Australian pronunciation, 17, 21, 25, 33, 65, 184.
ay, 16.
[ɒ], 4, 36
[ɐ], 4, 29, 31, 32.

[b], 5, 44, 46, 48 49, 57.
b, bb, 47, 48.
back-breath-stop—see [k].
back-stops, 44.
back-voice-stop—see [g].
back vowels, 14.
balance between weak and secondary syllables, 168.
Bleton, 85, 89.
breath consonants, 42 ff.
breath-stops, 45.
breathing, 6, 45.

c, 2, 51, 52, 62.
ç, 2, 62
Caen, 141.
careless pronunciations, 86, 142.
cc, 51.
cch, 51.
cet homme, 140.
cette année, 140.
ch, 51, 63.
Chrestomathie française, 71, 85 ff., 112, 121, 123, 125, 126, 129, 130, 131, 138, 142, 145, 162, 182
close *a*—see [a].
close *e* – see [e].
close *eu*—see [ø].
close French *u*—see [y].
close *i*—see [i].
close *o*—see [o].
close *ou*—see [u].
close vowels, 11.
closed syllables, 73, quantity of vowels in, 175-181.
Cockney, 17.
combination of speech-sounds, 69.
Comédie française, 66.
comparison of Fr. and Eng. consonant-systems, 43
comparison of Fr. and Eng. vowel-systems, 12.

Conservatoire, 66.
consonant-systems compared, 43-44.
consonants, kinds of, 42-43.
,,   quantity of, 181-182.
continuants—see *fricatives*.
cqu, 51.

[d], 5, 44, 46, 50-51, 57.
d, dd, 49, 50
defectiveness of French orthography, 1 ff.
denasalization, 80-81.
delayed elision, 135, 136, 139.
devocalization, 6, 147-152, 153
diagrams, 13, 27, 32, 44, 54, 57
dictionary with phonetic script, 21, 80.
diphthongization, Eng. habit of, 12, 13, 15, 17, 18, 20, 25, 26, 163, 173, 175, 178.
diphthongs (so-called), 39-41.
displacement of accent, 170-173.
double consonants, 156-159.
double signs, 118, 156.
double vowels, 162-163.
[ö], 5.

[e], 1, 4, 10, 11, 12, 14, 16-18, 29, 176.
[ɛ], 1,2,4,14,18,19-20,31,38,178.
[ẽ], 4, 34-35, 81, 175.
[è], 28, 30.
e, 1, 16, 19, 20, 30.
é, 16, 19.
è, 2, 19.
ê, 2, 16, 19, 178.
eau, 25.
ee, 14.
ei, 19.
ein, 1, 34.
elision of [ə] following a single consonant, 118

elision of [e] following a vowel, 117.

elision of .[ə] following two or more consonants, 125-132.

elision of [ə] in final syllables, 116, 125, 127, 128, 129.

elision of [ə] in initial syllables, 115, 122-124, 126.

elision of [ə] in inner syllables, 124-125, 126.

elision of [ə] in monosyllables, 115, 118-122, 126.

elision of [ə] in *ne*, 121-122, 145.
,, in *que*, 121-122, 145.
,, in series of syllables, 132-140.

elision of [ə] in single syllables, 114-132.

elision in verse, 143-145.

elision of consonants, 128, 141-142.

elision of [k], 141, 142.
,, [l], 141, 142.
,, other vowels than [ə], 140.

em, 1, 36.

emphasis, 17, 165, 169-173, 185.

e mute—see [ə] below.

en, 1, 34, 36.

et in linking, 103, 107.

êtes, 2, 178.

eu, 1, 3, 28, 29, 31.

eû, 3, 28.

eue, 29.

eun, 37.

eux, 29.

explosives—see *stops*.

extraordinaire, 140.

[ə], 1, 4, 12, 13, 20, 30-31, 163, 164.

[ə] elided—see *elision*.

[ə] not elided, 115, 118, 119, 122, 123, 124, 125, 126, 127, 128, 163, 164.

[f], 5, 57, 60, 80.

f, *ff*, 60.

falling diphthong, 39.

faon, 141.

Français parlé, 89, 105, 112, 119, 127, 129, 133, 136, 139.

French and English vowel-systems, 12.

fricatives, 42, 57-68.

front-voice-fricative, 67.

front vowels, 14.

[g], 5, 44, 46, 52-53, 57.

g, 51, 52, 64.

gg, 52.

glottal-breath-fricative, 68.
,, fricative, 57.
,, stop, 6, 44, 53, 57, 162, 164.

glottis, 9, 44, 45, 50, 52, 53.

glides (see also *transition*), 155-164.

gn, 56.

gu, 52.

[h], 5, 57, 68, 163, 164.

h, 68, 79,

half-long vowels, 7, 174, 179-180.

half-open vowels, 11.

half-wide vowels, 11.

hard consonants, 43.

hiatus, 162, 163.

high-back-narrow vowel—see [u].

high-back-wide vowel—see [ʊ].

high-front-narrow-round vowel—see [y].

high-front-narrow vowel—see [i].

high-front-wide vowel—see [ɪ].

Hyacinthe, le Père, 89, 104.

[i], 4, 10, 11, 12, 14-16, 28.

[ɪ], 4, 15, 18.

i, 2, 14, 20, 22, 40, 67

f̥, 14.

ɨ, 15

ɪe, 14

ɪl, 141-142.

-il, -ille, 67

ɪm, ɪn, 1, 35.

inconsistency of French orthography, 1 ff.

ɪŋɡ, 35

International Phonetic Association, 3, 113

Irish *r*, 65.

[j], 5, 15, 39, 40, 57, 67-68.

j, 64

Jacob, M , 85, 89, 110

[k], 5, 43, 44, 45, 51-52, 57.

k, 51

kinds of consonants, 42-43.

kinds of vowels, 9-10

Koschwitz, E (see also *Parlers
parisiens*), 71, 85 ff., 112, 119,
123, 126, 136, 139, 145, 158,
160

[l], 5, 43, 57, 61.

l, 61.

Legouvé, Ernest, 87, 95

liaison—see *linking*

linking, 78-113, 171.

,,   in compound expres-
sions, 84, 110

linking obligatory, 82-84.

,,   of adj and noun, 82.

,,   of adj. or adv. and complement, 101

linking of adv. and adj., 83, 101.

,,   of adv. and object, 99.

,,   of adv and subject, 102

,,   of adv and verb, 93.

,,   of article and noun or
adj., 82.

linking of auxiliary and past
part , 83

linking of a word with *et* and *ou*,
103.

linking of demonstr. adj. and
noun, 82

linking of direct and indirect
object, 103

linking of *dont*, 84.

,,   of *être* and complement,
83.

linking of *mais* and foll word,
107.

linking of noun and adj., 87-89.

,,   of noun-subject and predicate, 90.

linking of numeral, 82.

,,   of poss. adj. and noun,
82

linking of preposition and complement, 83.

linking of pronoun and verb, 82.

,,   of *quand*, 84.

,,   of rel. pron. and foll.
word, 109

linking of two adverbs, 100

,,   of two verbs, 90.

,,   of verb and adv., 93

,,   of verb and object, 96.

,,   of verb and pron., 82

,,   optional, 85-113.

,,   words not admitting of,
79

lip-back-voice-fricative—see [w].

lip-breath-stop—see [p].

lip-fricatives, 57

lip-front-voice-fricative, 59-60.

lip stop-nasal—see [m]

lip-stops, 44, 54

lip-teeth-breath-fricative—see[f]

lip-teeth-voice-fricative—see [v].

lip-voice-stop—see [b]

liquid *l*, 68

ll, 61.
l mouillée, 68.
long consonants, 181.
long vowels, 174 ff.
low-back-wide-nasal—see [ɑ̃].
low-back-wide vowel—see [ɑ].
low-front-narrow vowel—see [a].

[m], 5, 33, 35, 54-55, 57.
m, 54.
Maître phonétique, 113.
mid-back-narrow vowel – see [o].
mid-back-wide-nasal—see [ɔ̃].
mid-back-wide vowel—see [ɔ].
mid - front - half - narrow - round
    vowel—see [ə].
mid-front-narrow-round vowel—
    see [ø].
mid-front-narrow vowel—see [e].
mid-front-wide-nasal—see [ɛ̃].
mid-front-wide-round-nasal—see
    [œ̃].
mid-front-wide vowel – see [ɛ]
mid-palate-stop-nasal, 56.
mm, 54.
mn, 55.
mute *e*—see [ə].

[n], 5, 33, 35, 44, 55-56, 57.
n, 55.
narrow vowels, 11.
nasal *a*—see [ɑ̃].
  ,,   *e*—see [ɛ̃].
  ,,   *o*—see [ɔ̃].
  ,,   *u*—see [œ̃].
nasal consonants, 54-56.
  ,,   ,,   in linking, 80.
nasal consonant not pronounced,
    33-34, 35, 36, 37, 38.
nasalization, 1, 32 ff., 147, 153,
    154.

nasalized abnormal vowel, 37-38.
nasalized normal vowels, 34-37.
nasalized vowels, 10, 13, 32-38,
    175, 179.
neuf, 80.
non-elision of [ə], 115, 118, 119,
    122, 123, 124, 125, 126, 127,
    128, 163, 164.
normal accentuation, 165-169.
normally   accented   syllables,
    quantity of vowels in, 175.
normal oral vowels, 13.
normal vowels, 10-11, 12-13.
Northern English, 17, 19, 25,
    65, 66.
[ɲ], 5, 35, 43, 56, 57.
[ŋ], 5, 33, 34, 153.

[o], 4, 10, 12, 14, 25-26, 29,
    175, 179.
[ò], 30.
[ɔ], 2, 4, 14, 23-25, 31, 37.
[ɔ̃], 5, 36-37, 80, 175.
[ø], 5, 29-30, 175, 179.
o, 23, 25, 58.
ò, 23, 25.
ð, 2.
obligatory liaisons, 82-84.
[œ], 5, 31-32.
[œ̃], 5, 37-38, 81, 175.
œ, 1, 31.
œu, 1, 29, 31.
oi, 2, 20, 22, 58.
om, on, 37.
open *a*—see [ɑ].
open *e*—see [ɛ].
open *eu*—see [œ].
open *o*—see [ɔ].
open syllables, 73; quantity of
    vowels in, 175-181.
open vowels, 6, 11.
oral vowels, 9.

orthography, defective, 1 ff.
ou, 2, 26, 40, 58.
oû, 26.
où, 26.

[p], 5, 43, 44, 45, 47-48, 57.
p, 47.
paon, 141.
parce que, 141-142.
Paris, Gaston, 119, 120, 121, 122, 123, 126, 128, 130, 131, 133, 136, 139.
Parlers parisiens (see also *Koschwitz*), 71, 82, 85 ff , 112, 119, 127, 128, 129, 133, 136, 139, 145, 158, 160
Passy, Jean (see also *Chrest. fr.*), 71, 85, 92, 95.
Passy, Paul, 78, 88, 91, 104, 108, 112, 119, 122, 123, 126, 130, 131, 133, 136, 139, 149, 163, 171, 181.
peut-être, 140.
ph, 60.
phonetic alphabet, 3-6.
phonetic texts, 112.
pitch, 183-187
point-teeth-breath-stop—see [t].
point-teeth-lateral-voice-fricative—see [l].
point-teeth-stop-nasal—see [n].
point-teeth-stops, 44, 54.
point-teeth-voice-stop—see [d].
point-trill—see [r].
pp, 47.
Précis de pron. fr. (see also *Rousselot*), 71, 88, 142.
principal accent, 166-169.
progressive devocalization, 150-152.
puis, 140.
punctuation, 71, 184.
pure vowels—see *oral vowels*.

q, *qu*, 51.
quantity of consonants, 181-182.
quantity of vowels, 168, 172, 173, 174-181.
quelque, 141, 142.

[r], 5, 44, 57, 65-67.
[ʀ], 5, 43, 57, 66-67.
r, 65, 67, 112.
Rambeau, Adolphe (see also *Chrest. fr*), 71, 85 ff., 112.
regressive devocalization, 148-150.
regressive vocalization, 125, 152-3.
relaxed organs—see *slackness*.
r grasseyée, 66.
rhythm, 127-129, 167-168, 171.
rising diphthong, 39.
Ritter, M., 85, 89, 104.
rounded front-vowels, 27.
rounded vowels, 14, 27.
Rousselot, M., 71, 85, 88, 89, 91, 95, 99, 104, 109, 110, 142.
rr, 65, 67.
[ɹ], 5, 65.
[ʁ], 66.

[s], 5, 44, 57, 62.
s, 2, 62, 63.
Saône, 141.
sc, 2, 62.
sch, 63.
Scotch pronunciation, 15, 17, 25, 26, 65, 125.
secondary accents, 12, 167-168.
secondary syllables, 12, 167-168.
semi-vowels, 40, 79, 151, 163.
sentence, 69.
sh, 63.
shifting of accent, 170-173.
signs, phonetic, 2, 4 ff.

slackness of organs in English,
  12, 13, 16, 43, 45, 47, 50, 58,
  60, 61, 62, 64.
soft consonants, 43.
Sons du Français, 78, 171, 181.
sound-group, 70-71, 166-167.
sounds and symbols, 1 ff.
Southern English, 17, 19, 21, 23,
  24, 25, 30, 31, 65.
ss, 2, 62.
standard French, 7.
stops, 42, 44-56.
stress—see *accentuation, principal accent, secondary accent,
  weak syllables*, etc.
stress group, 72, 166-167.
subsister, 149, 150.
supporting-vowel, 125.
syllable, 6, 72-73.
syllabication, 64, 73-76, 156, 157,
  173, 175.
symbols, phonetic, 2, 4 ft.
[ʃ], 5, 44, 57, 63-64.

[t], 5, 43, 44, 45, 49-50, 57.
t, 2, 49, 62.
taon, 141.
teeth-blade consonants, 57.
teeth-(broad) blade-breath-fricative, 63-64.
teeth-(broad) blade-voice-fricative, 64-65.
teeth-(narrow) blade-breath-fricative, 62.
teeth-(narrow) blade-voice-fricative, 63.
teeth-stops, 44.
texts in phonetic script, 112.
th, 49.
tonic accent, 166 ft.
transition, 155-164.
  ,,   between   dissimilar
  stops, 161.

transition between identical consonants, 156-159.
transition between stops produced at same place, 159-161.
transition between vowels, 162-
  163.
transition from consonant to
  vowel in another syllable, 163-
  164.
tt, 49.
[θ], 6.

[u], 5, 10, 11, 12, 14, 26-27, 28,
  59.
[ʊ], 5, 27.
u, 2, 23, 28, 37, 40, 58, 59.
û, 28.
ue, 1; 31.
um, 1, 23, 37.
un, 1, 37.
unaccented syllables, 16, 18, 20,
  22, 24, 26, 27, 31, 167, 178-
  180, 183-186.
units of speech, 69-77.
unstressed syllables—see *unaccented syllables*.
uvula, 32 ff.
uvula-trill, 57.
uvular *r*, 66.

[v], 6, 44, 57, 60-61.
v, 60.
velum, 9, 32 ft.
Viëtor, Prof., 21.
vocal chords, 9.
vocalization, 6, 125, 147, 148,
  152, 153.
voice, 6, 9, 46.
voice-consonants, 42 ff.
voice-stops, 44, 46.
  ,,   quantity of vowels
  before, 177.
voilà, 140.

vowel-signs representing consonants, 2, 39, 40
vowel-systems compared, 12-13
vowels, 9-38.
,, in unaccented syllables,
12-13, 16, 18, 20, 22, 26, 27
vowels, kinds of, 9
,, quantity of, 174-181.
voyelle d'appui, 125.
[ʌ], 4, 13.

[w], 6, 39, 40, 43, 57, 58, 59.
w, 58, 60.
weak syllables, 12, 167-169
,, ,, quantity of vowels
in, 178 ff.
wh, 58.

wide vowels, 11
word not phonetic unit, 76-77

x, 2, 51, 52, 62, 63.
xc, 2, 62.

[y], 5, 28-29, 59.
[ɤ], 29
y, 14, 67
[ɥ], 5, 39, 40, 43, 57, 59 60.

[z], 6, 57, 63
z, 63
Zola, 85, 89.
zz, 63.
[ʒ], 5, 44, 57, 64-65

GLASGOW . PRINTED AT THE UNIVERSITY PRESS BY ROBERT MACLEHOSE AND CO. LTD.

BIBLIOLIFE

Old Books Deserve a New Life
www.bibliolife.com

Did you know that you can get most of our titles in our trademark **EasyScript**[TM] print format? **EasyScript**[TM] provides readers with a larger than average typeface, for a reading experience that's easier on the eyes.

Did you know that we have an ever-growing collection of books in many languages?

Order online:
www.bibliolife.com/store

Or to exclusively browse our **EasyScript**[TM] collection:
www.bibliogrande.com

At BiblioLife, we aim to make knowledge more accessible by making thousands of titles available to you – quickly and affordably.

Contact us:
BiblioLife
PO Box 21206
Charleston, SC 29413

Lightning Source UK Ltd.
Milton Keynes UK
24 March 2010